CAGE FIGHTER

CAGE FIGHTER

IAN FREEMAN

WITH STUART WHEATMAN

JOHN BLAKE

Published by John Blake Publishing Ltd,
3, Bramber Court, 2 Bramber Road,
London W14 9PB, England

www.blake.co.uk

First published in paperback in 2004

ISBN 1844540367

British Library Cataloguing-in-Publication Data:

A catalogue record for this book is available from the British Library.

Design by www.envydesign.co.uk

Printed in Great Britain by Bookmarque

3 5 7 9 10 8 6 4 2

Papers used by John Blake Publishing are natural, recyclable products made from wood grown in sustainable forests. The manufacturing processes conform to the environmental regulations of the country of origin.

Every attempt has been made to contact the relevant copyright-holders, but some were unobtainable. We would be grateful if the appropriate people could contact us.

For my father

'It was hard fighting knowing you were leaving me dad, but mum sat me down and asked me to do it for you. She said it would make you happy and proud. Looking back, I'm pleased I fought because I know you had the best seat in the house watching over me. I hope you're still looking over me and as proud as ever.'

Contents

Foreword

MY NAME'S ROY 'Pretty Boy' Shaw. I've fought against the best and become the best. I don't easily get impressed, and so when a special character comes along in the fight game I take notice. In the fight game you've got to be able to take as much as you dish out, otherwise you'll be gone in sixty seconds. Ian 'The Machine' Freeman is awesome and impressed me with his gentlemanly conduct right from the start. You can act as tough as you want outside of the ring, be as mean as you want, as angry as you want, but that don't impress me none. Politeness counts more than anything else and Ian is as much an ambassador for his sport mixing with the public as he is while fighting an opponent. Tuxedo warriors are hard as nails but when it comes to fighting an equally hard opponent not many stay around to walk the walk. Ian's top rated and he's got something not many people have got. As Ian says: 'Don't take my politeness as a weakness.' I say it's also one of his strengths.

Ian,

Box it clever,

Roy 'Pretty Boy' Shaw

Introduction

Dictionary definition of the word 'machine':

1: Apparatus for applying mechanical power, having several parts each with a definite function.

2: Person who acts mechanically or with unfailing regularity.

3: Ian Freeman.
(*The Concise Oxford English Dictionary*)

OK, so the third one doesn't actually appear in the dictionary. Yet. I'm sure they'll be knocking on my door soon enough. But the two definitions above are correct and they serve as a warning to any opponent in the ring. A lot of you might know it already, but here's how my name came about: I was training down at the gym and we were getting really into it. When I'm in serious training for a fight I want to be tested to the limit. I need to know what I'm capable of. So here's me in the gym with the rest of my training partners and we're really going for it. I take on one at a time, each for five minutes. There's five of them, so it goes like this: when I've fought the first one he sits it out and the second steps in, then the third, fourth and fifth. Then it's back to lucky number one again. These will be all-out battles: vale tudo, jiu jitsu, boxing, grappling – a whole mixture (mixed martial arts) that, amongst other names, carries the title of 'No-Holds-Barred Fighting'.

I was unstoppable, mate. In the end they were all too tired to carry on and gave in. One of them came out with the immortal line, 'Ian. You're like a fucking machine.' It just kinda stuck after that – Ian 'The Machine' Freeman, British Rings Rule Champion, CFC Vale Tudo Champion, Intercontinental Champion, Britain's Best Heavyweight Fighter, UFC Champion, Pancrase Super Bout Champion and all-round good guy. That's me – not being cocky about it, it's what I am.

I say 'good guy' and I can tell a lot of you are wondering, 'How can he do all that and call himself a good guy?' It's simple to explain: I'm a professional fighter; it's what I do for a living. It's just like being a traffic warden: they are not nice people at work, but as a person ... shit, never mind. You know what I'm saying. I've got the best job in the world and you wouldn't believe the job satisfaction I get. Street fighting is fine, but it's nothing compared to fighting in front of a packed audience screaming your name. I love the recognition of fighting in front of an audience, but I don't mind fighting in front of just two people if I'm challenged. For me it's the buzz, the excitement, the whole adrenaline thing.

This is the bit that a lot of people don't understand. The buzz I talk about is not the buzz of hurting people. If I got a buzz out of hurting people I'd be hiding in bushes, jumping out on people all over the place to give them a bashing and running away. It's not that kind of buzz – it's a test of skill and strength. In the ring it's controlled and you are testing yourself as well as your opponent.

There's another thing people can't grasp: it's controlled. We go for submission moves and, if they are applied correctly, your opponent will tap out – they will submit before they are hurt. That's when you have proved you had the skill to read them, know how they would react, maybe counter, maybe attack, go for submissions – whatever. Above all, it is a sport. We are trained athletes taking part in a sport that we love.

You can't be nice to people in the ring; you can't open the ropes for them to climb in like you would hold a door open to someone. You can't say, 'Sorry, did that hurt?' Get what I'm saying? You can be a good guy on the street *and* a bad guy in the ring. I'm a good guy on the street until I'm crossed. On the street it's personal; in the ring it isn't. That's where the difference is.

And please don't believe everything you read in the papers. I'll go into this in more detail later, but for the record: I haven't eaten anyone's hamster, I didn't meet Hitler on the moon and I don't eat babies for dinner (everyone knows they get stuck in your teeth). Just to prove when I'm not fighting or training that I'm just an ordinary down-to-earth bloke, there's one story I want to get out of the way before we get going. Now, I know there are people who won't like to admit it, but everyone is scared of little things that are probably nothing to others. You know the things I mean: spiders, bees, wasps, snakes, dogs, birds, judges, police ... the list is endless. Me? I'm absolutely petrified of moths. (Get the laughs over now and I'll continue.) I can't stand the bastard things. Fucking horrible little creepy fuckers. If I saw one now I'd be off like a shot. I reckon things like that have some sixth sense – they can tell you are freaked out by them, so they just go straight for you. No kidding. You say to yourself, 'I'm scared of dogs', and the ponciest little shih-tzu in the world will come and bite you on your arse in front of all your mates. I know someone who's shit-scared of bees, and you can guarantee that he'll be out with his girlfriend in some crowded place and one will chase after him; he'll start screaming and leg it – and look a right twat. They never go for anyone else, just him. It's Sod's Law, innit? Or Fucking Poor Bastard's Law, as it's more commonly known. Some people's phobias are deep-rooted things that go back to their childhood, so they're something you shouldn't really take the piss out of. But, of course, we all do.

There was this time when I was working in Bentleys nightclub in Sunderland. I worked there from the back end of the '80s to the early '90s. When I joined the team there I was only around twenty, so I was very new to the game. There was Stevie Watson the head doorman, a massive bloke, as wide as he was tall. Then there was Big John, and he was fucking big too, John Ord, Billy and Arnie Croft, Graham Baxter and my partner Geordie Watson, Stevie's brother. God knows what their mother used to feed them when they were kids; they must have slept in grow bags. Geordie's this big six-foot-two brawler with dark curly hair. He's like Captain Kirk, a real man's man, only he doesn't set his phaser to stun, he sets the headbutt to knockout (one other difference: he's got his own hair). And his sense of humour ... we had to hose him down every hour 'cos he was that dry we thought he might start to crack. He is definitely one of the best people to have on your side when things get a bit hot under the collar. And he would take anyone on. Anyone. He could wade into any fight and would always clear the house. When I was first partnered up with him, I think he was a bit, 'Oh shit. Here comes another' – you know, a bit pissed off at having to train me up, so to speak. The first ever night I worked there a big fight kicked off and we instantly bonded. We were back to back and in the thick of it. We could practically read each other's mind when something was about to go off.

At Bentleys they used to have all sorts of functions every few weeks. This one time I think they were displaying and modelling wedding dresses. The function was packed out. There were even photographers from the *Daily Mirror* there – quite an event, it was. So there's us lot, the doormen, in our dinner suits, keeping watch over the proceedings. A few of us were standing round the front of the stage, which was done up sort of like a catwalk. Even at a function like this, and bearing in mind the reputation Bentleys had, anything could kick off at any time – if you let your guard down once, you're fucked. While I was standing, I felt something by my side. Because we were all in line and nothing should be past us, I turned quickly to see what was going on. False alarm. It was just one of the lads, Stevie Watson. I haven't got the best hearing in the world and with all that was going on I couldn't make out what he said. I just assumed that he'd nipped into my pocket to borrow my lighter and thought nothing more of it.

Back to the usual stance and on with the job. As I was standing there, I felt something in my pocket again. It didn't feel anything like a hand this time; this was like something twitching and flapping about. Of course, I just delved straight in there to see what it was – the biggest fucking moth I've ever seen in my life! I shit a brick there and then. Within a second my jacket was off and I threw it to the ground. I was totally freaked out and stamping all over it like a madman. That was when I looked up and realised where I was. In that kind of situation you are oblivious to your surroundings, aren't you? All that was going on in my mind was to get this thing away from me by any means necessary. When I eventually looked up it turned out that somehow I'd managed to get myself up on stage. Christ knows how I'd got up there and only God knows what the audience was making of all this. I was giving that Michael Flatulence bloke a run for his money – legs everywhere, the full works. I'm sure I saw him in the crowd going, 'That bloke's got feet of fire, I say. Feet of fire, so he has.' And the poor audience probably thought it was all part of the show: 'And to your left, Mr Freeman is demonstrating the amount of damage our dinner jackets can endure, ladies and gentlemen.' I was expecting a round of applause when I got down – I suppose I was the half-time entertainment, after all. The rest of the doormen were going absolutely mental. They all knew what Stevie was up to and were all in on it. Bastards nearly gave me a heart attack.

We always had a laugh there, and taking the piss out of each other was second nature. In a job like that you've got to, or you'll end up going insane. They would keep bringing up the moth incident and there was this one bloke who just wouldn't let it lie. A joke's a joke and all that, but come on. Thing is with this bloke, he'd let slip one of his little phobias as well. Big mistake. It turned out that he was scared of seagulls.

If none of you have been to Sunderland, there's something I have to explain here: the place is absolutely crawling with them. And they're as big as light aircraft! It's right on the coast, so instead, of your usual gangs of pigeons shitting all over the place, Sunderland's got stacks of great big fuck-off seagulls that fly around and terrorise the shoppers. Bad place to be if you're scared of them – and an even worse place to be is locked in the staff room of Bentleys with one of them! All you could hear was screaming and crashing around; we didn't know if he was trying to murder it or if it was pecking *him* to death. When we eventually opened the door it was like a bombsite. It was completely wrecked: furniture all over, chairs and tables overturned, a real mess. You'd think Carol Smillie had just decorated. We're standing there with the door open having a laugh and this big ugly seagull just casually strolls out going, 'You've got a right lunatic on your hands there, mate', and he's sitting there crying his eyes out. Not an Alfred Hitchcock fan, then. Like I said earlier: phobias are something you shouldn't take the piss out of.

I think in those days we probably caused a few phobias of our own. You can imagine all these people going straight to the doctor's on a Monday morning, going, 'Doctor, I wonder if you can help. I've got a fear of huge fists and getting hit by them.'

'Well, when did this happen, Mr Smith?'

'Some time around half-past ten on Saturday night, I think.'

And as for taking the piss ... We'll never forget the time when Arnie Croft thought someone was taking the piss out of him. Arnie's small but well built. Small and stocky, no taller than five foot five, and talks with a stutter. One time this lad was trying to get in the club and he was off his head – looked like he'd just raided Oliver Reed's drinks cabinet. So Arnie's trying to tell this lad that he was perhaps a bit too drunk to want to go clubbing, but the lad was having none of it. Arnie's going, 'S-S-S-Sorry, m-m-m-m-ate, y-y-you can't c-c-c-c-come in', and the reply from the drunken lad was, 'P-P-P-Please, m-m-m-m-m-mate.' It was like listening to a conversation between Paul Hardcastle and Norman Collier.

It went on for a bit and Arnie thought that he was having a laugh, thought he was taking the piss out of his stutter, so he cracked him and told him to f-fuck off. I didn't know if the lad actually spoke with a stutter or if it was the drink ... until the week after. The same lad came back but wasn't quite as drunk as he was the last time – must only have had fifteen beers or so. He came up to us and asked, 'A-A-A-A-A-Am I b-b-barred from l-l-l-last week?' He really did have a speech impediment! We couldn't help laughing but we felt for the poor bloke. We let him in and he made sure to keep out of Arnie's way. It was p-p-priceless.

Lots of the boys look back on those times and call them the good old days. And they *were* the good old days, although there were some times when you didn't really think so. Being locked up nearly every night, for example, isn't really everybody's idea of fun. Nor is having around ten fights a night with up to fifteen people at a time, every night of the week. Or being covered in someone else's blood, having knives and guns pulled on you ... the list is endless. But to us, it's second nature. It's *first* nature. It's what we do – and we're damn good at it. You miss times like that, but you look forward to all the next ones.

There are a helluva lot of fond memories splattered up the walls of the pubs and clubs we worked in. I'm telling you, Russell Crowe wouldn't have a look in. We were, and very much still are, the Gladiators of our town and sometimes we really have had to fight for our lives. There are those who have retired or left the arena for different reasons. They will always be greatly respected and remembered amongst us all. What would we do differently? Absolutely Jack Shit. We love every minute of it and we wouldn't change a thing. We've all been part of a special era and helped to make the myths.

God bless the fucking lot of us.

Boyz 'n the Hood: the mischief years

***EVERY KID GETS** up to all kinds of mad things in the years that they can get away with it. Some people keep doing it. As a kid growing up in Sunderland, I took every day as it came without looking back. If having fun becomes a crime, then only criminals will have fun.*

I was born and bred in Sunderland, so that would make me a proper Makem. For those of you who are not from the North-east, a Makem is just a name for someone from Sunderland. You know, you've got Geordies from Newcastle, Cockneys from London and all that caper. It came about many moons ago – back in the shipbuilding days, I think. The story differs so much depending on who you ask, or who can actually remember, but it's something to do with the regional dialect: 'Ships – We Mak 'em [We make them], and you tak 'em [you take them]' ... something like that.

Anyway, 1966 is the year everyone remembers as the year we last won the World Cup – and it will probably *be* the last year we win the World Cup. It was a good time for England but what made it even better was that I arrived on the scene on 11 October of that very year. Football's not really my thing, though – the idea of chasing after some bloke to hug and kiss him just because he managed to get a ball between a couple of goalposts? Do me a favour. I'm also a Libra, so that means I've got the Scales of Justice on my side, which has come in pretty useful for me in my line of work (no, I'm not a policeman, but I have met a few). One thing I've got in common with my mate Dave Courtney, amongst others, is that I don't care too much about star signs, but I'm forever being mistaken for a Sagittarian. (That'll be fifteen per cent commission for boosting your book sales, cheers, mate.)

I was born with perforated eardrums, which was a real worry for my parents. I only have seventy-five per cent hearing in my left ear and fifty per cent in my right. It wasn't an easy thing to deal with at all, but I had to adapt to it and learn to handle it. At school I mostly had to sit at the front of the class so I could hear properly. I'm sure you are aware that kids can be cruel when they see something they don't understand. I used to wear a hearing aid while I was young and some of the kids in class would sneak up behind me and turn it up to full volume. If any of them are reading this, I'd just like to say that it *really* was *very* funny. Hilarious. Imagine yourself in that position … what a laugh you'd have.

It would have been good to have got support from people in the class, but it's just what kids are like. They target the different ones – the kid with glasses, the one with a speech impediment … even the kid with ginger hair! Once I got a bit older and into comprehensive school I stopped using the aid. I used what hearing I had, as well as learning to lip read. It was one of those things that I couldn't let beat me. It wouldn't hold me back. I don't think people appreciate the disadvantage that some kids are born with. Something they have to overcome before even starting out in life. Those kids, those people it happens to at any time in their lives, they are the real fighters.

I've got two sisters – Kim, the eldest, and Sue – and a younger brother called Colin, our kid. I think I would have preferred to be the youngest one, though, 'cos you get spoiled rotten but, more importantly, you get away with everything. Then again, when I think about the accidents that our Colin endured, it makes me glad I wasn't the youngest. I was always out to test people. You know, to see exactly how much I could get away with before I landed myself in trouble.

First we lived in an upstairs flat in Townend Farm, but soon moved to a nice big four-bedroom house in a place called Downhill ... which was just downhill: 18 Kingsland Square. It was brilliant. My parents, William and Trudy Freeman, had started a taxi firm up from scratch and later sold it on. After that my dad had a spare parts shop on Coronation Street (no, not *that* one), and my mam had the café next door.

My dad used to keep pigeons when we moved to Downhill and I loved it. I think it gave me a sense of responsibility helping to keep and look after them. One time my dad said we were going to have to let them out at some point to see if they would go away and come back. I wasn't convinced. They were all my pets and I loved every last one of them. The day came when we let them out and they just seemed to fuck right off. They couldn't wait to get away. For the rest of the day I kept checking and checking, but they didn't come back. I was absolutely gutted. Heartbroken. You know what it's like when you're young. They still hadn't come back when it was bedtime, so I went up and practically cried myself to sleep; I wasn't too chuffed with my dad right then, so I'd only said goodnight to my mam to get at him. Dad woke me up dead early in the morning, long before anyone else had got up.

Here's me all grumpy and huffing and puffing all the way downstairs until he took me outside and pointed up to the roof. There they were! They had come back! They were sitting there cooing as if nothing had happened and I was dancing around like Bez from The Happy Mondays. In all fairness, though, from their point of view nothing *had* happened. They had just stretched their wings for a bit and then come home. No problem. They were probably looking at me and wondering what I was on.

My mates and me used to hang around in the square all the time. There were four coal sheds we used as a sort of gang hut when it was raining. There was Cracker (Neil Jenkins), Punner (Lee Puncheon) and Brian Summers who used to knock around, and our Colin. We did all the things kids did back then: climbed trees, built dens, caught bees, played on bikes, went exploring and generally tormented the neighbours half to death. Without sounding like an oldie, they were great times to be a kid. The problem with kids today is that they have got *everything* and they still complain that they've got nothing to do! They've got absolutely no imagination 'cos most of them are all sitting about playing computer games. Too much cyberspace between their ears.

There's nothing worse than wasting time. I don't see the point in doing something tomorrow when you could do it today, or in half an hour when you could be doing it now. That's what I'm like. Tomorrow never comes and I've got no time for the tomorrow people. If you've got to do something, do it now – then you can't say you never did it or you never tried. If it doesn't work you've always got another day to think of another angle to attempt to sort it out. It goes the same for revenge: I always want it straight away, though sometimes it has to wait. Circumstances dictate the speed you can react, and sometimes you have to know when to hang back a bit. There'll always be times when you leave things too long and you don't have the same amount of passion any more. For instance, there is someone out there now who was in line for such a serious going over, you wouldn't believe it. But, because it had to wait, the passion to bash that person has died down to such an extent that he will just be knocked out instead of taking his meals through a straw for the rest of his life ...

You made your own entertainment back then and there was always plenty to do. I was a right little tearaway. Our Colin and me were always up to something. Once, he was bought an orange tractor and he absolutely loved it. Remember when you used to get toys one week and they would be the best things in the whole world until the week after when you'd get something else? Well, this tractor was the cow's tits for Colin. It was his toy of the moment. Our dad used to take us camping quite a lot and while we were there he'd take us shooting, so as a kid I had my own air rifle. One day I clocked the tractor in the garden and Colin was nowhere in sight. I thought it must have taken the doctors ages to separate the pair of them, so I didn't want to waste such an opportunity. I tied it to the washing line with a piece of string, bounded upstairs, hung out the window, took aim with the rifle. Ping ... *Crack!* I was like a fucking sniper. It was the dog's. ('Dogs': See '*Dog's Bollocks*' or '*the bollocks*': a British term for something that is amazing/the business. Originates from a dog being able to lick its own parts – hence the brilliance.)

Here's me sitting there like Scorpio in *Dirty Harry* – *Ping, Ping, Ping,* and there's all these bits of orange plastic flying all over the garden. After a few minutes I heard someone else bound up the stairs. You'll never guess who it was... His first reaction was, 'You'll get wrong for that', but he hadn't even seen what the target was yet. So I'm going, 'Here. Have a go.' He knew it was a bit naughty, but at that age when you're handed an air rifle and told it's all right to shoot it, guess what you're gonna do? By the time he set eyes on the thing it looked nothing like any tractor I've ever seen, so he aimed and pulled the trigger. *Ping, Ping* ... he loved it. He was getting well into it and falling around laughing – then he asked me what it was he was shooting at. I couldn't lie: 'It's your brand new orange tractor!' He stopped laughing, for some reason. There was that two-second pause that kids do just before they start to bawl their eyes out. And that's when I knew the little git was gonna shop me when our mam and dad got home.

I mentioned the camping with our dad. Another essential for a kid who's out camping is a knife. This is where I should tell you that my parents didn't go out and get us all these dangerous weapons and then train us in armed combat. They weren't international arms dealers, you understand. They had to draw the line when Kim had set her heart on a rocket launcher for her ninth birthday. The sheath knives we had were the real thing, proper knives for proper adventures, and weren't supposed to be touched when our parents were out of the house ... well, unless you knew where they were kept, that is.

Me and our Colin used to love playing cowboys and all that shit. Everyone did. At home we had the album of *The Good, The Bad and the Ugly* by Ennio Morricone. We used to play the record and act along to it. We would both be standing there looking at each other at each end of the room with the sheath knives fastened to our snake belts. We couldn't have been any more than eight or nine when this happened. It was all pure method acting, real De Niro shit, we wouldn't go for loads of dialogue, it was the actions we were concerned with. Even when you hear that music now you can't help but react to it. It transforms you.

We'd have both thumbs tucked into the front of our belts, sizing each other up and waiting for the music to take hold of us, and then we'd begin to mosey into the inevitable showdown. Our paths would cross in the middle of the room and we'd greet each other with a polite 'Howdy', as we changed ends. Then next time we passed each other it would be, 'Uh, huh', then next time we would throw a real dirty look. This would be proper Sergio Leone stuff: our eyes would narrow to a squint, I'd blow on my trigger fingers to limber them up; Colin's hand would be poised and dangling by his side.

Then the knives would come out. '*Draw!*' Quick as a flash my knife is out and, before we know it, it's sticking out of his leg. Colin's rolling about in agony clutching at it and screaming the house down. And I'm thinking it's just as well we didn't have arms dealers as parents or I'd be scraping him off the walls. All the time the record is still going – it's not really the right music for quick getaways so, instead of running away (as you always used to at that point), I felt myself swaggering away up the street in fast motion like Lee Van Cleef after too much campfire coffee. Great times.

When we were young though, we had a fascination with things like that. Nearly everyone I know has at least one scar from where they were messing around with a knife as a kid. Next time you're with your mates, ask around. It'll be like that scene out of *Jaws* when the three of them are in the boat comparing all their scars from shark attacks and things. At least I gave Colin something to show people, although the circumstances aren't as heroic as a shark bite.

One time we were out in the square indulging in a friendly game of Pass the Dart. And no, before you ask, I'm not going to explain the rules. We used to start close together and end up drifting to well over thirty feet apart, so each throw became more and more dangerous until one of you ended up doing the old King Harold impression. (Stop reading now if you can't work out who got the dart in his head!) He was lucky actually, 'cos this thing had just missed his eye by a fraction – or, rather, *I* was lucky it had just missed. All of a sudden this gadgey (*Gadgey*: according to our friends at *The Concise Oxford Dictionary*, a gadgey is a Makem term for a man, sometimes of a radgey nature. *Radgey*: going or gone a bit mental – i.e. getting radged up) came running out of his house and scooped Colin up in his arms. There was blood everywhere and he was really screaming this time. That's when I realised it was a bit more serious than usual. Poor kid. He reminded me of a badly deformed Dalek with the dart sticking out of his head. So I'm following along going, 'It's all right, mister. I'll take him home. He'll be all right.' It's when someone intervenes that you know it's serious. That was one of the first times I was aware of the consequences as well. I knew I'd get it ... an eye for an eye and all that. I was just praying my dad wouldn't come at me with a dart in his hand. I got a right old lashing. Don't try that at home, kids, there just isn't the room.

Colin wasn't always the innocent victim, though; he had this trick he would always pull to land me in the shit. Get this, the devious bastard. He'd spit up into the air and throw his head down so the back was now at the top. Then he would manoeuvre himself so that the spit landed on the back of his head! Next he'd run to my mam or dad and say that I'd spat on him. If that's not the mind of a genius at work I don't know what is. He should have been running the space programme. He had me stitched right up. How the hell can you get out of that? I'd get a right clip round the ear for being a dirty pig and he'd get the poor baby treatment. He would always throw me this sly look as well as he was being led away for biscuits or whatever, and so I'd be shouting that he spat on himself and I would get told off even more for making up stories. Some things you just can't win. I bet he lay there for hours at night plotting that one.

Now if you're thinking that I got off lightly in all this, just remember that I had an older sister who, at the time, was a proper, *proper* tomboy. We made the washhouse into a gang hut one time with carpets and everything. Our Sue was around fifteen years old and I would have been around fourteen. Within the gang there was a bit of a power struggle going on – we both wanted to be leader. Our egos were too big to be partners, so the scene was set for a hostile takeover. Next thing I knew she picked up a brush (of the dustpan and brush variety) and pounded it straight into my head, handle first. It snapped off, leaving this fucking handle stuck in my head! I think it freaked everyone out at the time. It was the most hostile takeover bid you've ever seen. We had just watched *West Side Story* that day and what a film that was: the Sharks and the Jets, I think that was my first experience of that kind of lifestyle and the romance and mystique that went along with it. Sue must have been a bit moved by it all as well.

I got my own back a while later when we were having what started out as a fun fight. They never did stay fun for long, though, did they? We were fighting and I chased Sue into the kitchen. She was quick off the mark and locked the door behind her. The door had a glass panel, and without thinking I put my fist straight through it trying to get her. Not one of my best moves, but Jack Nicholson would have been well proud. My wrist was cut and bleeding immediately. This was where I decided to go for the injured child routine. If in doubt, try owt. When you've got an injury, who do you go to first? Your dad doesn't go all soppy, does he? It's not that dads don't care. I am one and we do. But when you want the full sympathy vote you have to make it count, so you make a beeline straight for Mammy and turn the waterworks on at exactly the right time. Not that I had to act hurt – remember, my wrist was pouring blood and, believe it or not, it did hurt. The shops were only a few minutes away, so I found her in the middle of the supermarket and bawled my eyes out. I don't think that *Ian bleeding all over the place* was on her shopping list that day. But if I hadn't gone for the sympathy vote I might have got a bollocking for breaking the glass, you see.

I think as a child I was pretty much just your normal everyday kid. Find someone who didn't get into little bits of bother when they were growing up and you've found yourself a liar. It's human nature. Freeman Nature. We weren't brought up on violence and I had a very stable and loving upbringing. My mam hates violence. Can't stand it. We'd be in for it if we were caught fighting in the street or something. My mates knew this and would wind me up so much that I'd end up giving them a slap. Brian Summers was the main culprit, so as soon as I'd dished out a light slap he'd be straight round to knock on our door to grass. I'd get called home to have a rather heavier slap dished out. And this was my mate! I wish his mam had told him that it was wrong to grass on a mate. Absolutely no morals in those days!

Kids have the most mischievous minds in the world. Far more than they're given credit for. Our Colin with the spitting trick was pure calculated evil. Then there were other things, like wrapping dog shit up in paper, putting it outside someone's door, setting fire to it, ringing the bell, running away, then watching what happened. Everyone used to come out and stamp it out every time. That stunt is to kids' pranks what *The Third Man* is to films – an absolute classic. (Or would it be *The Turd Man*?) It goes back to what I mentioned about imagination. We were the best thinkers in the world. I may be wrong here, but I'll bet even Aristotle didn't come up with this next one: another belter. Let's do this one like Janet Ellis would have if they ever had it on *Blue Peter*. Clear your throat and assume the bubbly kids' TV presenter voice:

'First of all make sure mums and dads leave the room … OK, kids, this is what you do. Get some superglue out of the kitchen drawer and a tin of emulsion paint from the garden shed. Next you glue up the locks of the garage door of someone you don't like … That bastard at number 24 who kept your footy the other week is a prime target. Pretty tame, you might think, but hold on … Remember to take along with you the second ingredient: the tin of emulsion. Next, you pour it all over the path (cover a good area to be safe) in front of the garage door. This is where it is not good to have an adult present. Make sure your mate stands on the corner to keep toot. Once you have done that and are satisfied that there is no evidence – run!'

If you do it at night, then the paint will still be wet the next day and that's the beauty of it. Your target has to step into the paint and only then do they discover the locks are jammed. Do they then take their shoes off and go back in the house? Do they wash or bin the shoes? If they don't clean it properly, it ends up all over their tyres as well. The possibilities are endless and they have to deal with all these dilemmas before they can even think about the lock. You could even go as far as nicking the car first – now that *would* be funny – but that's not even a suggestion. You could just park it across the street with the locks glued. I'm not saying I've ever done this; I'm just saying I've heard of it.

Up into my teens I got into one or two scrapes at school as well, but again it was nothing serious. The only half-serious thing I did was with my mate Terry Willams. We were sitting in class once and we both excused ourselves to go to the toilet. This was just before bonfire night, so as you can imagine the streets at night were like Beirut. You weren't allowed fireworks in school. At all. But we decided we would give it a try. I didn't tell a lie, though – I made sure I went to the toilet before we embarked on our mission of mayhem. We had a packet of those little ten pence rockets that let off an almighty scream. (If you don't know the ones I'm talking about, you probably know them as those little *two quid* rockets that let off an almighty scream.) *Mini Rockets.* We made our way to the longest corridor the school had to offer and positioned ourselves at one end. We had a countdown, then ignition, and watched them screeching and screaming along the floor, bouncing off walls and classroom doors on the way. After lift-off we legged it back to the class and were safely back in our seats. That was when the headmaster came in to ask if a certain two boys had just been out of class at the same time ... Houston, we have a problem. We were given the cane for that one. Teachers always have a habit of overreacting, don't they? It's not like we were trying to recreate the gunpowder plot or anything; we were just having a laugh. They should start having prank days in schools so everyone can get everything out of their system at the same time and it's all over with. *Then* you can punish them all you want for being silly beggars if they do it before or after.

The kind of things we got up to was nothing like the kind of shit you can pull now and get away with: answering back, shouting, swearing, spitting, hitting, kicking – and that's just the teachers! Seriously, though, there is an alarming amount of violence that goes on towards teachers today and back then it was completely unheard of. In some schools teachers get threatened and some have even been killed just for doing their job. All they are trying to do is prepare you for life and make a difference. It's madness.

Terry Willams, Shaun Irving, Davey Mackle and Jimmy Humble were the lads I was hanging around school with at the time. All we were interested in was causing a bit mischief to make the days a bit more bearable. Mischief made school worth going to. If you couldn't have a laugh there, there wasn't much point in going in. I only ever bunked off once or twice and my dad and his belt convinced me that school was worth going to. The only time he ever hit me was for playing truant, and I'd deserved it. Normally he would just go along with what my mam said and, if he ever so much as raised his voice to you, you'd be bricking it for ages until you knew it was OK to come out of hiding. The mother will dish out all the minor punishments, like a quick slap or a good yelling, but, when it moves on to a more serious crime, it's the father's department. Like I say, a quick belt across your arse is an instant fuck-up deterrent.

One day a week we got to go to college in the morning instead of school. What an excellent idea. We'd get to school and then get taken over there on one of those luxury coaches; one of them ones with no air conditioning, boiling hot, state of the art, spring up your arse, wheels hanging off etc. Evel Knievel driving. And brought back after lunch. When I eventually meet my guardian angel I'm going to thank him big time. Terry Willams and me took Engineering. I'd go as far as saying it was the bollocks. One morning we got to the room and went to our usual seats. As I sat down I let my arms fall by my sides and my right hand fell into something. I looked down and there was this massive pot of oil and my hand was in it. It must have been from an oil change or something.

Next thing Terry knows I'm up on my feet and flicking it at him. Not all of it hit, but enough of it went on his face and clothes. I was laughing away without really noticing that he had come over for a quick dip. As I turned to face him he let me have it in true Batman style. Kerr-splattt! Right in the eye! I wouldn't stand for that and picked the whole tin up and was half chasing him, half threatening him. If you were one of the other kids watching this, you would have anticipated exactly what was going to happen long before we had any idea. The basics of it are that Terry got a good coating but so did someone else. Instead of a teacher, we now had the Creature from the Black Lagoon to throw us out of the class. How he managed to teach the rest of them I'll never know. Not only must he have *been* slick; he was also an oil slick. I know I've said that teachers have to put up with a lot, but this was just a bit of laughable banter. He took it reasonably well, we thought. That was until ...

Next day at school we were told that we were no longer welcome at college. Marvellous. I knew we should have feathered him while we were at it. He obviously wasn't as good humoured as we'd imagined. And what about my dad and the fuck-up deterrent? This is where my mam stepped in to save the day. Not only did she save my bacon; she effectively saved the entire pig farm. She had the bright idea that on a college day I had to get ready for school as per usual and go over to my sister's place for the morning, wait until after dinner and then go to school. Perfect. If my dad ever found out he'd go ape shit. Let's hope no one tells him, then. *Right?*

A great thing about my dad was that he used to stick up for me if I was blamed for something and he knew I had nothing to do with it. I'll have to fill you in with a bit of background information before I tell you this one.

Shaun Irving got knocked over once and it was pretty bad. He was hit after trying to cross the road in front of the bus he'd just got off. Both his legs were messed up, so he was in chalks for six months or so. When they were taken off he was unable to walk until he got his strength back in them so he was in a wheelchair for quite some time afterwards. It wasn't that bad for Shaun, though, 'cos he could lay it all on by saying he was a poor raspberry ripple and muggins here would push him around all over the place. Even I was susceptible to the sympathy vote.

I was pushing him along one day and we decided to go down a really steep hill for a laugh. Off we went and before we knew it a bloody police car had pulled up alongside us and we had this twat telling us to pull over. He was getting well into it. I'm sure he thought we were Bo and Luke Duke or something. He was doing all the actions of an enthusiastic TV cop. Once we pulled our vehicle over, we could not stop laughing. I wish you could have seen it. Shaun's looking around for his licence and registration and I'm thinking that this has got to be the first time in history that a wheelchair has been stopped for speeding. It turned out that the friendly bobby was as far from being friendly as was humanly possible. In short: a right cunt. I know some of you are thinking, Come on, Ian. A policeman being a cunt? Get away. (Before I go on any further here, you may be genuinely offended at reading such obscenities, but if you looked up from this book now and clocked him, you'd go, 'Christ. He's a right cunt, him.')

He just wouldn't believe that Shaun was wheelchair-bound. A real barrel of compassion this copper was. The next thing he did was force Shaun to stand up. Really. I was going off it and shouting at him that he couldn't walk, but he was having none of it. In the end Shaun was made to stand up and he just toppled over. Remind me again why the police never win any popularity prizes. This one was obviously no PR genius. As soon as he saw this happen he got into his car and took off. He didn't bother to apologise, let alone help; he just fled the scene of his crime. The only good bit was that I called him a wanker to his face and he didn't dare do a thing about it. Later on, Shaun's folks phoned to make a complaint but we didn't know who the copper was or anything about him (other than that he was a you-know-what, but if they had used that description there would still be investigations around the entire police force going on today).

So there's a story within a story. I was telling you about my dad, remember, and the time he stood up for me. Shaun was now out of his wheelchair and on crutches, which meant he could start going back to school. Me 'n' Hopalong gets to class one morning and there's a bit of a delay 'cos the store shed had been screwed overnight. It was some Technical Whatever class, and the store had, or had once had, all the equipment in it. The teacher walks in and he really hates us. We used to call him Cabbage Head, because his head looked exactly like a fucking cabbage – baldy, with a ring of hair round the back and sides. Not sure if that was the only reason he hated us but, because he did, he hauled our arses in front of the whole class and accused us of stealing all the stuff from the shed. If I've ever heard of someone having a laugh, it was now, but this bloke was deadly serious. He really meant it. I'm going, 'You're telling me that we came here last night and helped ourselves to the entire contents of that shed and made off with it?' He's answering back with, 'Yes, you did', and I'm saying, '*How?*' How the hell can you manage to rob something that is a three-man job with only two people, and one of them is on crutches? How do you carry the loot away? Why would we want all this stuff anyway? If anyone has any theories, please let me know.

I wasn't taking that kind of shit. Before he could ask me where I was the day JFK was shot, I was straight home and told my dad. He went totally ballistic. Firstly, he knew I would never steal. Never. He asked me just to make sure and I told him no. He wasn't one of those who would fly off the handle only to find out that I'd been guilty all along. Now he knew that we hadn't just committed the great store room robbery and was on the warpath. We went up to school and paid the teacher a visit. My dad didn't hit him or threaten him. He did it with style and class, and he made sure that Cabbage Head apologised to Shaun and me in front of the same class he'd accused us in front of. We left with the faint smell of teacher's pooh in the air. I already knew it, but right then my dad was an instant hero.

It was also in my early teens that I got my first experiences of court. Going to court is no picnic at the best of times, and can be a daunting one when you're only a youngster. I was first in at twelve years old but that was simply for being in the wrong place at the wrong time. The two local schools used to hate each other and would always be fighting up on Bunny Hill. This happened practically every week, so after the first few times it wasn't really a big deal any more. I happened to be walking past and heard everything going on, so I went over to see if any of the lads were in amongst it all. Before I'd even got close to the action, a police van pulled up and I was dragged in for being a part of it. There were all these kids in the back who I'd never seen before and to look at them it was obvious that they had been fighting, while I didn't have a scratch on me. I still use that excuse when I'm arrested, but it isn't quite as effective these days. They tried to do me for some sort of behavioural nuisance thing, but I was able to get off on account of being totally innocent.

A year later I had a more serious run-in. There was me, our Colin and a couple of others from the square and we were messing around in Sunderland town centre, in an alleyway just next to the train station. We were carrying on as usual and stumbled across these canisters of yellow spray paint. They must have been used for filling in bits of road markings we assumed. The messing around turned that bit messier. The only reason we didn't end up like four miniature La Las is 'cos the canisters were already virtually empty. There was no other use for them except to throw them at each other. See what I mean now about making your own entertainment? But you don't really find throwing cans at your mates that entertaining for long, so we tossed them over the nearest wall and forgot about it. As were walking away the station police collared us. Unknown to us the wall backed on to the station itself and beneath it was a glass canopy. Correction – there had been a glass canopy, about five minutes previously. It's not like we did it on purpose, though. We claimed accidental vandalism, but it was no use when it went to court. We were all ordered to pay for the damages. We went from throwing the can at each other to carrying the can for each other. Luckily we didn't get too much grief at home for it. It was mainly the shame of being in court that they didn't like – that, and the fact that I'd got Colin involved.

* * * * *

I was now turning into your average teenager. Build wise, one of the first things you'd expect is that I was this strapping, well-built lad. Wrong. I was a skinny kid to be honest and wasn't really much of a fighter as a youngster. When our Kim moved out, my dad set about turning the spare bedroom into a gym for Colin and me. He didn't force us into training or fighting, though, I think it's more of a curiosity thing that a lot of teenagers go through, wanting to hit the bag and lift weights. My dad didn't do things by half. He really went to town on the renovations. We had his old army kit bag full of sand and foam that we used as a punch bag, and we had a chin-up bar and weights bench in there as well.

My mam was less than enthusiastic about the whole thing, especially when she saw all the holes in the rafters of the ceiling the chains went through to secure the equipment. She couldn't really say much about it by then, though, and eventually she was fine about it. The golden rule to anyone is to consult with the woman of the house before doing any drastic handiwork – something that we'd overlooked. Having said that, I think she was a lot happier to have us in the gym rather than roaming around the streets at night. It was really good fun. We weren't that serious about training really, it was more of an after-school hobby, but it was by hitting this bag that my punch developed from a boy's into a teenager's. The sand in the bag used to drop to the bottom and it was rock solid and great for strengthening the uppercut. Dad was always at hand to help us along. He was the ABA Boxing Champion back in the forties, after all, so we had a bit of a genetic advantage straight away, a bit of a leg-up. Dad had been a PT instructor in his army days and always kept himself fit. When we were a bit younger in school he used to run fitness schemes for us in his spare time. Not like full-on regimental stuff, just showing us that fit can be fun. He was really good like that.

In school I started to show a keen interest in sports. I was on the school teams for cricket, cross-country, table tennis – everything. My main interest was rugby. I used to play scrum half and had a few unorthodox tactics up my sleeves. When we'd go into a scrum I'd look directly at people on the other team and blow kisses to them so I'd force them into coming for me and fouling. I loved to see them get so wound up and frustrated. They would lose their rag and that meant it would put them off their game. As soon as you lose your focus in anything, competitive or otherwise, you lose it completely. It used to work every time. I played rugby for Sunderland for a short time but soon found out that they were all toffee-nosed brats. They really thought they were something special, until they found it was a lot harder to look down a broken nose at someone. I ended up playing for Belford House. The lads there were excellent and I enjoyed playing there for quite some time. Another pet hate of mine: people who go around and think that they're better than others. I'm not saying that *everyone* who's into rugby and the whole culture around it are snobs, or think they are part of the elite or what have you, but a great deal of them have lost touch with reality.

My one and only fight at school was with Davey Spence – 'Spegga'. An argument started over a pencil, of all things. In class one day he nicked my pencil and said it was his. If it had been his, then there wouldn't have been a problem, but I'm the kind of person who won't sit back and take any kind of shit. Especially since it was mine in the first place! So after all the 'It's mine, no it's not, yes it is' malarkey, I snatched it off him and he wasn't too chuffed at all. This kid was the second-best fighter in the school and he said he was going to get me on the way home. That's how bright he was – he thought a pencil was worth fighting over. A *pencil*! You can't really argue with someone who has the intellectual capabilities of a bucket full of shit, but he also had the reputation that fighters only dream of. This is a lethal combination to come across at any age. It seems like nothing now, but when you're in the fourth year of a comprehensive and get threatened by one of the hard lads you shit yourself. Needless to say, I shat myself.

The argument was enough to keep me on edge until home time. I had that feeling of butterflies in my stomach and had real paranoia all day. He could have been anywhere; you look around and everyone looks the same in their uniforms. That's how on edge I was; even the sixth-form girls were starting to look like him. The bell went and as usual I walked home with Terry Willams. I couldn't relax. I tried to be as calm as possible but I was a real bag of nerves and was completely bricking it.

'Ian, you're gonna have to get stuck into him if he comes up to you. You can't just stand there and let him hit ya. He'll fuckin kill ya,' Terry told me. Nicely put, don't you think? He'd put it in the most basic of forms, but that's all it needed. The basics were that I was going to get a pasting. But when you're that age and in a fight you only have a few options really: the first one is you can hope that your older (and harder – that's always a bonus) mate walks round the corner and saves you. The problem here is that, unlike the song that goes with the TV series, friends are not always there for you (in those days they weren't, anyway). And that's when the rain starts to pour. In this case, though, there wasn't a mate in sight (except Terry, remember) so we'll move on to the second option: you let them knock you about a bit and hope they leave you in one piece; they'll soon get bored and move on to some other poor kid. Of course, they may not get bored straight away at all, in which case you're in for a tough time. The third option is that you might dare to hit them back, you know, retaliate a bit; the downside to this one is that you'll make them mad or madder and they'll really go to town on your arse and give it a right proper kicking. For any young kid to be in this position it can make your life at school a living hell: it's a tough call all right. If you stand up to a bully you've got to do it right or it can easily backfire. Remember all the trouble the lads in *Grange Hill* had in trying to nail that Gripper Stepson? Fuck me. It backfired a few times but they got him in the end. I don't mean to sound like I'm making light of it here, because I am so dead against bullies – anyone who knows me knows that.

So here we are, walking home, and Terry turns round: 'Ian, they're coming, they're fucking coming.' This is when I felt my heart dislodge and make its way up to my mouth – which, in turn, was doing a spot-on impression of the Sahara Desert. I was just thinking, Oh, God, here we go. Good old Terry offered to hold my blazer for me – I can't imagine what I would have done if he hadn't been there. I just had time to get my heart back in place when I heard this voice: 'Come here, Freeman, I'm going to punch your fucking head in.' He didn't waste his words either. He was no Shakespeare, you understand. If he had been, then my reply would have been, 'Nay, as they dare. I will bite my thumb at them, which is disgrace to them if they bear it.' But as you can see, it wouldn't really have worked wonders for my chances of survival, would it? (To anyone not into Shakespeare, that quote is from *Romeo and Juliet* and it's supposed to insult your opponent. Can't think why we talk so differently now ...)

At this point I probably should mention the fourth option from that list earlier: the fourth option is an elaboration on the third – you go a bit further than daring to hit them back. You do what bullies anywhere in the world can't handle. You stand up to them. You've really got to turn it on. You hit them hard and you hit them fast. Now you can guess which option I decided to take.

It was obvious what was about to happen with Spegga and I didn't see any point in trying to run away. I decided to stand my ground and face my fears. If I did run, I'd be running forever. I took my blazer off and handed it to Terry, and turned round just as this hard case drew near. I caught a glimpse in his eyes straight away, I don't even think he was expecting me to turn. From that millisecond I knew he wasn't worth shit. You can always see it in people's eyes and this was an early lesson for me – right then he'd lost the fight. He probably knew it as well. I knew I had to get him first and so I just went for it. I squared up to him and punched him in the face with my right. It had to count and I couldn't allow him any chances. He didn't even have time to put up any defence. That first one sent him staggering backwards, so I followed in with a left and another right and sent him packing. The left one popped his nose and the second right-hander made sure he was floored. I moved in for the kill and beat the living shit out of him. No method, just pure madness: rights, lefts, headbutts; I hit him with everything I had. In no time at all I was on top of him, punching fuck out of his face, when I heard his mates shouting, 'You better let him up.' I looked over my shoulder and there were three of them shouting at me. I saw Terry still there clutching my blazer (cheers, Tel). I don't know why, but I did what they'd asked! I actually stopped punching into him and let him stand up.

Well, to say he was standing up is a bit of an exaggeration. I mean, he was on his feet sure enough, but he couldn't exactly stand. There we were, facing each other; he's out of breath and red in the face with fist marks and all these little white stringy bits in his mouth from where he's trying to catch his breath; and I'm standing there, cool as fuck, just measuring him up for round two. I don't really think he knew what was going on by now, so I just lunged at him, got him back on the ground and hit him with the full artillery. I almost felt sorry for him for a bit – no kidding, he looked like he'd just run a marathon and got hit by a bus as he crossed the finishing line. If it weren't him, though, it would have been me lying beneath him and he would have been dishing it out. With that in mind I couldn't show any sympathy.

That was it, basically. His mates didn't even try to do anything once I'd decided he'd had enough. They had just watched their great white hope get a right old slapping, so with their leader lying there they didn't really have enough brains between them to react. There's another trait that bullies and their cronies have – they're all usually sackless bastards as well. I got my blazer from Terry and walked the rest of the way home nursing and rubbing my fists. And I had a few scuff marks on my knees from where I'd knelt down to hit him. Small price to pay, though – his face was covered in scuff marks (and I'm sure I burst a few zits for him as well). It was an excellent feeling: the blood pumping and that rush of pure adrenaline you get. I was on top of the world. Now, I don't want anyone to get the wrong idea from that little story. Violence isn't always the best way to settle something, but sometimes it's the only way. This lad and his mates simply wanted to beat me up and they only went after me because there were four of them. Sure, I could have approached him and said, 'Let's talk about it, I'm sure we can work this out', but what do you think would have happened? I was in no position to claim diplomatic immunity. I had to nip the thing in the bud. The best part of it was that I earned respect after that and certainly had no more trouble from the so-called hard case. He started it and I finished it. I definitely knew I had something special after that day. It had come to me so naturally. Respect was something I'd get used to later in life ... but you always have to earn it. Funny thing was, the next day one of his mates who had shouted for me to let Spegga up got me a Mars Bar from the tuck shop. Can you believe it? What a crawler! I've got to name him and shame him:

Johnny Hughes, you slimey-arsed bastard!

I know what you're wondering ... of course I ate it. A Mars a day helps you work, rest and bray, after all.

Looking back it was like it was my first ever bout: there was Terry my corner man offering advice and holding my top. The fight itself, when I stared him out then took him straight to the floor. The referee telling us to get up. Then taking him back to the floor to finish him off. Weird. That was my only fight at school but, as I say, I was never a fighter back then. It must have been in me – I proved that – but the difference was I didn't have that instinct to fight then. Now I have. It certainly put an end to any bullying straight away, but there are kids up and down the country and all over the world that are not so lucky. They have to go through it every day. I really feel for kids who are victims of bullying and I hope that one day they can overcome it.

What a way to make a living

AFTER SCHOOL YOU have the choice of putting what you've learnt to some use or going on to learned more. This is why your parents tell you to stick in there. After leaving school I was ready to do my real learning. It's a big, bad world out there and it's survival of the fittest. You can't stay a kid all your life. Like it or not, money makes the world go round.

That fight with Spegga took place right before I left school. It marked a big change for me. People always tell you to stand up to bullies, but it still takes a whole lot of balls. Luckily, mine are fucking huge. To me, it marked a different type of graduation, I was entering the big, bad world and at least I now knew I could handle myself. As we were getting on a bit, the lads in the square were starting to drift apart. I still saw them around – but that's when you tend to find you have one mate and the rest become acquaintances.

* * * * *

I left school at sixteen years old and was working fiddle in a scrap yard. My first job! I was now (un)officially a working man. I was working on the aluminium bailer, cutting all the shite off the aluminium and making it into bails. I suppose every glamorous lifestyle has to start somewhere ... I'm proud to admit that I was a hard worker back then. Not that I was shoved up chimneys when I was five or anything, but I wasn't scared of hard work. After that I moved on to the iron bailer (no prizes for guessing what that involved) and other odd jobs in and around the yard. And so began my career of scrapping for a living.

It turned out that the boss was a right piss-taking (and fat) twat and was trying to use me. I was earning five quid a day – that's five quid for working your sixteen-year-old bollocks off from seven in the morning till a six-at-night finish. It was like slave labour to me then, and the feeling was made worse when I found out that everybody else in the place was on fifteen quid a day. It didn't seem fair that I was on a fiver. I told him so and asked when I was going to get a rise – his answer was that I'd get a tenner the following week, which turned into the week after, and the week after that and so on. As I said: a right piss-taking twat and there was no way I was going to take any more, no way at all.

In the end he said, 'OK then, you prove to me that you can work as hard as everyone else and you'll get the same pay as everyone else.'

Fair enough, I thought, I could do that. I knew I could make him eat his own words (he'd eaten everything else in sight) and I wanted to see him choke on them. Every fortnight in the scrap yard there used to be a count on how many kilos were being smelted and put into ingots. This was my chance to prove myself and for the next two weeks I worked like a dog – no, make that a pack of dogs ... on speed. On the next count I had beaten the yard record. Imagine that! I was a young lad and had just broken a record set by some gadgey! I couldn't believe it. All that hard graft had paid off and I was pleased as punch. I'd proved a lot to myself and to my boss – or so I thought. I went over to him: 'Do I get my rise now, then?'

Did I fuck get it. He said, 'You'll get it next week.'

'Well, fuck you, you fat bastard, I'm not coming back,' I shouted as he hit the floor.

No, *no*. I didn't hit him. I know that's what you were expecting. Come on, I'd just broken the yard record, for God's sake – I was knackered. I just shoved him as hard as I could, which must have been hard, because he went over like a huge Weeble and he didn't even get the chance to wobble; my hands were covered in horrible thick grease and dirt as well. Some of the lads watching had a right good laugh at his expense as he crashed to the floor; he'd treated them like shit as well, so I was only doing what they had no doubt been dying to do for ages. The thing was, this bloke was a friend of my dad. My dad was a bit of a boy back then, as you've probably guessed, and was known a bit around town. When I got home and he heard what happened, he dragged me back there kicking and screaming. It was right embarrassing. Here I was on top of the world; I'd beaten the record, made the boss look a right arse, got laughs *and* respect from the others – my dad brought me right down to earth with a bang. When we got there I can remember this fat bastard with two dirty handprints on his chest (from where I'd shoved him). He was still red in the face and was saying, 'No, I don't want him back 'cos he swore at me.'

So, obviously, I didn't get the job back. My dad had made me keep my work gear on as well, in case he let me start back, so I felt a bit of a twat standing there with my haversack over my shoulder. I think he had to save face in front of that lot who had just been laughing at him, you know, as an example of what would happen to them ... They probably would have been as bothered as I was if he had sacked them. If my dad wasn't there the temptation to hit the bastard would have been too hard to resist. It wasn't much fun that job, and I was glad to see the back of it. You could say it was crap working in scrap.

I didn't really take another job for a while after that. It wasn't that I'd turned hippy lazy or anything. I didn't need a great deal of money to get by on and so I took life easy on the dole for a bit. I'm sure there's a lot of people out there who are familiar with having to sign on. It's the pits. They are very skilled at making you feel useless – but don't worry, it's their job to do just that. They have this short-sightedness where they can't see past the edge of their desk, if you know what I mean. I'd go to sign on first thing in the morning so I could beat all the queues and it was like stumbling on the set of the latest *Living Dead* movie. The staff, I mean, and I'm not kidding. Wandering around trying to look busy; sitting staring into space. They are either half asleep and just want to get through their day hassle free, or they are the type that will scrutinise every last detail about you. Just keep in mind that no matter how bad the place is, how bad it makes you feel, you only have to be in the place a few minutes every fortnight. The ones that are trying to grind you down and catch you out are the ones who are stuck there every day nine to five. Apparently it's even worse now. But don't think that because I've just defended you that I condone what you're doing. I was just getting a few things off my chest. Why should everyone else support you? Get a job, lazy-arsed parasite!

While I was signing on I was just enjoying myself really. No commitments, no pressures, doing exactly what I should have been doing. I was the original 'Wanderer' from the song. Shaun and me both had motorbikes so we used to roam around (and round and round and round and round ...) all the time. I had a YB 100 and, as I was a smoker back then, most of my money was going on cigarettes and petrol. It was great, but there were a couple of people who didn't think my *Easy Rider* lifestyle was so great: my parents. And now, of course, I can see exactly why they were concerned. Back then it was, 'Do whatever and worry about the consequences later.' I'm a parent now and to think that any of my lot would end up doing that kind of thing is worrying. I don't think I'd like the idea of my son tearing around on a motorbike the way I used to, either. Not just because I didn't have a care in the world, but also because roads seem to be a lot more dangerous now. A few years ago, I witnessed a motorcycle accident and it really had quite an effect on me. It stayed in my head for a long time afterwards, seeing the guy lying there and everyone being unable to save him. It's a horrible thing to have to watch and it sends all kinds of questions through your head. It was on the A1 motorway – there had been a crash and people were slowing down because of it; that was when a car ploughed into the back of a motorbike. The driver couldn't have seen the bike in time. The rider was knocked off and died there on the road. He'd been travelling with his brother, who was in front of him – he'd ridden back to find him. I later found out that his name was Christopher McCourt and he was in the Army. It was horrific ... Fucking awful.

The wind upon your face
Riding free like a bird
Nothing but good memories
Not a care in this world

On this long road of freedom
You no longer travel on
I saw you drift away
Now you're gone, gone, gone, gone, gone

You were only a stranger to me, to me
I never knew you at all
You became part of me, of me
I saw you fall

All this sadness I feel, I feel
Like a friend would feel, feel the same
I could not call out to you, to you
Never knew your name

The wind upon your face
Riding free, free like a bird
Nothing but good memories
Not a care in this world

On this long road of freedom
You no longer travel on
I saw you drift away
Now you're gone, gone, gone, gone, gone

I saw you fall.

'Unknown Soldier', Ian Freeman

* * * * *

I was just taking each day as it came, one adventure after another. The future was something in the distance, like a spot on the horizon that I was never quite going to reach. I didn't really give any thought to the future; I had no plans, only what I'd be doing the next day. From my parents' point of view their son was doing nothing with his life, but from my point of view I was doing everything every day. I was happy, but then again I was wasting a lot of time and I couldn't really expect my parents to support me while I was. It was time to knuckle down.

I needed to get myself a job. And rightly so. At that time I thought that having a motorbike, a packet of cigarettes and the open road in front of me was freedom. When you get yourself a bit of life experience you realise that it's money that gives you freedom. It gives you chances you couldn't take with only half a packet of Bensons in your back pocket. It was my sister, Kim, who helped me get another job. She was working in a shoe shop at the time and a vacancy had come up there. I was a bit reluctant to take it, but she'd gone out of her way to put in a good word, so I thought why not give it a go. You've got to knock on every door. You don't know you'll like something until you try it.

I was seventeen years old and working. Coming to terms with it was a shock to the system, but when my payslips started coming in things started to brighten up. That's when you realise that riding around like Dennis Hopper all the time doesn't get you the little luxuries like buying clothes, going to the pictures and impressing the ladies. Still not all glamour and excess, but I felt I was moving up the ladder all the same. At first I was based in Gateshead and then Wallsend, though I was working for the same company in both cases. Wallsend is in Newcastle and Gateshead is just over the river Tyne, only a kick up the arse away from Sunderland. In the space of a year I went from assistant to assistant manager, but still I was really only a kid. Not bad though, only eighteen years old and in a better job than Al Bundy, the patron saint of all shoe salesmen.

The boss was a *proper* perv. He'd pull stuff that you wouldn't dream of getting away with these days. OK, it was probably just a bit of laddish banter, but this bloke had his passport ready and was sitting right on the border of Weirdsville. He used to angle the mirrors so you could get a good look up women's skirts. Seriously. At the back of the shop there was a cobblers, which essentially became the bird-watching hut. Now, this wasn't the kind of place where you would stumble across Bill Oddie with his flask of soup – this was the *other* type of bird-watching hut. It had a hatch with an innocent-looking opening that was the perfect tool for any conscientious pervert. You could get behind the counter and bend down to look through a gap – this took your eyeline directly to the mirrors, where you could see up every skirt. Looking at this thing from inside the shop you couldn't tell you were being watched. The women's shoes section was placed strategically in front of the hatch and you could always look from one mirror to another and get an eye full from almost anywhere. He may not have been the brightest bloke in the world, but he could outsmart Pythagorus when it came to angles.

> In the air, on top of a tram, a girl is sitting. Her dress lifted a little, blows out. But a block in the traffic separates us. The tramcar glides away, fading like a nightmare. Moving in both directions, the street is full of dresses which sway, offering themselves airily, the skirts lifting; dresses that lift and yet do not lift. In the tall and narrow shop mirror I see myself approaching, rather pale and heavy-eyed. It is not a woman I want – it is *all* women, and I seek for them in those around me, one by one ...
>
> *Henri Barbusse, L'Enfer (The Inferno), 1932*

That quote just about sums it up. The job itself was basically chatting up women for a living. *All* women. That's really what selling is when it comes down to it: it's flirting and flattering. You give the customer your undivided attention, you let them hear exactly what they want to hear, you flirt to some degree and you get a sale. You may be telling them a right load of balls and not mean any of it, but that is why you are there. It's escapism in a way: lads love it when they go into a shoe shop and a good-looking girl comes over and helps them. You feel special like you've been singled out from everyone else and you can't help but fall for her charms. If you are browsing around and a lad tries to help you it's like, 'Piss off and stop hassling me.' Women are no different. They love attention as much as we do. It's human nature, innit?

I'm the first to admit that I was damn good at that job. Everyone (especially the ladies) who came in I saw as a challenge; something I had to conquer. It was always a race to get over there first. The shop was a good place simply to hang out in. This one woman used to come in just to listen to the tapes we played; I still managed to sell her pairs of shoes. If they were older I could be the little loveable rascal or I could be someone they wanted to mother and take care of. If they were more my age, I could go for all-out flirting or 'silent mysterious'. You had to adapt to each and every situation, read what was going on in an instant and apply your skills to it. I loved it – loved working with people and learned the whole psychology of people, reactions and communication along the way. This was real education. It was a great way of developing my perception of people: never preconceive, you'll always be proved wrong.

Another scam the manager had was when the shoes were a fraction too tight. This is when we would take them into the cobblers and use our special shoe-stretching machine – or broom shank to you and me. We'd be riving at them with the broom handle and then take them back through, trying to disguise being a bit out of breath.

In the end I was paid off but I tried not to let it bother me too much; there wasn't enough work for us and we were all let down as gently as possible. One of those things when head office makes the decision and the workers bear the brunt of it. The shop went into liquidation and Malcolm, the boss, was relocated back to Gateshead. Before that happened, I had so much time off anyway that I never really counted myself as working there. Something happened to me prior to that, something that meant I didn't go to work or leave the house for a very long time. Something that only my family knows about. Until now.

The day that changed my life forever

MY BOSS MALCOLM and me were enjoying a boozy night out in Newcastle after work. It had been just an average day as usual in the shoe shop, but in the pubs it was a really busy night. Come to think of it, even back then *every* night in Newcastle was busy. The bars were jam-packed and I was absolutely mortal drunk. It was nearing last orders and this is where the enjoyment stopped for me. The drink seemed to creep up on me and hit me like a truck. I was only eighteen years old and not used to drinking at all, and here I was in the middle of Newcastle with someone who was used to drinking a lot of beer. I just couldn't handle it at all.

In the toilets of Bar 42 I took a long look in the mirror and knew it was time to call it a night. I assumed that both my eyes were red 'cos to see straight I had to keep one of them shut. I must have looked a sight. I came out, slurred some sort of goodbye and made my way up the stairs and out the door. The streets were just as packed as the bars. It was all the Madonna wannabes and massive fuck-off hairdos of the '80s everywhere you looked. I was staggering all over the place but managed to make the short distance to the Monument Metro station.

Now there I was, standing on the empty platform at Heworth. The journey from Newcastle was completely lost – not even a distant memory. It was that old 'Metro Time Machine Syndrome' that everyone seems to get. The gentle buzzing of the lights and the music still ringing in my ears created this weird, confusing state. Mix all that with the drink and you know what I'm talking about. It was like a different world – one I was not familiar with.

The Metro doors closed behind me and the train left the station. At first glance it could easily have been a group of lads just messing around on the opposite platform, and to them lot that's all it was. My eyes slowly began to focus and I could finally see what was going on. The group of lads messing about was, in fact, four skinheads, and they were kicking the shit out of what appeared to be a human figure on the ground. It was a horrible sight to see, like they were all just laying into a punch bag. There was a bombardment of Doc Martens literally raining down on this figure, this person; braces swinging, the shine of their bomber jackets and bleached jeans were a blur as they kicked and stomped all over it. They were shouting and laughing as they put the boot in to the poor bastard, and there were these almost haunting cries filling the station. Makes me shudder to even think about it. From my side of the platform I drew parallel to them: 'Hey, man, what the fuck are you doing?' It just came out. Pure emotion spurred on by anger. With no one else in sight I was the only fucker who could do anything about it. The skinheads stopped and legged it upstairs. Once they'd disappeared, the punch bag began to move. It got to its feet and walked unsteadily over the track to the platform I was on.

'You all right, mate?' The punch bag looked to be in his early twenties and was in a bad way. He said he was all right, but then again he couldn't see himself – he looked a thousand fucking miles from all right. He shook my hand and mumbled a thank you. It was obvious that he wouldn't realise how bad he was until the morning. After thanking me once more, he left.

The platform was empty again. I was still drunk but the shock seemed to sober me up a bit – or so I thought. The lights were still buzzing and they dazzled my eyes as I looked around to find my bearings. It was late and I had to catch the last bus home to Sunderland. I was smiling to myself as I climbed the stairs, gripped by a warm feeling to know that I had helped out someone who looked like they were in serious trouble.

I got to the top of the stairs, through the barriers and out into the night. Then I saw them ... it was the fucking skinheads. They definitely looked hard as fuck, no doubt about that. I stopped dead – about to head back into the station, when the ringleader looked over and clocked me. Shit. Too late. Fuck! Get outta there quick. I took off, tearing down the street as fast as I could with these bastards hot on my tail. I could feel my teeth banging together with every dodgy stride and I seemed to be getting nowhere. It was like I was running through treacle.

Panic and sheer determination were the only things carrying me. I was totally out of breath and lost. All I could do was run, but where the fuck was I? I had absolutely no idea. It was dark and cold. I could hear them gaining behind me, the boots getting louder like they were closing in on their prey. I bolted down an alley. It was a dead end.

Realisation sunk in and I slowed to a walk. I was fucking doomed and I knew it. Hands on knees and doubled over to catch my breath, I turned to confront the inevitable. I was like a trapped animal. My breath was coming out thick and fast. Then I heard the gang of boots stop running. Now I was trapped and *they* knew it. They turned the corner and I faced them to see sadistic grins approach – they could see the panic in me as my eyes darted round for escape. The moon lit the whole alleyway with an eerie whiteness; it made the whole scene seem even more surreal. The figures with white faces, dark shadows falling across their eyes making them look colder and inhuman, began to move in. They just lurched forward and took turns to bray the shit out of me. It was no contest. I couldn't do anything to stop what was going on. I might have stood half a chance if I was sober and there was only one of them – but bullies don't work alone, do they? Within seconds my face was cut and bleeding: I was winded and I was hurt.

Another roundhouse punch connected. They had all the time they needed to hit with pinpoint accuracy. I could see every punch, every kick, knee and elbow long before impact. It was like a scene from *Raging Bull*: black and white and going from real time to slow motion and back to real time, only I wasn't watching it – I was living it. All I could do was brace myself, I tried to put my hands up to protect my face but they just buckled under the immense force. My face was numbed and I could feel the throbbing of my burst lip and the taste of my blood. Sweat stung the cut on my forehead and the blood mixed with it and ran into my eyes, blinding me. I wiped at them furiously to prepare for the next flurry. In an attempt to shield myself I naturally went to the floor. It was too easy for them when I was standing and I didn't know what else I could do. They stopped for a second, one of them telling the others to back off, then I felt these hands clasp my collar and round my neck. I was hurled to my feet and from them I was held against the wall. I was headbutted in the face, smashing my nose and cracking my head off the wall behind me. The blood spilled down my face and clothes as I slumped down. I tried to stay low but there was no safe position to retreat to. The pain was intense; shooting right through my nose, into my head and down my spine.

How much longer would this go on for? Why did nobody help

me? I was down on my hands and knees and spat blood on to the damp paving. It looked like sticky black ink. I was kicked on the chin, snapping my head back. Before I could catch my breath a fist came lumbering down and caught the side of my head. By now I was practically unconscious. I really didn't think they were going to stop. It was like they were trying to torture me to within an inch of my life – possibly further. I picked myself up, only to have another fist crunch squarely into my nose. The pain shot through my face and the tears in my eyes obscured my vision even more. My whole face was numbed and throbbing. I was back to my hands and knees again and trying to crawl forward to safety. My back, head and shoulders were stamped on a few times and then I just gave way under the weight and my chin scraped on the floor as I hit it again.

Finally I was turned over. This huge skinhead sat astride me and took aim. It was the ringleader – a big, muscular and ugly fucker: He had the look of an escaped psychopath. For the first time I looked into his eyes and looked straight into pure madness. He looked completely deranged; his hands smelled of tobacco and then came the smell of something else on his breath. There wasn't time to pinpoint it. His fists drew back and began to pound into my face. The huge open mouth with strings of saliva from top to bottom, spitting and sucking in breath with each blow. The rest of his gang was egging him on. He grabbed my neck and raised my face up to his while he and one of the others searched my pockets. I was absolutely powerless to stop them. I felt myself crying inside as I could feel the hands rifling through my pockets. They took my watch and my money. Someone else moved in to snatch my ring and broke my finger as he rived at it. The huge bulging eyes and mouth were all I could see as this was going on. Anything of value was taken. Anything.

Blood was everywhere, it really was. Still this face was within inches of me; the expressionless, cold eyes scanning each cut and graze they'd inflicted. It was like he was inspecting his own handiwork. I don't know what he started to say, whether it was before or after, but I started to cough uncontrollably. Blood caught in the back of my throat was pushing its way out and splattering all over the fucker's face and shirt. My chest was still heaving as the bastard started lashing out and screaming all over again. Eyes bulging like a crazed animal, with only one thing on his tiny mind – he was poised to beat the remaining bit of life out of me. Simple as that. He was out of control. He dragged my face forward; smashing his head into it again and again. The first one fucked my nose up even more, the second made sure of it. I really didn't think there was anything left of it, to be honest – I certainly couldn't feel it and I couldn't breathe out of it, which was why I ended up gasping for breath and coughing up blood in the first place. It was smashed to fuck, along with the rest of me. Still coughing my guts up (by now there was vomit), I felt something hard smash me just above the right eye. It could have been a fist, head or boot – I was oblivious by now and back on my hands and knees. I was just trying to keep myself up and remain conscious. This was their cue to kick into me again. This time it was a real kicking – it was all of them, and they were fucking relentless. It was like we all knew they were gonna finish me there and then. I think I had tried to curl up into a ball, I don't know for sure. My instinct was screaming and pleading with me to get the fuck out of there. It was one after the other – *thump, thump, thump* – into my back and kidneys and head. They were silent with concentration. It was serious.

Where the strength came from I'll never know. I somehow rose to my feet and charged through them. It was my chance. My only chance. Any more punishment and I don't think I would have made it. I had to get out of there or they would have fucking killed me. My legs buckled as I tried to keep upright, desperate and determined, I staggered forward and dived through a privet hedge. Anything could have been on the other side of the hedge, but 'anything' looked the best option. I really didn't care. It could have been a thirty-foot drop for all I knew, but I had to risk it. A thirty-foot drop I knew I had a chance of surviving. I heard their voices behind me. Whether they had let me go or I had escaped I'll never know. Were these bushes here before? Nothing made sense. I didn't know what was happening. I was so tired and ready to drop. I was through the hedge and in someone's garden. The last thing I remembered was seeing lights and a house and knocking on the door. Someone must have opened it, but by then I had blacked out.

* * * * *

This was to be the turning point in my life. A lot of people have something that happens to them and it changes the course of their life, sometimes without them realising it. Well, I knew all about mine. That incident with the skinheads changed me and changed my life completely. Simple as that. I suppose it's hard for someone to understand if it hasn't happened to them – on second thoughts, make that *impossible* to understand. When it happened to me I was just your normal eighteen-year-old lad on the street. I didn't claim to be a hard nut and I hadn't been exposed to any real violence until then, it just wasn't a part of my life. Yeah, I mentioned the scrap at school, but this was a different thing altogether.

Something like that completely messes your head up – and I mean real psychological messiness. For ages I was asking myself all the 'what ifs' in the world and in doing that I was torturing myself even more. Deep down I knew there was nothing I could do to stop those people. I can look back at it now and realise that it was depression. It wasn't just the material things they had taken; they had taken my confidence, my self-respect and my self-esteem, like I was stripped of my personality. I remember just sitting around the house or lying on my bed. Not wanting to go out or do anything. During that time I lost touch with my friends, I couldn't bring myself to contact any of them. I was a real recluse. My family were great: they did everything they thought possible to help and I love them for it. I think it was really hard for them to watch me go through something like that and not know what to do. In that situation the right words to say are impossible. Your family will love you through all the bad times and will help you through anything. I think it's the things they can't see that are going on in your head – the mental problems as opposed to something physical that they can see – that make them feel helpless. It's probably the only thing in the world that they can't protect you from. It hurt them to see me suffering like that.

Those of you familiar with depression may be able to relate to this: it was like I had no energy and I had no will to get up in the morning. I was like a zombie. What was there to get up for? What was the point in getting ready when I wasn't going to go out? Then, when I did drag myself out of bed, I felt so deflated and exhausted I may as well have stayed there. But the more time I spent alone and in my room, the more time I spent in my own mind. I was locked in some kind of vicious circle where I was constantly torturing myself with all these thoughts. At the worst of it, my life wasn't worth shit to me. I didn't feel suicidal, but I didn't feel like going on. There didn't feel like anything in my life worth going on for. It was like I was in limbo. Depression is a massive build-up. It can send some people to a place from where they never quite return. I really had to battle with my mind to come out of it and I was getting myself into a hole. I needed to step up a gear to get out of it. It was a real struggle to stop myself from going under altogether, but I had to do it. I couldn't let those lowlife bastards beat me.

Getting out of that kind of hole is not an overnight thing. You can't just wake up and suddenly be OK. Each and every one of those problems that have built up in your head all have to be resolved and the only person who can do it is you. It took me well over a year before I can honestly say I was over the worst of it. I had scratches on my wrist where I'd had my watch ripped off and until those had healed up they were there to bring the whole thing back every day.

From then on I was a fighter – not just in the literal sense, but a fighter all the same. I had to be. Fuck or be fucked is the only way to describe it. That's how I've lived my life ever since and that's where all the rage comes from, or used to come from in my early days as a doorman. Anyone who fucked with me after that I just went for as if they were one of those skinheads. I really didn't care. I had no feelings for anyone. I wasn't beating up that person; I was beating up one of those cowards. A lot of people may not have understood my reasoning, but it was my way of dealing with things. Right then I think I could easily have killed someone with my bare hands. That's how dangerous and out of control they had made me. Sometimes I would be punching into someone who was already unconscious and would have to be dragged off. If they could do it to me, then I would do it to anyone. One thing that really gets to me is that in all the years since that happened those skinheads could actually have been in one of my pubs. One of those shitbags could have been standing next to me without me knowing it. *That* makes my fucking blood boil.

When I'm asked why I never wear a watch I always skate around the real reason. Since that night I can't bring myself to wear a watch, a ring, a necklace or even carry a wallet. That's how much it affected me. For Christmas after I'd had it stolen, my parents bought me a new watch to help me get over it. As soon as I opened the wrapping and saw what it was I cried my eyes out.

I couldn't bring myself to wear it. Those items have too many bad memories for me and I feel, that if I never wear them again, then it can't happen again. It won't happen again and I'll never let it happen again, that much I know. Ask me what I'd be like if that hadn't happened and I haven't got an answer. Just don't ask what I'd do to those skinheads if I saw them now.

I despise bullies. People who pick on someone smaller or weaker cannot be classed as human. They're scum. I'm the one who's hard as fuck now and I'd tear each and every one of them a brand new arsehole if I ever set eyes on them again. I don't blame the drink for that night; I blame a bunch of pricks. Maybe if I wasn't drunk I might not have got involved, who knows. It was just a reaction to the situation. The thought of them coming after me hadn't even entered my head. In the end it comes down to a bunch of cowards doing what cowards do. I went through hell to get here and I'm never going back. That incident eventually made me determined and strong. I think, if you can sink that far down that you can't get any lower and somehow pull yourself out of it, you're the strongest person alive. And that's not physical strength. That's strength of character; that's being emotionally strong.

Every time in this book that I talk about someone I've beaten up at work, someone who's angered me, crossed me or my family – remember this story each time. Remember what I went through and how it nearly destroyed me. If there is something positive hidden beneath the kicking I got that night, I'd say it's that it made me who I am today: the best no-holds-barred fighter in Britain – now working my way to being the best in the world.

Step up to get your rep up

I NEEDED TO get out of that mess and that's exactly what I did. This was the point in my life where I needed to change. There was no turning back. I needed to be strong and I needed to train. I would never let anything like that to happen to me again as long as I lived.

There came a point in my life where I had to say to myself, 'I'm either going to give up on life or I'm going to get on with things.' This was where I had reached that make-or-break time of my life. This was not the type of thing you could just snap out of, but I took steps to hopefully do just that. The first decision I made was to get my own place. This was a year on from the skinhead incident and I was slowly but surely starting to get my life in order. It was time to move out and get some order going. I felt that, if I could sit around in my parents' place for so long, then I could end up doing it forever. If I was on my own I would have to motivate myself, and that's what I had been lacking for so long. Motivation.

I got my own place in Townend Farm and set about getting back into the swing of things. It wasn't exactly a palace, but it was mine. One thing I used to do to try to cope when I was down was to do something I enjoyed every day. It really is a good way of coping. Think to yourself about all your hobbies or interests and do one of them every day instead of sitting around and thinking about all the bad things in your life. It does help. Get yourself to the cinema, draw a picture, go swimming, ride your bike, whatever. Occupy your mind with something you like and it will work towards pushing the bad stuff from it. Mostly for me, this would involve smoking and drinking. And my diet! Jesus. Thinking about this now it's a wonder that I didn't have a heart attack before I hit twenty years old. I used to live off a sack of potatoes a week, but I'd only ever make chips out of them. It makes me want to barf just thinking about it. That's a helluva lot of chips, mate. At least Jamie Oliver would have sorted some jackets one day, mashed on another, then had some boiled, sliced and diced the next. Something pukka. Not me. They were all peeled and bunged in the chip pan. The only adventurous meals I had were eating chips while watching the Discovery Channel. When I fancied a decent meal, I'd go over and visit my parents.

There were so many changes going on in my life. I was still drinking quite heavily, but it wasn't like I was out of control with it. It was something I liked doing. My brother-in-law Keith and me used to make home brew as well, so there was always plenty of it around. For my nineteenth birthday we had a party round at the flat. It was absolutely mental. Well over fifty people crammed into a one-bedroom flat is not easy. Keith was the barman in the kitchen, which was also the DJ booth. He was playing everything from The Drifters to Culture Club. We'd started making another load of home brew especially for it, but got all the timing mixed up. It didn't have time to ferment properly, so it was either drink almost-ready beer or none at all. No prizes – you know what we did. We got through a whole forty pints of rancid, warm beer. Shaun and me weren't really knocking about any more, but he was still at the party. He used to hang out at the ice rink so he brought a load of people from there back with him on the bus. He didn't even know most of them, and I certainly didn't, but our strict door policy was that we'd only let people in who had beers with them.

In no time at all everyone was pissed and having an excellent time. Or at least I thought they were, till I saw the state of the bathroom. The toilet was full of puke and so was the bath; then people started using the bath as a toilet, but the plug was already blocked with sick, so it began to fill up. By the morning I had a bath full of pissy-puke – imagine cleaning that with the mother of all hangovers trying to kick your head in. At first I was a bit unsure about all these people in the flat who I didn't even know. You know what it's like: do you trust them? Will they smash the place up? Will they nick anything? But soon enough everyone was too drunk to even bother carrying on like that; Keith had made sure that everyone was well served, so I could relax a bit.

I must have relaxed a bit too much because I drank like there was no tomorrow. I was caught up in the party spirit. Everything I saw was a complete blur and everything I said was a complete slur. Then it happened. I can't say how it happened because I honestly don't know. I ended up having sex with one of the girls there. It was just silly fumbling around in a dark room. We had no idea what we were doing and I don't even know how we managed to do it. The state I was in I didn't think it was physically possible. It was one of those dumb drunken experiences where the little head is thinking, Yes! I'm well in here, and the big head doesn't know where the hell he is. And we all know that the little head has a one-track mind. It just seemed like one second I was in the middle of the party, the next I was having sex, then the next I was back in the party. It was so confusing that from my point of view it could never have happened. I knew *something* had happened, but not enough of it to piece the whole event together. It's like I was missing a few pieces of the jigsaw and couldn't quite make out what the picture was. Like one of those dreams when you can't quite remember what happened – you can almost explain it, but not quite. I didn't know who she was, what her name was or anything. We didn't have a relationship prior to that or afterwards. It's not like we had even shared an intimate moment that we would both remember. It just happened and then that was it. Over.

The next day I got complaints from the old couple who lived opposite. Because it was a communal foyer area, people had spilled out of my flat in the early hours and had continued being sick and using anything in sight as a toilet – including the old couple's door and letterbox.

All this drinking, partying and living off chips may give the wrong impression of my lifestyle. I did say there were changes going on, but I wasn't becoming a slob. Honest. This is when I'd started lifting weights a bit more seriously. Just a little at first, but enough to say that I was in training. I had an EZ Bar and would do squats and things in the front room. Anyone who trains will know that most of the time it's best to train with someone. There's the advantage of spurring each other along and helping to get those final two reps out, but, more importantly, they are right there to spot you. There I was, standing and raising the weights over and above my head, pressing the weights behind my neck. All was going well until I hit that point that a lot of you will be familiar with. You've gone over your limit and can't do another repetition. I was struggling like hell to raise the thing but had no chance. I'd move it a couple of centimetres only to lose it again. Shit. What would I do? I'd had similar accidents before where I would just drop the weights, but it split the carpet every time (and this was my own carpet now). So I'm looking around for somewhere safe to unload the weights. Ah-ha – the table! I had to lower my head down while turning my face so that my cheek was on the tabletop. Next I rolled the bar from the back of my neck over my ear and other cheek and finally to the table. It was an absolute nightmare. If you want to know how much it hurt, try putting your head in a vice and tightening it up till your face turns purple. That's about as close as you can get without popping an eye out.

Another accident I had was when I was bench-pressing. As if I hadn't learned my lesson already, I was benching on my own. On this occasion I got to the point where I couldn't push the bar up for another rep. I was hammered. Lying there with the barbell crushing my chest, trying to muster enough energy for one last press – I would still be there now if I hadn't thought fast. When you're stuck in that position, there isn't a lot of choice; you're pinned to the bloody bench. So, if you haven't guessed already, I had to roll the thing down my body to escape and unless, you've ever had to roll 100 kilos over your own bollocks, you'll never understand the pain. My chods were like pancakes. They wouldn't have looked out of place on a plate with Jif lemon juice on them. I was in so much agony that I was nearly sick. I'm sure there's plenty of you who can empathise here. But how *do* you describe the pain? It can't be explained. In fact, Tom Cruise is in talks at the minute for *Mission Impossible 3: Describing the Agony of Bashed Bollocks.* Let's see if he does his own stunts in that one. I suppose you could say I asked for it, trying to be clever and all that, but no one deserves to have to do that kind of punishment to themselves. I had the old cowboy swagger back for a few hours after that incident, I can tell you. The only sensible thing was to start going to the gym.

I started boxing when I was around nineteen, coming up to

twenty years old. I know how naughty this sounds, but this was when I found I had a real talent for hitting people. I started at Hylton Castle Boys Club – the Boysy to you. It's one of those places you only hear about now. A dying breed. It had that kind of distressed wooden look that people were going mad for a few years back, so in one sense it was ahead of its time. Distressed would still be a word I'd use to describe it, though. It stank of stale sweat, sawdust on the floor, everything like that. The ring itself was at floor level, nothing fancy, with buckets in the two corners to spit or puke into. The Boys Club was used for all sorts of things; it wasn't a purpose-built gym, it was somewhere to hang around – if you could stand the smell, that is. I still go there to this day and it's still got the same atmosphere; they've kept it real.

When I started, I would train with the younger lads before the seniors came in. The lads I trained with ranged from around sixteen to just over eighteen. I was quite conscious of the fact that these lads had been training seriously for some time. Up until that point I'd been training more as a hobby, but now I was ready to throw myself into it. Training lasted for something like an hour and a half. We used to do circuits, bag work, speedballs, skipping, sit-ups, all the usual stuff.

The dog's? Absolutely. I really immersed myself in the whole thing. Boxing and training became all I was interested in. I was even beginning to drink and smoke less as I found myself getting fitter and stronger and, whereas I used to be skinny and awkward, I was now becoming muscular and confident. The physical side of it was gradual, of course, but the mental side was going on all the time. I was returning with a vengeance. The theory of doing something you enjoy every day was actually working.

After the hour and a half, the seniors would come in and start warming up before their training and sparring. Sometimes I used to hang back a bit and watch in awe. Some of these blokes were amazing – tall, small, fat, thin, but all had this fighting quality and determination. They were all good mates but as soon as they stepped into the ring they would turn it on. The best way of explaining it is the way Mickey (Burgess Meredith) described it in the *Rocky* films: 'Eye of the Tiger'. That's exactly what it was: instinct, animal instinct. They would pound each other to a pulp and then go out for a pint afterwards.

So I'm sitting there watching one night after a training session. The coach was standing behind me. I would always try my best to impress upon him that I could fight. Try to prove myself and all that. He was sort of studying me as I watched this one guy laying into the bag. I could sense I was being watched and he soon came over. 'Get yourself together and get in the ring. Let's see how good you are,' he said.

I didn't really know what to do, so I just strolled over to the ring, but kept an eye on him all the time. That was when I saw him go over to the bloke I'd been watching. Oh, *fuck*, I thought. Anyone but him. I was trying to talk the coach out of it even as we were stood there in the ring. Slightly nervous? I had to keep looking on the floor behind me, 'cos it felt like I'd dropped one right there and then. I kept saying that this bloke would knock my block off, but the coach insisted that he wasn't there to do that. That made me feel a bit more at ease – until I turned to face my opponent. He had a face like a welder's bench, uglier than sin itself, and that made him look even scarier. Even John Merrick would have turned and ran away screaming if he'd clocked this bloke's boat. He was not the type of person you'd want to bump into on a dark night, or come face to face with in the ring for that matter.

We started and I came straight out from my corner and tore into him. I needed to do some damage quickly. If it were proof he needed, I'd give him proof. I was hitting on pure, raw, nervous energy. I'd seen the way this bloke was letting the bag have some vicious uppercuts, so I kept well back and picked him off with rights and left jabs going through his guard. Sure, I was getting hit back, but it meant nothing to me; I couldn't be hurt. They were bouncing off me like I was wearing armour. His punches were just something that were stopping me connecting with more of my own, a minor annoyance I had to ride out. Then it was back to work on him, switching from the stomach to the face: the low noise of the damp leather on skin was going *dupe, dupe, dupe* as the combinations were hitting him thick and fast.

I may have looked like the coolest, most calculated fighter in the world, but it was the whole fear of the situation that had enhanced my awareness. Underneath the cool exterior I was bricking it. He knew that he couldn't do a thing against me and he managed to get in close enough to go for the clinch. We were both out of breath with the ferocity and pace and were leaning into each other to try to tire the other one out that bit more. When we were dragged apart, his nose was popped and bleeding down over his mouth and on to the ground. That was when the coach stepped in and stopped the fight. The guy I had just been tearing into took his gum shield out and congratulated me.

It was at this point that I was most frightened. He was big and a few years older than me. I really thought that he'd be waiting for me outside afterwards. Yeah, that proved that I could fight, but proved a bit of naivety on my part, and luckily I was the only one privy to this information that was flying around in my head. This type of fight is controlled, remember. It wasn't personal at all: it was sparring. Not a full-on fight. If it had been a street fight in the first place and I'd got the edge, then he probably would have been waiting for me, or would have borne a grudge.

I was beginning to earn respect from fighters in the gym, but, more importantly to me, these were the older and more experienced fighters who were taking notice. This is what it was all about. Doing a good job and earning respect.

It was when I started boxing that I found out that I was a really good hitter. How else do you find out something like that? You chose to do something for a living that you're good at, right? Well, this was definitely something I enjoyed and anyone who's ever fought me will tell you that, when I hit you, you know you've been hit. Hold on, that isn't strictly true ... they'll tell you once they come round and are helped up, that's when they know it. I already had a fair idea from my school days that I could fight, but this was the real thing. Now I wanted to fight – that's the big difference. I needed to prove something to myself more than anything else. I needed to prove that I could not be held back – I had to bounce back and become someone. It became the Ian Freeman calling card to get straight in there and do maximum damage in minimum time. In the early stages I was still fighting on nervous energy and it worked for me. I was being put against sparring partners who were a lot older and who had been training for a lot longer, so I had to overcome my nerves and my fear as I entered the ring. I think at this stage that it was one of the best things for me, the fear factor. It meant that I was always on my toes and ready for anything that was thrown my way. After a while it seemed to subside. People could see a confident and fearless fighter in the ring and, because to me the process had been so gradual, I hadn't really noticed the transition myself.

I was working out in Arthur's Gym at the same time I was boxing at the Boysy. You get gyms now where people basically go just to swan around. This one was a real working gym. I used to go in and it was a good atmosphere, everybody helped everybody else. Again, like the Boysy, this was one of the old school. The smell of sweat hit you as soon as you walked in and you could hear grunting and crashing of weights from outside. You had free weights as well as proper machines; it was always busy, with people training and not just standing around in brand new gym clothes and talking.

Everyone was there for a purpose. People went in there and they trained hard. It was good to be in that environment. You weren't intimidated by your size, what you were wearing or by how much you could lift. It had no distractions at all; it was straight in and training with no nonsense. Some of the blokes who used to train there were amazing. Absolutely massive. Because of the type of place it was, this was where most of the hardmen of Sunderland would train. There would be club doormen, bouncers and boxers there all the time. It was a real who's who of faces and fighters. This is where I felt at home. I was amongst my own, and pretty soon they would all know me. This was the right environment for me to grow and blossom.

Everyone at the Boysy soon realised that I was a good fighter. I built up a reputation in the ring and was knocking people out left, right and centre. There was no one I wouldn't fight. I've always said that fighting for me is something I look forward to. This is where I discovered my love for it. This is when I became the new, improved Ian Freeman. Any fears I had in the ring had subsided. It was my sparring partners who now feared me and I couldn't wait to get in there and let rip on anyone. I was completely hooked by the whole thing. I would eat, sleep and breathe boxing. It was my addiction. I was a different person all together. At Arthur's Gym I was getting to know a lot of the boys. These were people who had reputations as fighters and were beginning to look at me as one of them. I wasn't a kid any more, I was a twenty-year-old fighter with a reputation all of my own.

One of the most important things to anyone is their acceptance into a particular group. Whatever sporting or leisure activity you take up, you are always the newcomer until you get noticed or prove yourself somehow. Up until now I was still on the fringes and would always hear the lads talking about this fight and that fight and who got chinned last night and where and how much damage was inflicted. Then one day they started to talk about someone else; someone they had heard of who was going to be the next big thing. That's when they started talking about me.

Since a lot of the lads got themselves down to the Boysy anyway, it was mostly the same people who went to Arthur's. That's how most of the stories found their way there. It wasn't long before I got to know the owner, Arthur Beautiman. Arthur worked the doors around town and on one occasion he wanted the night off. He knew I could handle myself and I think he'd heard that I wanted to get into something like that line of work, so it just seemed to be a natural progression. He asked if I'd work the night for him and I agreed. Just getting asked was a big thing for me, because it meant that, to start with, I was being taken seriously. I jumped at the chance; it was like my big break. His name carried a lot of weight and to me it signified my acceptance into this particular group. And, if Arthur had seen something in me, then it wouldn't be long before the rest of them would.

* * * * *

My first night of filling in for Arthur was at Scott's in Sunderland, and on this night there was some bother. It wasn't anything serious – a fight had broken out inside the bar and me and Derek Stephenson, who I was working with at the time, just ran over, dragged the two blokes apart and chucked them out. Simple as that, really, but along with it came this huge adrenaline buzz. They were shoved out on to the street viciously and I was willing them to start something. I was ready to take them both on. That first time was a bit like fighting in the Boysy, but I felt like I was in full control. There was a tiny touch of that same nervousness that I had had in the early days of boxing, but it gave me the edge I needed. I was confident. I knew I was there because I could do the job and, while I was filling in, it was my job and I didn't feel like I was keeping it warm for someone. That's how much heart I put into it from that first night. It was *my* patch. Even if it was just for a few hours at first. It was like that from the word go. You see things going on and it's your job to stop it or to sort it out. My first night on the doors and I broke my cherry! I was like the cat that got the cream. The dog's? You better believe it. I abso-fucking-lutely loved it. If I had messed up on that first night, then none of what I'm doing now might ever have happened. When working a door you have to get stuck in otherwise no one will want you on their door protecting their premises. Stands to reason, dunnit?

Arthur soon got to know that I was staunch from the glowing report I got from Derek. He knew I could live up to my reputation and by doing that night's work I had enhanced it. That meant that he now trusted me to fill in for him any other night he wanted to take off. This is what I mean about it taking time: bouncers, or doormen as they are now called, belong to a very exclusive club. Not everyone is suitable for membership. You can find a way in, usually through a friend and reputation, but you have to make your mark. You're the new kid on the block, after all, and if no one can trust you, then no one wants to work with you. It also makes the bloke who you filled in for look a right twat for vouching for you, which won't go down well with him at all. If you lose your bottle when something kicks off you are putting your partner in serious danger. That is when the exclusive club will blackball you. And you can rest assured that you'll never work in this town again, as they say. You can never be just an OK doorman. You are either good at it or you don't do it.

After covering that night I thought to myself, This is a piece of piss, this. It was just so easy. It was like money for nothing, I really couldn't believe it. It was something I could get used to. Sure, it could easily have gone the other way, but I fitted into the role perfectly. And I'm not trying to brag or sound conceited by these remarks. Some people are good at things that others are bad at; even now it's very rare that you can walk into the job and be offered weekend work straight away. It just doesn't happen. You have to fill in for people here and there until you get yourself noticed. Once people see you can do the job then you might get asked to do a bit more, then a bit more. I couldn't wait to get more work. I was still quite young and started to earn good money for a night's work. I thought it was the business, know what I mean? I had suddenly found my niche.

I moved on to a full-time position at Greens. Still in Sunderland, this place was owned by the same people. They knew me and knew I was quite capable of doing the job, you see, so they came straight for me. Pretty soon after that I was back working at Scott's. This was all in the space of only a few months, so you can see that it wasn't the most stable work to get into. When you're trying to find your feet you'll take just about any grief along the way if you think there will be steady work as the outcome. You know the old Catch-22 situation you've all found yourselves in when trying to find work? Well, it's true with doorwork – to an extent. You'll find that you have probably taken some degree of shit to get where you are now. Everyone who starts off in this business uses their early years to work out the score and become streetwise. This is where the University of Life cliché enters the picture. You have to learn fast. You've got to know when you're being taken for a ride. While I'm on the subject, the manager at Scott's would probably do things a little bit differently these days, I reckon. Some people never learn. Get this ...

I was on fifteen quid a night, which was quite good money back then. Being ever so naughty in those days, I wasn't exactly one hundred per cent honest. I was working under someone else's name so I could still be entitled to certain benefits from the good people at the DSS. Oh, come on, it's not like I was doing a Nick Leeson. I was just out for a bit of extra pocket money. I was working weekends here, a prime-time slot that carried a lot of responsibility with it. This is when the manager decided to take the piss. He was a bit of a knob, this bloke. He was only nineteen years old and really fancied himself; he thought he was the cat's ass. One of these Yuppie types who would drink Perrier and like certain things because he read that he had to in Cosmo-bloody-politan. He had long, greased-back hair, went by the name of Coggy and didn't believe in doing himself any favours, as you will soon find out. I'd go as far as saying he had a death wish.

He knew that I wasn't being honest with the Benefits Agency. In those days everyone was at it, you had to be. He tried to be subtle about it at first. One weekend I wasn't paid and he said that there had been some sort of mix-up with paperwork. How spineless is that? He couldn't even tell me the reason. OK, I thought, I can ride this one out and see what happens. It could have been a mix-up and, even though things smelled a bit fishy, I gave him the benefit of the trout.

It got to the stage where he owed me sixty quid. That was for two weekends and he was still making excuses. Now this was quite a tidy sum to live off then and I wasn't prepared to let it go. On the Friday before my next shift I phoned him up. 'Am I going to get paid this week?' I asked.

'Like I say, you haven't got a leg to stand on,' came the reply. 'What do you mean by that?' I was beginning to lose my rag.

'Well, you haven't been using your real name and basically you haven't got a leg to stand on.'

He insisted on digging his own grave. I put the phone down and went straight round there. It had got to the point where actions were going to have to be deployed. I'm no one's fool and no one is going to take me for a mug. If this sounds ever so slightly familiar, it's because it's almost identical to what happened with Fatboy Fat over at the scrap yard. Some people, eh? All this Coggy fella had to do was say he didn't want me to work there and pay me what I was owed, but that would have been too simple. It turned out that he was putting it through the books as though he was paying me but he was pocketing the money for himself. He must have had a lobotomy for breakfast instead of scrambled eggs.

I got to the pub and asked the barmaid where he was. In the office? Nice one. I let myself in and oddly enough he wasn't a fraction as cocky as he'd been on the phone. He was sitting behind his desk shaking as I gave him one final chance and asked for my money. 'You haven't got a leg to stand on ...' The wrong answer again! That was his third strike, if he was on *Family Fortunes* he would have got the 'Uh-Ugh', and in my book you know what that means.

I told him to stand up. Suddenly, he couldn't understand what I was saying – complete Selective Language Recognition Disorder I think it's called, which is usually brought on when someone finds themselves well out of their depth. After we got through the rigmarole of: 'Stand up.' 'What for?' '*Fucking stand up*!' He eventually stood up and I put him straight on his arse. He found himself downwardly immobile. He didn't know what had hit him, but before he even had the chance to work it out I grabbed him by his greasy hair and dragged him out of the office. The only reason I didn't knock him out cold or follow in was because I wanted him conscious. He was beginning to realise that he was the one who didn't have a leg to stand on. I had a good handful of hair twisted around my fingers and wasn't going to let go, no matter how loud he screamed. Just as well I am a bit corned beef in one ear, 'cos the glasses out in the bar were beginning to shatter.

I dragged him into the bar and then behind the counter to the till. I knew there was a safe in the office, but I didn't want it to look like I was screwing the place. He was definitely the type who would have tried to stitch me up like that. I just wanted what I was owed. The rest of the staff looked on as I continued to drag him around. If he was a well-liked and respected boss, surely *someone* would have stuck up for him, or at least looked concerned for him. Their only concern was that they would be mopping up the trail of blood when I'd finished with him, so you can see the type of person he was.

When we reached the till I told him to open it. He looked up at me and said he couldn't. I wasn't in the mood for him now. If I'd had to crack it off his head to open it, I would have. If I'd had to bite every one of his fingers off before he told me where the key was, guess what I would have done? With his hair still in one hand I made a fist out of the other and drew it back to pound his face in. As if by magic, he remembered how to open the till – and Jesus! He had the key in his pocket. (I should hire myself out as a revision buddy, a new sideline: 'You will remember who assassinated Franz Ferdinand or I'll punch your Goddamn face in.') I took the sixty quid and made sure I counted it out in front of the barmaid. I wanted to punch him again, but he wasn't worth the bother. All right then, he was, and I did. I think the police were called but they didn't know my real name and, because I hadn't been anywhere near the place that night, they wouldn't have had a leg to stand on if they questioned me.

Soon after that I was hit with something. Something that knocked me for six. The girl I'd had sex with at my party turned up to tell me she was pregnant. Of course, I barely recognised her when she came to the door, I had been mortal drunk when it had all happened. You've got to understand that this situation is a very tricky one to deal with. I am not a callous and cold-hearted person, but I needed to know for sure. I didn't know this girl at all, so from my point of view the child could have been anyone's. For all I knew she could have been looking for a way out of something. It made me real angry because I felt like I was the scapegoat. Another part of me was saying that it wasn't meant to be like that. It couldn't be true – we'd only done it that one time. The outcome of this was going to affect me in a big way and I couldn't just take her word for it – I needed proof. I told her to get all the necessary blood tests and, if I really were the father, then I would not shy away from my responsibilities.

In the time that passed waiting for the results I was on tenterhooks. It was a long time of turmoil for me. The baby was over half a year old when I found out for certain that she was mine. If we had been in a relationship then it would have been something we could sit down and plan around. We could have weighed up the pros and cons and decided what actions we'd take, but here we were, two strangers having to discuss the future of this tiny little life that we had created during a moment of drunken stupidity. I was learning the news that I was a father for the first time and it should have been the happiest moment of my life. I didn't know how to feel or how to react. Even when I found out the girl's name and that she lived quite nearby I was still unmoved. I was happy but was heavily restricted by the circumstances I was thrown into. It possibly could have been a time to start a relationship, but it would have been for the wrong reasons. We didn't fancy each other. We didn't know each other. What would have been the point? It's really hard to articulate something like this. In doing so I cannot use the word 'mistake'. As a result of what happened I now have a beautiful daughter called Kayleigh, who I love dearly. I wouldn't change that. The only thing I would change would be the circumstances under which she came to be born, because I think that children should be brought up in a happy and stable environment. She has a stepdad now but I never did or will neglect her in any way or deny her anything. She is my daughter.

Watching the world go by
Growing before my very eyes
I never noticed
That you have changed
But you're still only a baby to me

No more bedtime stories
No more candy lollies
Hide and seek
Secrets to keep
But you're still only a baby to me

You are all grown now
But I'm not sure how
It seemed like yesterday
Not that far away
You were still only a baby to me

No more playing in the park
No more frightened of the dark
Bikes to ride
Tears to hide
But you're still only a baby to me

Now that you have grown
I know it won't be very long
For you to start a family too
Knowing what you'll have to do
Because you were, yes you were
Once a baby to me

'Only a Baby to Me', Ian Freeman

Fuck or be fucked: that is the answer

***SOMETIMES YOU DO** things you are not entirely proud of. On the doors I'd use excessive force and I didn't care who got hurt along the way. This is by no means an apology, but it may help you to see what was going through my mind at the time. The beating I took from those skinhead cowards affected me to the point that I showed absolutely no mercy when confronted by one, five or ten men. I still live by it, but in a more controlled way. Put me in a mood and I'll put you on your arse.*

My life was changing at a dramatic pace. Not only in doorwork, but also in my personal life, with the birth of my daughter. On the doors I was going from strength to strength. I was starting to make some great friends along the way and found that, once I was known, then there was plenty of relief work to be had around town. The strange thing was that I didn't really set out to become a doorman. Even when I first started I don't think I really intended to do it ... it just happened, a natural progression, something you just find yourself falling into. OK, I suppose not *everyone* suddenly finds that they are working as a doorman, but a lot of people who do it find that it wasn't top of the list in their career plan at school. They may have been out of work and perhaps they were asked if they wanted to work a night for a bit of extra cash. That's how it starts. Before you know it you're looking for full-time work doing just that. I know I didn't expect to follow it through. Obviously, because it was such an easy job and the pay was good, I just stuck with it. I felt sure it would lead somewhere.

Once I did get into it, there was no stopping me. I could not be stopped. I used to get feedback from other doormen. They would say things like, 'You went in there well' and 'You done good there, mate' – it was like the job became even easier. It's great to get praise and recognition in anything you do. Another incentive was that each time I was filling in for people on different doors, the pay was going up and up. I was building up a reputation in no time at all. It was soon common knowledge that I was solid. The moment you show anyone any fear is the moment they know you can be beaten. I've never backed down from anyone and I've never been beaten in any street fight. I've never been knocked off my feet and I've never been knocked out. There's a lot of people I've seen who think that working the doors *is* going to be easy but, once they get there and something kicks off, you can see them panic. It's certainly not a job for everyone. You can definitely find yourself in some frightening situations and not everyone is cut out to deal with it. Just ask any doorman. I know this may sound hard to comprehend, but you have got to be prepared to risk your life. There will definitely be times when you are fighting for it. If you're not prepared mentally as well as physically, then the very least you can expect is serious injury. Each and every time you hear me describe my work the words *trust* and *respect* will always come into it. I have continued to work for certain people over the years because I would put my life and my family's lives in their hands. If it sounds like I'm repeating myself, it's because I don't think that level of commitment can ever be overemphasised. It can't be understood unless you yourself are in a similar position to me. To know that your friend would stand with you in any situation is something that not many people can be confident of. My lads would take a bullet or a blade for me and they all know I'd do the same for them.

It's something you have to adapt to. I adapted and took to it. I could handle those situations, but at the same time I saw a lot of people who couldn't. If we could all do it there would be more people working the doors than there are drinking in the pubs and clubs we protect. For me it wasn't just doing it; it was doing it, being good at it and enjoying it. Any trouble that went on was like the drug and I was feeding my habit. Getting in there and fighting was my addiction and I was getting stronger all the time.

I mentioned earlier about my anger and aggression while on the doors. Again, I'm the only one who fully knows my inner feelings, but I'll try to give you an insight as best I can. It's important that people know the reasons behind my actions. The thing that really made me feared on the doors was that I would fight anyone. This is where my philosophy of 'fuck or be fucked' comes in. I'm sure there are people who wouldn't agree with this, but for me it was the only way. Any sign of danger and my defences were straight up – the button was pushed. Sometimes I would be breaking up a fight and would get hit with a stray punch. That would be it. I'd explode. All the memories of getting mugged by the skinheads that night would come rushing back and God help anyone who got in my way, because I was bringing hell with me. No one would ever hit me again and get away with it. That's how much it affected me. I would hammer the shit out of anyone. It was like demonic possession. The rage and anger would be there in a second.

I know how much this will affect all of you, but it may help to see where I'm coming from: imagine your girlfriend, boyfriend, husband or wife is being raped or sodomised in front of you. Right in front of you and you can't do a thing to stop it. Then they have their throat sliced open and you are forced to watch them suffer and die, choking on their own blood. Imagine seeing your mother or father, son or daughter tortured by some sick bastard and you can do absolutely fuck all about it. Imagine them screaming out for you, the mental torture as some evil cunt is enjoying it. Their cries set to haunt you forever ... Then imagine that the person who did it is in the next room and you have ten minutes in there alone with them to get out all the aggression that you feel. You are granted just ten minutes, then. That's it. You'd love to think that you wouldn't turn to violence as a solution or lower yourself to their level but, believe me, each and every one of you would stop at nothing to punish them. Imagine the beating you'd give them, the speed with which you'd go about it. Imagine that feeling when they are begging for mercy, making them suffer, making them pay, the wild, savage beast you'd become in those minutes. Those were my feelings. That was going through my mind. All the time. I hit everyone with that kind of rage.

I know people have said that I was volatile then ... but that's not even close. I was a fucking animal. I hated people and people hated me back. Even friends would be scared of me. Good friends knew deep down that I would never hurt them, but those I didn't know too well were just as likely to end up in hospital as everyone else. I was getting barred from clubs all over the place; at one time I was barred from every nightclub in Sunderland for what I had done. I could snap in an instant and if I was fighting you there was no one on the planet capable of stopping me. I would only stop when I wanted to and even I didn't know when that would be.

There is also the fact that, when you start off as a doorman, you have everything to prove. And that's what you do. You go all out to prove that you can fight. No matter how many fights you have on the doors, there are people who have been working them a lot longer than you have and you want to rise above these people. They have years of experience under their belts and you are the rookie.

I don't have to go out of my way to hit anybody now, 'cos I know what I can do. I know I'm up there now and things are a lot different to what they used to be. You couldn't talk to people then – in most cases violence was the only answer. To get some tosser out of a bar, you had to use force and a great deal of the time it would need to be excessive force. Ever tried telling a drunk they are in the wrong? Ever known one to be totally reasonable? But at the same time *I* couldn't give a fuck about reason. If someone did anything that constitutes bad behaviour I would smash them to bits. My head was so messed up that I was the one that nobody could reason with. If you tried to, then we would get into an argument and if you ever raised your voice to me you got hurt. You would never win an argument against me. Never. There were those people who didn't go out just looking for a fight, but it was those who did that spoiled it for everyone else. Because there were so many like that, the ones who weren't looking for trouble were still handled the same way. There would be no questions because I wasn't bothered what the answer would be. You were just another excuse to let out some of the anger that had been boiling away for the last twenty minutes. Just the excuse I needed to fucking torture you in front of whoever you were out with.

* * * * *

On the streets, respect is the main word. You don't have to make enemies. That is something I know today. I'm known as a gentleman now in any of the circles I operate in. A gentleman gets respect; a thug doesn't. It's not like I was a bad-mannered guy in the past. I was brought up right. It was the conditioning of my mind and the way I reacted to the slightest amount of trouble that gave me a bad reputation. It was a build-up of a lot of things that caused me to act the way I did. I would show no remorse. Now the mere mention of my name will stop any trouble. People know I don't think of fighting as a chore, it's just what I do, whether it's in the ring or no. If someone wants to fight me, I will gladly oblige.

One of my problems has always been that I like to know a job is being done properly and this usually means I'm there doing it myself. This is where the bad guy image comes from. In the past, it may have seemed to some people like I'm steaming in to whoever for no apparent reason. That would never happen now. I do delegate, but I like to be hands-on at the same time. Case in point: there was one bloke very recently – to protect his name, let's call him Des Ball. He found out first-hand that I send the best people round when it's time to delegate. Des had been causing bother in the bar at a golf club. I was approached and asked if I could sort this bloke out. Des was a big guy and was smashing the place up, taking drink and generally making it an unpleasant place to be. He had once worked behind the bar, but because he was nicking things he was sacked. That's when he decided to go in there and threaten people. I got a call from the owner asking if I could help out. I went round to see Des and have a word with him. I told him who I was and that he wasn't welcome there any more. At first I don't think he knew who I was, or whether it had all sunk in or not. I left him my card and told him to ask around about me. That was it. He'd been told. Half an hour later I received an apologetic call from him saying it would never happen again.

'No bother, Des. Make sure it doesn't,' I said.

Sorted. But a while later, he was back to his old tricks. He was drunk and was abusing the owners of the club – a middle-aged man and woman – again, and he was threatening to kick off. It needed to be handled quickly and quietly and I wasn't around to do it. I sent Carl and Ian round to shut him up. Carl smacked him full force on the jaw. Say goodnight, bozo. He was out of it. To make himself look even more stupid, Des actually shat himself when Carl knocked him out. I got a call from Carl saying he had these grey tracksuit bottoms on with all this stuff running down the leg ... my own fuck-up deterrent! I know he'll never try that again – he knows I'll tear him apart.

* * * * *

I can ensure that there will be no trouble. That's my guarantee to anyone. While the police don't necessarily like it, I can control things better than them without violence and I think I've kept a lot of trouble out of town without resorting to the police. People feel safe and protected with my team and me around. If they didn't feel safe, they wouldn't be asking for my help or for me to run some bully out of town. My name or presence can stop a fight. Does the mention of the police turning up once the fight is finished have the same effect? Can they get there as quickly as my boys or me to put a stop to bullying? I don't think so. It happens that there is a great demand for my expertise, whether it is to collect a debt, repossess property – anything. Even fifteen grand's worth of tools ... if you happen to have them stolen. People know I can be persuasive.

At first people would approach me with stupid things like recovering debts of fifty to a hundred and fifty quid. Sure, it doesn't seem like much, but these people must be desperate enough to ask, in which case I will listen to them. In the early days before I was well known, I would show a lot less restraint. Whatever amount was owed I told them I wanted it within seven days. That's when people cough up. I didn't have to be nice and I certainly didn't want to be. Now I get involved in recovering large amounts. I delegate. Any job like that is as important to me as it is to the person I am recovering it for. I'm too high profile to do my own running around now. Fame means caution and I prefer not to take any risks. That type of work spreads through word of mouth. You may not know me or how to get in touch with me, but someone will know how to reach me. Then I would meet you and explain my percentage. You don't need to know how the money ends up in your pocket. I will assure you that I will get it and, if you are still happy with the arrangement, then I can put the wheels in motion. One way or the other, I get the money. I have a ninety per cent success rate. I think that pretty much speaks for itself.

Bentleys gonna sort you out

ANYONE WHO USED to go to Bentleys will remember what a hole it was. Working there I made some really good friends and some enemies along the way. Many of the friends are still around, but not all of them. I was straight in at the deep end and felt right at home.

After doing all these one-off nights and filling in for people all over Sunderland, I was offered the job of filling in at Bentleys. It was Arthur Beautiman who got me in there. This was where the real work started. I worked there for only a short while before I was offered the full-time position. This was the latter part of the '80s. I was twenty years old at the time.

Hands up who remembers *Road House*, the Patrick Swayze movie? People everywhere were going mad over this film during the Bentleys era. It was probably the first film made about bouncers and, in true Hollywood style ... it got it completely wrong. It wasn't *that* bad, I suppose – it certainly made people more aware of us, if anything. It did glorify the job – and the violence – in a sense, but these guys were only having one fight a night whereas we were having anything up to ten. And it made it cool to be a bouncer. All of a sudden it was the coolest thing in the world, the best job you could ever imagine having, so the film was definitely a good PR exercise: get the girl, kill the baddies and save the entire town while you're doing it. Easy. Not much to live up to there, then. Cheers, Pat.

The reality of it was that we didn't have any stunt co-ordinators to stand in or to plot certain fight sequences – we did it all on our own, by instinct and by thinking on the spot. When a gang of blokes confronted you and were after your blood, you didn't wait for the director to shout 'Cut!' and go off to your dressing room. You stood your ground and fought until you were the last man standing. The Double Deuce was nothing compared to some of the stuff we saw and got up to in Bentleys, and Patrick Swayze and that old gadgey, Sam Elliot, instead of Geordie and me? Don't even go there!

They say it's a mad, mad world and I'm sure the 'they' in question must just have been on a bender in Sunderland. In those days there were no CCTV cameras around so people knew they could get away with stuff. You go out now and towns and cities are watched over all the time by Big Brother; back then it was like the Wild West and we were like Butch Cassidy and Sundance – absolutely mental. The Hole in the Head Gang, if you like. I've always said that fighting for me is something I look forward to. It's my work, my profession and my business; it's the equivalent of asking someone to step into my office, only when you step into my office I beat a new shade of shit out of you. Most of you nice people reading this will probably never be asked to step into the office, though. Joe Public has to be very naughty indeed before he gets an invite. In the words of Michael Barrymore, it's usually only my kind of people. You know what my state of mind was like then, so now you know that you didn't have to step that much out of line before the office door was opened.

As you know, I was teamed up with Geordie Watson, who was there to show me the ropes. I already knew the score, but Geordie was very experienced as well as respected, so I wasn't going to go in there acting as if I knew it all. I knew I didn't know *everything*, but if anyone could help me get there it was Geordie. I now worked in the biggest nightclub in town, and it was also the roughest. It was like a lunatic asylum at the best of times, but on practically every weekend it was rougher than a lorryload of badgers' arses. It was always packed wall to wall but I bet at least half of those people were only there because they knew they would see a good fight or ten – maybe more, you never could tell. We should have been charging the punters more for the entertainment we were putting on! We could even go in there on our day off and you could see the people tense up or take their feet off the chairs. Everyone knew we wouldn't take any shit. Normally I would walk in front of Geordie, so, if anyone gave any snide remarks or said anything, he was there to see it going on and we would put a stop to it there and then. We clicked immediately. We were the best partnership in Sunderland. Forget Quinn and Philips; Watson and Freeman are the best strike force Sunderland has known. We were unbeatable from the start.

After the very first incident broke out Geordie knew he could trust and rely on me. If there were ever any doubts, I made sure I quashed them that first time a fight kicked off. In a club, a fight can easily be over within twenty seconds. Those twenty seconds can be the longest you'll ever know. They are also the most crucial. You have to take control and you have to stick together, no matter what. When that first fight kicked off, Geordie was surrounded and was fighting his way out; he looked round to see where I was. This is how he could tell what I was made of – loads of people in that situation would hold back and think twice about jumping in. Not me. The reason he hadn't seen me straight off was because I was right behind him doing exactly what he was doing. We were back to back, punching our way to freedom. Do you know what it feels like to be in the middle of ten blokes laying into you and you only have your fists to rely on? That's when you need your partner. That was when we bonded. Each and every fight you get into in a pub or club could be your last; that's the harsh reality of it. If you can't do the job, don't expect to live very long, because a group of people kicking and stamping on your head will only take a few seconds to kill you. You have got to be on top every fight, every night of every week.

We got our picture taken on the steps of Bentleys in the first few weeks of me working there and I've still got it to this day. Us standing there with our dinner suits on. Actually, those dinner suits have reminded me: there's a great little story I've got to tell you. I think this took place just before Sunderland was actually able to call itself a city, so it was still a town. With a university. The university now got a capacity now of around 12–13,000, but there was still a huge student population then and, being the biggest nightclub around, we had student nights every week. Recipe for disaster, you think? Sometimes, yeah. Students and drink don't mix that well to start with, so, when you add a team of short-tempered, arse-kicking, take-no-shit doormen, sometimes there can be trouble. And, contrary to what you might think about us types and students, we do actually like them – medium rare.

There were a couple of fancy dress nights at Bentleys. They were always full of surprises. Most of the time they were OK, we could have a laugh with them. It was like all the extras from *It's a Knockout* on a piss-up. You used to look around and there would be Wonder Woman trying to get stuck into Black Beard, cowboys lusting after Indians and it was criminal what we found

Captain Caveman trying to do to old Mary Poppins in the bogs one night. They would start off all fresh and up for it and by the time they got a few cider and blacks into them it all turned to mush. If you just walked in off the street you'd think you were having some kind of nightmare acid flashback. How many times have you seen a six-foot banana being sick on Dracula? Or Starsky copping off with Hutch? I think it was the first time in my life when I said, 'I've seen it all now', and actually meant it.

One time the Blues Brothers were pissed as farts and started causing bother. Geordie and me ruled the roost and, as much as I like Dan Aykroyd, he's still in line for a good clout like the rest of them. We had told them to cool their jets a few times but they were having none of it. We restrained ourselves to the limit. The night was getting on and we were probably being a bit more lenient than usual. Just recently Tom, the boss, had given us a bollocking because on one of these nights we had thrown out more punters than there were inside. There were about two hundred people inside and four hundred standing outside, banging on the doors. We were in the thick of it all going, 'Right, whose next?'

It got to chucking-out time and as usual it took a good half-hour to clear everyone out. All the students hugging each other good night and arranging to meet in the David Baddiel bar after skipping tomorrow's lectures, and all that shit. This was the time when people would take offence at being asked to leave and would try and start something. Tom and Jerry even got a good slapping one night.

Here we were clearing them out, when who should present themselves? Yep, you guessed it, the stars of that all-singing, all-dancing cult movie and all-time classic *The Blues Brothers*. And they were up for it all right. They'd pushed us too far and now there was no going back. We always took the battle outside. We used to stand to watch over everyone from this raised-up area just in front of the back doors. Very conveniently placed, you might say. So the Blues Brothers are all suited and booted and in our faces and we had no other choice but to take it outside. These huge fire doors would get closed behind us as we took whoever it was outside, and that's when they were introduced to Boozy Alley. No, not Kirstie's piss-head brother, it was an alley behind the club where all the boozy idiots who caused bother were taken. Hence, Boozy Alley. This way no one could be brought into anything as a witness. Once the fight was over there would be three knocks on the door, which was a signal to let us back in.

Picture the scene: you've just let us four out to have a fight in the alley. It happens every night, so you think nothing of it as you wait for the three knocks and you let us back in. What you weren't expecting was for me and Geordie to walk in with such style. We swaggered in cool as fuck wearing the Blues Brothers' hats and shades! We already had the dinner suits on, so we looked the business. At one point I thought Geordie was getting too much into character and was going to start doing backflips all over the place. The rest of the doormen were pissing themselves laughing. Those Blues Brothers might have started off suited and booted, but it suited us to boot them around a bit.

Because of Geordie and me, Boozy Alley saw more action than Hamburger Hill, only it had a few more bodies lying around during our shift. We had a competition going on with the other doormen. As you can probably imagine, this was no conventional competition. What do you take us for? I mentioned the back doors of the club where we would take anyone who wanted to fight us. Once whoever it was had been knocked out, that was when the fun started. The knocking them out was just a formality – once they were unconscious they unknowingly became part of the Bentleys Olympics Team. We would grab an arm and a leg or back of the waistband and back of the collar and give it the old 'One ... two ... three', and see how far we could throw them. It was brilliant. It all came about by accident when we threw someone out and then someone else in a similar way soon after. The second one landed a bit further, so the next time we threw someone out we would try to beat the last throw. It soon got to the point where we were marking each throw with our names next to it and had all the doormen joining in. Sometimes, if we were throwing two out at the same time, we would weigh them to see who was the lightest for a good distance. We would even have arguments over who belonged to who! If there was only one lad getting thrown out we would take turns; one of us would throw him first, mark it and then he'd be dragged back for another throw. Some of the lads even started bringing their kids' chalk or crayon sets in to use as markers. I know there's a saying 'What you don't know cannot hurt you', but this lot was oblivious to it and I'm quite sure it wasn't an improvement on their health. We should have added, '... unless you are being thrown by your arms and legs across the length of a back yard to beat the record'. Believe me, you did not want to end up in Boozy Alley. These people would sometimes land face-first or head-first and, if the rest of their body fell the wrong way, who knows what could have happened. But who cared. They were being thrown out for a reason and any indignity they suffered as a result they had only themselves to thank.

There was one bloke who had really been working himself and wanted to fight me right there and then in the club, which wasn't my style. If an arsehole wanted to spoil everyone's night out by starting a fight, I wasn't going to help him injure an innocent bystander. A club should be a safe place for someone to enjoy a night out, but people like these guys make it unsafe. That's why it always went outside. At first they would always think you were backing down by saying, 'I don't want to fight you', when really it could have been finished there and then without anyone knowing about it, let alone the aggressor. In that situation we couldn't risk anyone else getting hurt except the bloke who was in our sights. Outside, he didn't even get the chance to draw breath let alone think about throwing a punch. He was on his back in a second. I did the usual knock and Geordie came out to give me a hand in throwing him. Now this bloke was a big, heavy charva. ('*Charva*': described by the *Concise Oxford Dictionary* as another word for 'gadgey'.) We didn't think he'd go very far, if at all. We had a couple of swings then launched him; he was like the bouncing fucking bomb. He must have gone over twenty feet. I didn't think he was going to stop. I thought he was going to demolish the town; he was like a giant space hopper full of pies and beer. What a sight. He bounced, skidded, rolled and cracked his head off one of the bar staff's cars.

So now I always laugh when I hear people say, 'I wouldn't trust him as far as I could throw him.' I think that's one of the reasons I never use that one, because I've got a good idea how far I could throw him and there are only a few people I'd trust that much. We got rumbled about throwing people as well. Not because they were getting injured and were complaining, but because of all the bodies that were piling up. So, always wanting to keep Britain tidy, we threw them, marked the spot and then put them in the skips or the bins that were nearby. We didn't put the Bouncing Bomb gadgey into a bin though; we would have needed a blowtorch to get him out. One of the good things was that, once they came round, they just assumed they were so drunk that they'd passed out in a bin, climbed out and went home. They had an amusing story to tell their mates and so did we.

* * * * *

When I say we could have anything up to ten, fifteen or even twenty fights a night, I know you're sitting there searching for your bullshit detector. It's true, though, and here's how. You know the background about how rough the place was – it was a cross between the bar from *Star Wars* and something out of *Mad Max*. And, apart from Bentleys, we had to monitor the other bars in the area as well. All the ones in our jurisdiction, so to speak.

If a fight had broken out, the DJ would get on the microphone and shout, 'Reejay ... Liberties', or 'Reejay Bill's Bar ...', 'Top Bar ...', 'Dance floor ...', 'Reception', practically anywhere there was standing room the chances were that someone would fight there. You had to leg it to wherever the fight happened to be. You could be in the middle of a conversation or anything and would have to take off there and then. Remember, someone could be in serious danger, so we had to get there as quickly as we could – any wasted time could be fatal to whoever was in trouble.

Sometimes we'd get to where the bother was – let's say it was Bill's Bar – and we'd hear, 'Reejay dance floor'. This wouldn't mean there'd been a mistake. It would mean we'd have to sort Bill's out in seconds and race over to the dance floor to sort another one out. That's when you can have well over ten fights in an hour – and, believe me, it did happen.

There was this time when a whole load of boxers rolled into Liberties. There were about twelve of these blokes and, as soon as they walked in, they had this arrogance about them. They had been to some sort of convention or something and they thought they were the bollocks. Must have taken the name of the bar a bit too literal, if you know what I mean. They were all wearing dinner suits so, for most of the punters in the place, they couldn't tell who was who. We could instantly tell that something would happen. If you enter with that kind of attitude, it will only worsen as you drink. The drink acted like the fuse to a bomb; it was the build-up to the explosion. This type of person in a nightclub, pub, or anywhere for that matter, is a liability. And anyone entering one of my bars with that attitude can rest assured that it will be kicked out of them before the night is over.

Sure enough, as the night progressed, things went pear-shaped for them. They'd come in thinking they had something to prove and now they were trying to prove it. Scuffles started inside so we went to work in sorting it out and escorting people off the premises. We had actually tried to reason with them, but it was obvious they had only come in for a fight. All we did was put them outside, but they wanted to fight. They kicked off with us and after they started throwing the first punches there was no going back for any of us. And what a battle it turned out to be! It was good because, unlike your usual drunks, they were trained fighters. So, instead of it being over after one punch, they did manage to stand their ground for a bit. But, because of this, it meant that they got a *proper* beating, not just a slap and a 'Come back next week and behave yourself.' It was good for us to enjoy a prolonged fight for a change and we gave them a lesson they wouldn't forget in a hurry.

One of them took a cheap shot at me. Big mistake, mate. If you do that sort of thing you've gotta do it right otherwise you're in for a serious kicking. He hit me first and that's when I turned psycho. I cracked him so hard that he fell against the wall behind him; that was the only thing that kept him up. He was so dazed that he turned to run away and just ran straight into the wall. This bastard was mine. I grabbed him by his jacket and the back of his head and rammed him into the wall. As his face hit the brick I heard it split open like a fucking melon. I smashed him into it again, cracking his teeth and his nose and then scraping his face along, shredding it to ribbons. The wall was covered in blood and his face was a swollen mess of flesh with skin hanging off and grit embedded into the wounds. From there I dragged him to the ground. His whole body gave up and I dropped him. It was a frenzied attack. I did him in the space of three seconds; all one move – he could do nothing to stop it. You know, the *him or me* frame of mind ... and it's never gonna be me.

I turned to the next one and hit him with all I had. I felt his jaw crack under my fist. The noise would send shivers through you. It was like I took his life there and then. As I hit him his teeth bit through his tongue and the blood oozed out of his mouth as he went down. His face turned white as the blood drained from it. Every time I hit someone they went down; it's the only possible reaction to that amount of power. Once I'd dropped them there was no way on earth they were ever getting up. I made sure of that. I had so much strength that even if I did take a hit it just added to my rage, as if I was absorbing it and then hitting them twice as hard. I felt no pain. In that kind of fight anyone nearby was in clear and present danger. If I'd had an iron bar right then I would have smashed skulls in and dug the bastards' brain out with my hands. I felt that close. Possessed. For me all they were was something in my way that I had to get rid of.

They had stepped out of line big time and were now finding out the hard way that we would not put up with their shit. This was where you got the chance to see everyone's speciality: Geordie must have knocked out at least five by sticking the head on them. He was like a fucking battering ram. There was one who was obviously unconscious after the first one but, because he'd jumped Geordie from behind, he nutted him and nutted him. Not even his mother could have recognised him after that. Stevie used his strength. He was so powerful that he could lift people by the throat in real Arnie style. He knocked one of them out then *threw* him at another. A creative genius if I've ever seen one. You never really noticed what the others were doing until they were in need of help. Once I was in a fight I was blind to everything except my opponent. I would be aware of things going on, but it was more like a blind rage. I would notice them out of the corner of my eye, but I never really had the time to see what moves they were doing. It was only after fights when the others would tell you what they done, who they'd hit and how much blood there was. That's when patterns started forming and you could tell what their specialist move would be.

By the time the police arrived it was all over. The usual scene awaited. A lot of them had managed to crawl away in all the excitement, so there wasn't that many left to talk to the police about what we'd done to them. There was one lying on the ground who was beginning to regain consciousness. One of the coppers goes to Stevie, 'Who's that bloke there?' and Stevie just told him he was one of ours. Good, eh? Because he was one of the only remaining boxers and wearing his penguin suit, he could have been one of us for all they knew. They asked if we wanted him taken to hospital but we said he'd be all right, we'd deal with him ourselves ... last thing we wanted was for him to regain consciousness in front of the police.

* * * * *

The one thing that fuelled all the fighting was the drink. Of course, that sounds obvious, but back then the level of drinking was phenomenal. The café bar and coffee-house culture of today was unthinkable in those days. To meet up with your mates and suggest going out for coffee? You'd never show your face ever again. People hadn't even considered watering down beer yet and all everyone seemed to be interested in was drinking as much as they could and then fighting as many people as possible. We are definitely a more civilised society these days. To put a table and chairs in the street out the front of a bar meant that by the end of the night they would be used as weapons – whether they were thrown at someone, went through the window of the pub or a shop or were smashed up and the legs used as bats. To put up a table and chairs now is cool and will attract possibly the more image-conscious type of person. Back then, there really was that Wild West anything-can-happen atmosphere.

Drugs were not a major problem then, either. I don't think people were that interested – they would rather get monged on twenty pints of beer. For all the bad press that the rave scene got in its early days, you would never see any of them fight. They were the happiest people around. People would be hugging, talking at a million miles an hour and chewing around four stone of gum. The next day their jaw would be sore, but from all the chewing and talking, not fighting. Of course, with drugs being a big thing now there are people who mix them with drink. That's when things usually go off. They would probably be fine just on drugs, because they'd be in their own little world, but give 'em a drink and they change. Some people just can't handle drink at all and turn violent and unreasonable. If this is backed up by a drug like speed, they can be a right pain in the arse. You can knock them down and they get straight back up! You could pull their arms out of their sockets and they would wriggle around shouting abuse and try to nut you. When they're ripped to the tits like that, they don't seem to notice the damage they are taking. In one of my clubs there is blood up the wall of the doorway from this type of incident. It only happened around two years ago. I'm not going to say he was on something, but God help him if he wasn't. Bulging eyes, foaming at the mouth – I mean, I know he was an ugly-looking spud to start with, but this kind of thing just wasn't natural. And he would not stay down. I was giving him a real beating, absolutely hammering him, but he kept getting up and coming for more. I thumped him again and again, cracking his nose wide open. It just shattered. You could actually see into his face after that. Where his nose used to be was a gaping hole and the blood sprayed out and up the wall. People were gasping as he kept staggering to his feet – they couldn't believe the state he was in. His top lip was also split and I thought the two wounds were going to meet just below his nose. If it got to that point I could have literally peeled his face off. I've never seen damage like it. Someone was sick on the spot, just watching. I couldn't punch him in the face again 'cos my fist would have torn right through it. I could have finished him for real without a problem. No amount of special effects could ever recreate it … it was disgusting.

People like him were just plain stupid. We had this one bloke in who was stupid enough to bring a knife in and start showing it around. Anyone taking a knife out with them on a night out must have serious problems – and you can guarantee that it *will* bring them serious problems one way or another. This bloke was about as bright as an eclipse. The club was a cattle market most of the time and I didn't want it to turn into a butcher's. I'd got word that he had a knife in his back pocket and I went over to confront him about it. This was a mistake – I went by myself when I should have taken Geordie. Probably the only time I'd not had him with me. I saw the lad at the bar and moved in. I asked him if I could have a word with him and he was straight on the defensive. The shitbag had just bought a pint of cider and, when I put my hand on his shoulder to lead him to a quiet place, he threw it in my face. Cider in your eyes stings like soap … I was blinded and wiping at my eyes with the sleeve of my jacket when I saw his arm coming for me. I grabbed him by the hair, dragged him down and stood on his face. I kept him down like this till I could wipe my eyes properly and that was when I saw the knife in his hand. I went berserk. Who the fuck did he think he was? I picked him up by his belt and collar and rammed him into the bar as hard as I could. Underneath the bar used to be loads of mirrors and I just kept ramming and ramming the bastard's face into it till they were all completely smashed. His face was literally in bits. Half of it looked like it was hanging off. There were bits of mirror all over him and blood was running down all the cracked bits at the bar. Behind the mirrors it was solid, so each time I rammed him into it, his face and head were being ground into all the tiny razor-sharp shards of glass. Once I felt his body go limp I dragged him out into Boozy Alley. The other doormen only knew what was going on once I'd dragged him out, 'cos when you open the doors it sets off an alarm in reception. They came running out as I was going ape shit with this lad. I threw him against the wall and he collapsed into a heap. I was shouting, 'The *cunt* had a knife', and sure enough one of them went back in and found it on the floor.

The next thing I knew he'd gone to the police to get *me* arrested. He must have been having a laugh. The police came in to see me and I told them he had pulled it out on me and I was acting in self-defence. I even gave them the knife so they could run a fingerprint check on it. They found his prints all over it and asked if I wanted to press charges. There was no way I was gonna do that; I wasn't as low as he was.

Speaking of low ... Monday nights were a pain in the arse. They were always good for a fight. Yes, really! Fighting in Sunderland wasn't just a weekend hobby. They were at it every day of the week. Monday night became known as Dog Night; this is where the low bit comes in, 'cos there was no limit to the depths people were willing to sink just to get laid. All the single parents had just cashed their benefit money in and were blowing it all on drink.

They were all responsible parents back then ... not. It used to be embarrassing at times. The night got its name because most of these slappers were the real dregs of the barrel. These were the type of people who had fallen off the ugly tree and hit every branch on the way down; it was only when they'd hit the ground that someone came along and beat them with the ugly stick. There was this woman who used to come in every Monday – in fact, I think we named the night after her. No kidding, she looked like a horse eating a toffee apple through a letterbox. We'd take the piss a bit but it was all good-natured; we knew when not to step over the line. There used to be loads of fights on Dog Night, because they would all be drinking like there was no tomorrow. They used to make themselves sick on purpose so they could drink more and then, if two stunners had eyes for the same hunk, we'd have a real dogfight on our hands.

There were other nights that definitely were not Dog Night. We used to have things like roadshows and other events like the wedding dress thing I mentioned earlier. The night the *Sunday Sport Roadshow* rolled into town was another memorable event. Now, these women must have been wearing ugly-stick repellent from an early age. Some background information for the people out there who are unfamiliar with the *Sunday Sport*: now simply called *The Sport*, it's a newspaper unlike any other you can possibly imagine. It is basically soft porn and is compulsive reading matter for any self-respecting workman on the street. This is the sort of thing that makes the tabloids look highbrow. It's packed with near-naked women in all kinds of different poses. I'm sure you can picture it now. At the height of its popularity it hit the road and the women in the paper would make appearances at nightclubs all over the place.

That night proved to be a real nightmare for us. The place was packed wall to wall with pissed-up, testosterone-fuelled blokes all dying to get near enough to the women for a quick grope. As they made their way from the dressing room to the stage, we had to make sure the tit jamboree could get there in one piece. There was Stevie on one side and me on the other as we walked the procession through. The rest of the doormen were doing a Moses so we could get through.

Then it just erupted. There was a bloke who was right behind Stevie and had been screaming abuse at him because he couldn't see properly. Not that many people could with Stevie in front of them, but that was when he made the mistake of taking a cheap shot – the coward bastard hit Stevie from behind. I think at first

Stevie let it ride because he thought it may have been an accident; when he shouted and hit him again, he knew it was for real. Stevie turned and decked him. He didn't need to suss him out first because he knew that no matter who it was they were getting hurt. From that moment, any interest in the women was well out the window. Attention had turned from the most basic of instincts (sex) to its closest rival – fighting. When you have to hold a crowd back there are always a few of them who will shout at you and give you a sly dig because they are safe amongst the rest. But when a fight breaks out between the crowd and us, those are the ones who are at the top of the hit list every time. Once Stevie had decked the first one we were all at it. We were wading into them lashing out at wherever the fists were coming from. I was straight in and punching for all I was worth. You could feel the connecting punch but in something like that there isn't really time to size up each and every face in your way. Basically, if they are in my way they are gonna get hit; if they weren't part of the fighting, there was no way they would be in front of me. By the time I'd looked up to see where I was, I was in front of the bar. There were puddles of drink and broken glass all over it; then I saw a bloke standing there looking straight down at me.

I started towards him and yelled at him to get the fuck off the bar. I couldn't tell if he was stupid or brave, but he was defiant. Again I yelled at him. You've got to imagine that there was a near riot going on and any time I spent just standing having an argument was leaving me wide open for attack. I had to move quickly. I went for him and he raised his hands up doing all kinds of kung fu moves. The cheeky bastard. He was in the dominant position up there, so I needed him on my level. I swept his legs with my right arm and he came crashing down on to his back. A couple of elbows and forearm smashes took the wind out of him. From that I folded him up like a deckchair and took him outside.

On the way out I opened two sets of doors with his head; I didn't hear a peep from him after that.

The next day Stevie and me were called up into the office to have a word with Tom. It turned into quite a few words actually, and the gist of it was that he wasn't happy. We were told that we were out of order and there was video evidence to back it up ... Run VT: it was mental! There we were flanking this gorgeous babe on the way to the stage and Stevie suddenly turns and plants someone. On his way down he takes about six others with him because of the sheer force of the punch. This starts the whole thing off and to see it from the angle we had was quite impressive. It was like a Mexican Wave of violence that spread across the whole room. Then, of course, we pan across nicely and see a lovely shot of yours truly in the confrontation with Chuck Norris on the bar. This is where the manager pauses it and turns to me, 'Why did you drag that poor lad off the bar like that?' he asked. Eh? Poor lad? Is it usual behaviour to stand on top of the bar? I pondered.

'Well, he was on top of the bar, wasn't he?' was my reply.

Run the tape on a bit ... Pause ...

'Well, what was he saying to you when you were shouting at him to get down?' asked Tom.

'Nothing,' I said. 'He just started doing all this kung fu business at me with his hands.'

The tape played through to when I took him outside and moved out of shot. The boss turned back from the screen to me. 'The reason why he didn't say anything is because he is deaf and dumb. He was telling you that he wasn't fighting and was already trying to get down. It wasn't kung fu at all. It was sign language.'

Well, that certainly did it for Stevie. He burst out laughing and couldn't stop. I was trying not to but sometimes when you try to stop it just makes it worse. My shoulders were jumping up and down like I was operating a pneumatic drill and my eyes were tight shut until I couldn't keep it in any longer. I exploded. I was roaring with laughter and Stevie was crying by now. Eventually Tom even cracked under the strain. We couldn't believe it. We wound the tape back a few more times and laughed louder each time. He's got to be one of the unluckiest men around – sorry, mate, I didn't know, but you still shouldn't have been on the bar, should you?

Other than that one, we were almost charged with inciting a proper riot one day ... as if? This one was a Showman's Guild Presentation and the outcome was that they wanted to charge me, Stevie, Geordie, Richey and Derek for three hundred and fifty assaults. That was everyone in the room (including staff, I think). I know we were quick, but assaulting three hundred and fifty people – that's seventy each, a bit excessive even for us. I was quite chuffed that they thought enough of us to even charge us with it. Cheers. Although they would like me to admit to it here, I can't. As unbelievable as it may seem, we didn't go to work to start fights. Even if we did, we'd get sacked. To have a night with no incidents would have been a pleasant surprise to us, but we knew it would never happen. It was quite a mad one and we all ended up carrying the fight on when we arrived at the casualty ward in hospital. People were getting patched up all over and we'd be running in to give them another bashing. Did we ever go to the police complaining we'd been jumped on? I could never understand the mentality of them. They start huge fights with the sole purpose of beating us and proving themselves around town. To beat the best, they would be the best, so to speak. Then, when they started on us and found they couldn't do it, we'd get done for assaulting *them*. Correct me if I'm wrong, but even Mr Spock would find that one illogical. We didn't get charged in the end – we were like Tefal: nothing would stick.

There were a few times when I got into battles and then went for round two in the hospital. It saves a lot of bother in the long run if the fight ends up in hospital. One of those times was a fight with a known hard man and drug dealer in the area. I was standing on the door at Bentleys. It must have been around ten o'clock, 'cos I was alone – Geordie was off on his break. A lad came up to me and asked if he could have a look inside. Sure, I said. He had his head in the doorway past my shoulder and as he withdrew he punched me. He must have had a ring on, 'cos it cut me just above my eye. Then he ran off up the street. He'd caught me off guard, but I went straight after him. He might have a head start, but he wasn't going to escape. I caught up with him round the corner on Crowtree Road, just in front of the leisure centre, and brayed fuck out of him. He was the only thing on my mind, not the fact that we were in the middle of the road, and a bus came within inches of hitting me. I just carried on hitting him until another doorman pulled me off. Once I let him up he was off again. I went back to Bentleys, checked my eye out and got a taxi to hospital to get it stitched up.

So there I was, sitting in hospital. It was quiet at that time of night. I heard the door open behind me and standing there was the same kid I'd just been fighting with! I still didn't know who he was at this point. I went over to him – 'Outside now!' He started yelling at the woman behind the counter that I was the one who had assaulted him, 'That's him, that's him!' he kept saying.

I told him, 'Get outside. I'm gonna fucking assault you again.'

He said something like, 'Why, have you brought a gun with you?' That was the last thing he said before I knocked him to the ground. I was straight on top of him and punching into his face. No sooner was I on top of him than I felt something solid round my neck from behind. It wasn't like a forearm. It turned out to be a policeman using his truncheon to drag me off. Once I realised it was the police, it stopped there. We were both questioned about the fight and I told the copper what had happened. We went over to the club, looked at the video footage and one of the police asked if I knew who the bloke was. I said I didn't care. He told me the bloke's name, but I still wasn't bothered. I later found out that, the week before, he had been in the club and had kicked off. He was bashed and thrown out, so he'd obviously came back for revenge. Seeing me alone on the door was his chance and he was only looking in to see if there were any others around before making his move. I knew nothing about it – it had nothing to do with me. As soon as I was involved, though, he certainly knew all about it.

Psychoanalysis

WE KNEW WE had a certain reputation when we were given our new name tags to wear. We'd wear them with pride but thinking back it was like the Devil himself had already brandished us:

Pleased to meet you, hope you guess my name ...

My main man, Geordie, was also head doorman at Gillespies and drafted me in to work with him. We were now best mates and had been through a shitload of trouble together. We trusted each other with our lives. That's the only way I'd describe it. I knew that Geordie would be prepared to die for me in a fight and he knew that I'd do the same for him – that's how tight we were. Sure, it may sound overdramatic, but the doormen among you will understand and I think the rest of you may have a good idea by now. I worked with Geordie at Gillespies on a night and later on we'd be on the doors at Bentleys. It was hectic but because we enjoyed it so much it just didn't feel like work. That's a great position to be in – there are not too many people who love their job that much, are there? And of course, I was getting paid for it as well. Life was sweeter than a bath of sugar.

On the odd nights we weren't working we were out and about in town. Nights out for us, as Geordie would put it, would be 'Fighting and fucking', or usually one of them at least. The likelihood was that it could only really be one or the other. When embarking on the latter, we were like a couple of tomcats out on the prowl. Geordie was the Nigel Havers of Sunderland – straight outta charm school, he was. Me? I've always been a magnet! As for the former, everywhere we went we would get a warning before going into the pub. Everyone knew us and what we were capable of. We'd get all the looks from people as we entered – people we'd kicked out the week before would still have the fresh battle scars to prove it. Sometimes it was that bad we would expect the needle of the record to scratch off and everyone staring at us in silence with tumbleweed blowing past.

We would still go in single file in case anyone tried anything. In our position you can never let your guard down. This one night we were sitting in Chambers having a drink when some lads decided to have a go. One thing when you have a reputation is that there are always people around who'll want to take a pop at you. This night was no different. There were around six or seven of them and one of them started it all off by throwing a bottle over. It's all a bit hazy really; the bouncers came over and calmed things down. The lads had disappeared and we were told they were outside – then, when we got out to look for them, the doors were shut behind us. Bastards. We were convinced it was a set-up and were more pissed off that we'd fallen for it than anything else. We hung around for a bit and moved on for another drink. We were still looking for them that night and went back to Chambers to watch for them. We saw plenty of people but were not exactly sure what the lads looked like and it wouldn't have been a good move to chin everyone in sight on the off chance. And by then we were slightly the worse for wear, so we let it go. Geordie even found half of the bottle that was thrown at us – it had landed in his top pocket! The urgency to get our revenge on the lads subsided. It wasn't as if we had taken a beating; it was just a scuffle that was over before it started. We were barred afterwards, so they got what they wanted. Didn't let it spoil our night, though; we got what we wanted as well – remember what our intentions were when we went out? Yep! Twice.

* * * * *

At Bentleys, Stevie was head doorman and had been trying to partner us off with different people. Geordie and me used to start off with the other bloke in tow then walk round the back to the doors where we used to stand, meet up and just kind of stay together for the rest of the shift. We couldn't be split up and didn't want to work with anyone else. At Gillespies, Geordie was the boy so we didn't have to answer to anyone. We ruled. Other staff there were getting nametags – know those badges that shop assistants and the like wear? All the bar staff ended up with them. Then one day we were given ours ... *Psycho One* and *Psycho Two*. We were the bollocks. Geordie got *Psycho One* – he was the original psycho after all (and still is). We were flattered by the gesture and wore them at Bentleys as well. We hardly ever took them off.

We'd seen plenty of action on the frontlines at Gillespies as well. Bearing in mind that most people would be regulars at Bentleys, we knew who was sound and who was likely to start something. There was this one bloke I had barred from Bentleys who tried to get in Gillespies. I didn't – and don't – like him. Full stop. After a while he was allowed back in and I made sure he knew he was on a warning. In just telling him this I wanted to rip his fucking voice box out and show it to him. His eyes said it all. His smug facial expression. I could picture this bastard's head above my mantelpiece like a trophy. Only the stupid tend to fuck up after first being barred and given a very serious warning. Just how stupid this bloke was, I was about to find out.

He came into Gillespies one night with some tart and another couple. I clocked him straight away as they walked in. He was wearing a suit and was obviously trying to be something he wasn't. Him and a suit went together about as well as Ozzy Osborne and Britney Spears out on a date; putting one on him was like trying to polish a lump of shit. I used to stand at the top of the staircase as you come in; it is separated midway by a small landing with the top half going off at a right angle. Sure enough he looked up and saw me and my instincts told me something would happen at some point during the night. I stared back at the fool, itching to get at him. As the night drew on he ditched the jacket and tie. This could be a sign that he was a bit drunk and relaxed or a sign that he was about to make his move – personally I think it was the drink giving him the balls to approach me.

He came up to me. Right in my face, and talking so much shit it was unbelievable. He was going, 'What the fuck did you bar me for in the first place?' Why he had to ask I'll never know. He knew exactly why he'd been barred but, because it had been festering away in his tiny little mind for so long, it sounded as though he wanted some sort of apology from me or something. As if I'd say, 'Sorry, it was all a misunderstanding. My mistake.' Know what I mean? As mentioned earlier, I cannot argue. If you argue with me I will argue back and, if you break eye contact, I know you know what will happen if it goes any further. If you do take it further I can guarantee it will be the last argument we ever have. No one has the right to talk or shout at me like that. It is my right to stop you, and that's what I'll do.

So, as he's rambling away, I'm thinking to myself, Oh aye, think you're fucking *something*, do you? He was looking for a fight, no doubt about it, and now he'd just found one ... *Bang!* Down he went. I cracked his stupid face open and watched as he rolled down the first flight of stairs and hit the rail of the platform at the bottom. As I went down after him, the other couple and this bloke's bird were looking up. She had tight hold of his jacket, just as Terry had for me all those years ago. It was obvious that this was his attempt to put on a show for them. Well, he was, wasn't he? A right fucking show. Seeing him fall beneath me was brilliant. This was what it was all about. Nothing could ever recreate that feeling when I'd see someone go down and I knew it was all over. I was following him down and wanted to stamp his head into the steps ... not my style, though.

I got to the landing, picked him up and knocked him down the first flight of stairs all the way to the bottom. When he rolled down on to the floor I wouldn't give him a chance to stand up. His hands were stretched out and I ground his knuckles into the floor with my foot. I wasn't just kicking him and hurting him – I was trying to break his ribs or smash his pelvis, wanting him to suffer afterwards as well as during the beating. I grabbed hold of his hair and dragged him out. On the way I clocked Geordie doing the 'Oh no, not again' face, shaking his head and half-grinning. I dragged this bloke outside and left him. Geordie propped him so he was sitting up against the window. The funny thing was that the ambulance service was on strike then, so a great big bloody fire engine pulled up at the pub with the siren blasting. *Everyone* was out in the street. This was definitely a first. One of the firemen got out and had to give him oxygen. When he came round he nearly shit himself. He thought he'd been in a fire.

You wouldn't believe some of the shit we saw at the club, though – and I mean *shit*. The amount of times we had to deal with people who had locked themselves in the toilets and passed out – it was a nightmare. We went in one time and this bloke had to have been on something. You've never seen anything like it. He was absolutely stark bollock naked – but that's not the weird bit. He had made a nest in the corner of the room and was trying to lay an egg! The toilets were quite big and had an old attendant gadgey who used to give us a shout in that kind of situation. The Bird Man was harmless, though, no bother at all, and it gave us something to laugh about. It's when you get people who have shit themselves that you begin to wonder if you're in the right profession. It was worse than babysitting. People would be passed out in a cubicle with their pants round their ankles, on the floor – they'd missed the toilet completely, shit all over and to top it all off they'd throw up when they were unconscious. We would have to climb over, unlock the doors, clean them up (yeah, right) and take them outside. This one lad was absolutely covered in vomit, piss and shit and God knows what else ... a real catch he was. After arguing over who would carry him and trying not to barf ourselves, we got him outside and propped him up. Every now and again the police van would pass and they would ask if we had anyone for them – the reason they used to ask was so they had an excuse to go back to the station and have a coffee. Straight up. So we offered them this unconscious thing, stinking of shit – and they weren't even interested! The *bastards!* They would rather go without their break than deal with him. What a time to get choosy about who you throw in the van. So we were stuck with him at the front for ages. He still hadn't woken up and it was obvious that he wouldn't be with a girlfriend, so we searched him for identification. We got his address and he still had twenty quid on him, so we flagged a taxi down. All going well: Geordie goes up and asks if he'll take us to the address, then when we go to put Shitty Arse in he just drives off with the door still open and us standing there, cursing him. We should have just thrown him in one of the bins round the back, but it wouldn't have been fair on whoever got chucked in next. In the end we had to chip in and pay another £20 to cover the cleaning bill and to get him home safely. I know people can go a bit daft and a bit childish after a drink but this lad should have been wearing Huggies. The council doesn't even charge that much to remove other rubbish. If this brings back any memories to anyone, we want the twenty quid back or your name goes into volume two.

Even more unbelievable is that the women were worse for this sort of thing than the lads were. No kidding. You've heard of damsels in distress; well, these were damsels in piss-dresses. It was absolutely disgusting. Slumped in the cubicles with their trolleys covered in shit, and we'd be slipping all over trying to get them out quick enough to avoid the smell. There was one lass who used to swan around Bentleys like she owned it. She really thought she was the dog's. And, without going into too much detail, the above happened to her. Absolutely honking it was. The following weekend, we were talking to the lads on the doors at Annabell's and who should appear with her mates? She was exactly like you'd expect an arrogant movie star to act, all prima donna centre-of-attention stuff. So here she is walking in and there's loads of people, men and women, behind queuing up. So I went over to her and said, 'I know you …' She's off on one, loving the attention … 'You're the one who shit herself last week and had to be carried out the club.' She must have lost her thirst after that, 'cos she stormed off with everyone laughing. If she hadn't thought she was above everyone else, there wouldn't have been a mention. Some people used to thank us the next week and we'd have a joke about it with them. Other people think their shit doesn't stink, but believe me …

This one time I was carrying a girl out and Geordie was opening the doors for me – why did *we* always have to do it? So we're moving through everyone, Geordie is seeing that no one gets in the way and I happen to glance down to make sure she isn't being sick on me. Well, you know the type of skimpy tops girls go out in, don't you? Here's one reason why they shouldn't ... Her top had slipped down, not loads but just enough for the left one to get a bit of fresh air. It had popped right out! I got Geordie over and told him to put it back in, but he was having none of it. (No 'feeling a right tit' jokes, please – too obvious.) If anyone was watching or happened to see him doing it they would think he was trying to take advantage of her, so the best bet was to keep moving. We propped her up at the usual spot, but gravity just wasn't playing ball. It was still on show. There weren't any female staff around at the time, so we had to find her mates to help her out.

It was always good to have daft little things like that happen to help lighten the mood. I'm not saying *they* were daft little things, just in case she's reading, but it's always nice to have a laugh, innit?

It was when I was working at Bentleys that I met the Ex-Mrs Freeman, Tracey Chambers. She started hanging around with Geordie's girlfriend, so they would be around most of the time. Now if there was ever anything to laugh at ... I must have had some feelings for her at first, but whatever was there soon turned to complete misery. When the bad times outweigh the good, your whole vision gets sort of clouded – I look back now and can barely remember a day we didn't fight. We've all heard of love/hate relationships – well, this turned into hate, hate and more hate. The inevitable happened: bitter marriage and sweet divorce. It only lasted a year. Don't tell me you've never made mistakes – I won't believe you.

* * * * *

I was now entering bodybuilding competitions. The first show I entered was the 1989 North-East Coast competition – and I won.

The dog's: first show, first prize, couldn't be happier. When I won it I weighed 12 stone 10 ounces. I was perfectly toned and thought I was at my peak. Everything was natural and that's what people couldn't understand. Once I put my mind to something I go for it with all my heart. It's not that I can't handle defeat and love to win (although who doesn't?); it's that I love to achieve. I love to compete and test myself in anything I do. If I set out on something, I like to see how far I can take it. As a bodybuilder I was committed. I entered two more competitions: in '91 it was Mr Yorkshire – 'Ay up, Ian Freeman takes first prize' – and also that year I came third in the Mansfield Classic, which was a really big show. I know I said that the Bentleys' events were getting worse, but I also entered the *Mr Bentleys* bodybuilding competition. There'll be certain people who won't expect me to mention it – OK, nuff said!

When we were together, Tracey used to do car boot sales on a Sunday morning. As if she wasn't annoying enough, she would get up at five in the morning when I'd just got back from work. What can you do? Well, you can get your dad to take her there for a start. He'd pick her up at quarter-past ridiculous in the morning, then a lot later on I would take my mam along when they were finishing up. My mam and dad would travel back in their car, and I'd take Tracey back. Happy families.

We were behind my dad one Sunday afternoon, going along Gateshead High Street. There were four sets of traffic lights down there and it was like a ghost town. You kept in the right lane to go straight on and the left lane if you wanted to turn left. A car cut in front of my dad. It came completely from nowhere, the only other car on the road. In cutting him off, he hit the front of my dad's car and pulled into the left-hand lane. I was behind them at this point. I watched as he cut in front of my dad twice more; I was going absolutely fucking mental.

At the next set of lights the bloke had turned to my dad and was giving him the V-sign. I knew my dad would have something to say. We were all in line now. Him in the front, my dad and then me. I saw my mam and dad having words and could see what was going to happen. He got out and approached the car. I was thinking, Here we go, as the other bloke made to get out of his. In the words of my mother, 'He got out of the car and I didn't think he was ever going to stop standing. He was that big.' Christ knows how he ever fitted into the car.

Once I saw this going on I knew I'd have to do something.

This bloke was huge – long enough to be continued – and he looked dangerous with it. I just wanted to tell the both of them to get back in their cars and to stop being stupid. As I got out, the bloke grabbed hold of my dad. Imagine the feeling of seeing someone grab your own dad like that. This is the guy who has been your hero all your life. This is the point in your life that you see your dad is not Superman after all. He looked normal in comparison to this giant. I felt the rage build up; *no one* would touch my dad like that. Who did he think he was? The way it worked out was as I was approaching my dad was facing me and the bloke had his back to me. I'm sure he was lifted off his feet. There was no time to be fancy; he needed to be stopped. I speeded up and I punched him with all my might. I connected with the right side of his face and it dropped him instantly. It had to be done with one punch and I made it count. He bounced off the car bonnet and slid down on to the road. My dad was now free so, while the geezer was out cold in the gutter, he gave him a quick hoof in the ribs before we legged it. Luckily, there were no other cars in sight. If I hadn't been there, I hate to think what would have happened, and my mother would have been forced to look on helplessly. I was mad enough to do some real damage, but the middle of the road was not the place to do it. I even had to drag my dad away!

A few weeks later a mate of mine told me about this story that had got out. The hard man of the area was getting out of his car to do this old gadgey in: apparently he had hold of him and was about to hit him when the old man clobbered him with a left so fast that he didn't even see it. He was out like a light. So it turned out that my dad was now the hardest in Gateshead. And probably helped invent road rage along the way. What a nutcase. My dad was a real character like that. It took balls for him to go up against a bloke of that size, but I think any other dad would do it. All dads are supermen and all of you would do anything for your dad. It rips your heart out to think that any harm can come to them; it may be through illness or whatever, but there will be a point in your life when you realise he is not invincible – that's when he knows you've grown up. That's when he can let out a sigh of relief to finally know he doesn't have to slay dragons or wrestle lions because you love him for the man he is.

* * * * *

Because I was getting so big, and with my reputation also growing, you'd think people would have learnt a bit of respect. Bollocks. Some people are just plain stupid – or they don't know what respect is. It goes one way or the other with the big lads – they'll introduce themselves and have a friendly chat (remember that friends are a lot better to have than enemies) or they will cop an attitude and take a pop at you. There isn't much in between – that's where all the two-faced bastards hang out and swap their bitchy stories all day. A lot of it comes down to jealousy, I guess. One time, Geordie and me were enjoying a night out and this absolutely huge charva started shouting the odds. I'd never laid eyes on him in my life, but he had a problem with me being there. The jealousy theory? I know Geordie's all right looking – if he really fancied him he just had to ask him out; it's not like I was his pimp. Maybe he felt threatened in some way. He must have thought he had to prove something – the biggest fish and all that.

We could see right away that he was a bodybuilder. He was like a gigantic bulldog; in fact, he was the one that the line '... a face like a bulldog licking piss off a nettle' was based on. True story. I was prepared to leave it. I didn't respond to him and tried my hardest to ignore him. It became harder to ignore him when he was standing right over me and practically casting a shadow ... and his breath ... Jesus. Of course, you don't have to fight to be a man – we all know that, but he didn't. To be a man was to beat me, as far as he was concerned. He had bad attitude written all over him. I was on a night off for a change; do electricians sit at home on a day off playing with cable and light fittings? I don't think so. Geordie said that I'd have to sort it out and I agreed. He'd certainly crossed the line and I had to do something about it. There was one way I could get him out of my face for good. We took it down a side street; there was me, Geordie, Bigger With Attitude and a couple of his mates. We came to a stop and prepared for battle. You'll never guess what the dork did next.

He stood there and ripped his shirt off! Just like the Incredible Hulk! We were half expecting him to turn green, but he just stood there tensing, posing and roaring like an idiot. I turned to Geordie and we gave each other a 'What the fuck?' expression.

'Oh, I'm well impressed with that, mate,' I said as I walked towards him. It was all over in seconds. I let rip with a right-left-right combination that sent him straight to the floor. That wiped the self-satisfied smirks from his mates' faces. They backed off as he landed, allowing me to move in to give him a proper slapping. He was gonna pay big time. I stared him in the eyes, drew the big right back and measured him up. I was gonna make this piece of shit bleed for every other kid he'd bullied. Before I could hit him he was up on his knees with his hands up in surrender: 'Please don't hit me!' he was screaming. '*Please* don't hit me!' I stepped closer and brought my fist up higher. 'No. Please don't. I'm *sorry*!'

Well, that was it. I couldn't hit him after that, could I? He may not have managed to turn green but he certainly produced a familiar shade of brown.

People like him give bodybuilders a bad name. If I hadn't reduced him to tears like that he would have gone around for the rest of his life using his size to intimidate people smaller than him. It always takes something like that to happen before they learn. Sad, innit? Making him beg like that was probably a lot worse for him than the kicking he was about to receive. He was all ego, all reputation and all mouth. Taking that away from him meant he couldn't present it in front of someone else. If I'd just beaten him up, he might have just moved on to some other kid, thinking it was a one-off. To beat someone up psychologically hurts a lot more than a physical beating and the scars last a lot longer. We couldn't keep our laughter in as we watched such a promising start turn in to the biggest disaster since the *Titanic*. It was pitiful ... the shirt I mean, what a waste.

I knew I was high profile when things like that started happening. It was all confrontations that I couldn't avoid. I'd be the biggest tosser on the planet if I just woke up one morning and thought, Today I think I'll walk around town, shout, abuse, threaten and start fights with anyone I feel deserves it. Am I wrong? I didn't start the fights, but boy did I stop them. I've never hit anyone who didn't do something to provoke me – and that's the way it will always be.

* * * * *

We should have got Bentleys sanctioned by Terry Wogan and raised thousands for Children in Need from weekend Fightathons. We even had a car drive through the place. This happened after we had kicked some lad out for being a right proper nuisance and he was giving it the full *Terminator* routine, vowing he'd be back and we were all like, 'Yeah, yeah. See you later, then.' Little did we know that he'd make such a grand entrance. The back doors that we used to stand next to and watch the punters from were big fire doors. Double doors, with two steps forming a raised-up area in front, where we had an excellent vantage point. We were in our usual position when we heard the revving and screeching of a fast car approaching. With absolutely no time to spare we dived for our lives. Geordie went one way and me the other and this car came crashing through the doors and came to a halt in the middle of the club. Everything seemed to slow down, though it was over in three seconds flat. There was dust and smoke everywhere, with a gaping hole where the doors used to be. We were all a bit dazed and were checking to see if people were OK. In the confusion, the driver's door opened and he made a mad dash for it. Oh no you don't! We were right after him down the alley – he would never get away. And he will never take a beating like that again and live. He was literally centimetres away from driving into us – and then there's all the others in the club he just missed.

We took turns in letting him know how we felt. We didn't want to stop. We punched his face till it was just a bloody mess – his nose was smashed and you couldn't make out that he had eyes; there was just a swollen mass with little slits where they used to be. In the night light, blood always looks like oil or ink and his face was leaking with the stuff. We were punching him and breaking bones. I held his face up to hit him but it didn't feel like a solid face any more. This wanker had come too close to killing us. Once you'd got hold of him, when do you decide he's had enough? You and a fair few others could be dying while he was bragging to his friends about what he'd done. Imagine what would be running through your mind when you caught up with him. I lost all control. It was rage and revenge that was controlling my actions. We left him lying in a heap against a wall, but it just didn't seem like enough was done. Even hanging him there and then would have been too good for him. People would still be in a state of shock back there and he wouldn't know the full extent of what he'd done. Even if he had killed anyone it wouldn't have mattered to him. He was that close to unconsciousness that he couldn't even cry out in agony, then he just passed out. We left him and went back to the club to help out. After that there was a bollard put up in front of the back doors to be on the safe side. We couldn't take any more risks like that; there could have been dozens killed that night.

Big Shaun Kelly was also working the doors at Bentleys. A real big bloke – bodybuilder – massive. You would easily lose count of the people you had to carry out or wake up because they were unconscious with the drink; they would be lying around all over the place. Shaun used to drag and hurl them around like rag dolls. Well over the top, and people were starting to notice. I was acting as head doorman from time to time and the management had left it up to me to fire him when I was working relief for Stevie. I told him he'd have to go; the management thought he was out of order and that was it. Off he went.

Pretty soon he was working in The Borough, which is just up the road from Bentleys, and for me to get to work I had to drive past there. As I drove past we clocked each other and he started shouting all kinds of rubbish. He was shouting that he was going to kill me. The window was wound down and I asked him why. He said it was 'cos I had sacked him. What a jerk-off. If he was looking for someone to blame he only needed to try the mirror. 'Tell you what,' I said, 'I'll go and park up round the back of Bentleys. Meet me round there in a few minutes and we'll see if you're going to kill me.'

Well, me being me I drove round the corner, parked up and went to confront him. We ended up brawling in the middle of the road. I was all over him like a Kappa shell suit. Next thing I knew a WPC appeared in front of us. I never did see them but she must have had some set of balls on her. With this woman in the line of fire, it finished there and then. I was pissed off 'cos I didn't get the chance to smash his bastard face in. More police arrived and we were arrested. I knew the officers quite well, so it wasn't like we were cuffed and stuffed. It was more of an informal arrest. Shaun was being put into one police car as I was led past him to another. As I got near I broke free and started giving him another bashing. I was dragged off him before being carted off to the station.

I didn't ask for a solicitor – didn't think it was necessary. In those days, it was usually a slapped wrist and then sent home. Usually. A few hours went by and I was wondering why we hadn't been interviewed. I rang the buzzer and a copper came to the cell door. He told me that the WPC had been assaulted and she didn't know which one of us had done it. Bloody marvellous – best call the cavalry in then. I sent for Mr Halliday of Gateshead to come and work his magic. Martin Halliday is still my solicitor. He helped me out in the past over a daft little incident, and in the turbulent years following that he was always around and helped out on many occasions. And this time in particular I was really grateful.

Because I was already on police bail for assault, I was kept overnight and up in court the next day. On the way in, Martin told me the charges: assaulting a police officer, affray and I was already on bail so there was no way they would let me out. He told me I was going to be remanded. I understood. What's gonna happen will happen. The WPC's statement was read out. It was along the lines of she stood between Mr Kelly and me. Mr Freeman on the left and Mr Kelly on the right. She had a swollen outer left knee, in which case it was obviously me, according to the evidence. Technically it couldn't have been Shaun; he could only have hit her right knee or the inner left. I was bollocksed. I

Top left: My bodybuilding days – ripped!

And it paid off – me as a bodybuilding champion (*Top right*)

Bottom left: Becoming British Champion was only the start of my success. It only got better from there.

Bottom right: Frank Mir too frightened to get back on his feet.

I'm no poser, but I was proud as anything to be the Vale Tudo champion.

Top left: British title with my best pal, Carl Simpson

Top right: Invincible! In the ring and in my prime – The Machine is a force to be reckoned with.

Bottom left: 'No pain, no gain.' Never a truer word spoken – me training hard, as I always do!

Bottom right: Training is always no holds barred, the only way to prepare for what's to come.

The Machine wins again and salutes the crowd – without them, there is no match.

Top: Frank Mir takes a big right hand.

Bottom: Travis Fulton feels the heat of The Machine's ground 'n' pound move.

Top: Proud to be at the top. The Machine with the UFC championship belt.

Bottom left: A work of art. Ten hours of sheer pain.

Bottom right: One of the guys being picked up in the gym.

(*Clockwise from top left*) King of Pancrase and UFC Champion Bas Rutten. UFC Middleweight Champion 'The Huntington Beach Bad Boy' Tito Ortiz. Me with Tedd Williams at UFC 27. Scott Adams and Me at UFC 24.

Top: Me and my wife, Angie. Without her I wouldn't be where I am today.

Bottom: Mam, Dad and me with the British title.

was asked by the judge if I could have hit her accidentally. I said possibly, but not intentionally – I mean, you can hit anyone by accident if you want, but hitting women – whether policewomen or not – just wasn't my style. I was fined. That was it. A fine was fine by me. Because of that, I now have assaulting a police officer on my otherwise squeaky clean record. What a shitter. Martin Halliday made me look and sound like an angel. By the time he finished telling them about me I was checking my shoulders to see if I had wings. He was brilliant, took everything in his stride and handled himself perfectly. A real gent and a top boy. He was to come to my rescue a few times in the future as well, but we'll get to that in due course.

* * * * *

You always make stupid mistakes until the right woman comes along, don'tcha? Think back to all the ones you've been with and at the time you were the only one who couldn't see what everyone else was seeing. But, of course, no one else can point things like that out to you. It's only after you break up that people feel it's safe to tell you. Tracey was the mistake that I ended up paying for. We had a child together: Ian. Two Ian Freemans – imagine that! When he was a child, he was just ammunition for Tracey. It was horrible. We split up; she used and manipulated things through a bitter separation. And again I am not directing the word 'mistake' towards my son here – the mistake I made was getting involved with and then marrying the woman. Ian's early years were the worst for any child to go through and I wish none of it had happened. It's easy for me to sit back and tell you that Tracey was to blame for everything. You can infer what you want from what I tell you, and you know it's only my side of the story. But, when I tell you that I ended up with custody of my son, you can probably begin to build up a picture of what she was like. She ended up dumping him. She had him and gave him up. The year we spent together is exactly how you'd imagine hell – possibly not all the time, but enough to call it a day after such a short while. It was after we split up that things got really bad. We had a year together, which we spent fighting with each other, and then two years fighting over our son.

It was a real tug of war, with Ian in the middle. Tracey let me have him for nine months then took me to court to get him back. They gave him to her because she was his mother. Big mistake. It turned out that she only gave him to me as a ploy to get me back, thinking that I couldn't cope with him by myself. After getting custody, she thought that would get me back as well, because she thought that I'd miss Ian too much and go back to her. I missed him dearly but I wasn't gonna go back to her. She would phone me up and ask if I wanted to see him. Once I got round there and rang the doorbell she would appear at the top window with Ian in her arms and give me the V-sign. She used to do this all the time. Once I booted the door in and took him. I knew it was the wrong way to go about things, but I wanted to see my son and she had pushed me too far. I knew the police would be on their way. That's what she wanted. I would spend the day with him and take him back knowing full well what would happen when I returned. I got arrested, but it was worth it. She did her best to screw my head in.

My mate Reggie Conlin and his mother were great to me in this time of trouble. Reggie's a stand-up guy. Not so much in the action these days, but proved that he's got a heart of gold and showed that he knew the true meaning of friends. I had Ian one Christmas and I was literally left with nothing for him. This was at a time when I had basically rescued him from Tracey. The things I had seen him go through used to break my heart; no son of mine should go through that and I did everything I could for him. I was doing my best and was being a mother and a father to him. Reggie and his mam rallied round and helped me make Ian's Christmas a special one. I used to sit with his mother for hours at a time talking, sometimes crying. She loved me like a son and did everything she could to help. I felt things slipping away again. My temper would take hold and would control me at times instead of me controlling it. She knew all about my rage during that difficult time. She once said if I didn't learn to control my anger that I would end up killing someone. I can look back now and agree. When the demons got hold of me like that I was like a monster. I just couldn't give a shit who I hurt.

I extend my gratitude. Reggie and his mam didn't have to do what they did. They did it out of love and kindness. I'll never forget how they helped me with my little boy.

Why did you give up our little boy
Never loved and resented in care
This little child with arms open wide
Needed love but in your arms never there
Why did you give up our little boy

Legal battles and angry words
Courts of law for a long time to come
This little child with arms open wide
All he wanted was to have a real home
Legal battles and angry words

Please let there be, some justice for me
Please give me what is rightfully mine
Let him be loved, he needs to be loved
And stay with his daddy till end of all time

Frightened to lose this bundle of joy
Fought for him all of the way

This little child with arms open wide
Now has a family with him today
Frightened to lose this bundle of joy

Happy not sad in his life from now on
No more tears or going through pain
This little child with arms open wide
Will never be lonely again
Happy not sad in his life from now on

'Our Little Boy', *Ian Freeman*

It was shocking how Tracey would use her own son to get at me. She didn't care who got hurt along the way as long as she knew she had wound me up. One time she called me to say I could come and take Ian for the day. The usual happened. I went straight round, excited at the prospect of spending time with him. I should have known better. She wouldn't let me in. I stood knocking for a while and got sick of it. I shouted at her and walked away. She only wanted me to do something so she could have me arrested and I wasn't going to give her the satisfaction. The amount of times she had me charged for affray is criminal itself. I was in court on that charge so many times that it became a routine.

Unknown to me, she was looking after someone else's kids at the same time she pulled this one. The other woman just happened to be married to Shaun Kelly, the bloke I'd sacked and had had a fight with. The next thing I hear is that Shaun is pissed off with me for swearing at his kids. Tracey had told him that I went into the house and was shouting and swearing at them. Bollocks. It didn't and wouldn't happen. I do not go around shouting at kids; it's ridiculous.

I got word to Shaun to come and see me. I told him I didn't want to fight him and that it was Tracey causing trouble between us. She wanted us to fight; she'd pay to see me in a fight with someone as big as him. Shaun wasn't having any of it. He wanted a fight. Typical. This was only because I hadn't gave him the bashing he deserved outside The Borough and he probably thought he had half a chance. It was the WPC that saved his skin that time as far as I was concerned.

I told my mate Les to get round to the pub where Shaun worked and arrange a fight. If he definitely wanted to go through with it, there was no way I'd back down. Les arranged it. Monday morning, ten o'clock, Arthur's Gym. Fine, I thought, let's do it.

I went down to the gym with our Colin and Reggie. When we got to the reception area, Arthur came running over. His nerves were shot to shit. I told him I didn't want to fight with Shaun but that I was there to set the record straight. Arthur went to get him. You could have cut the atmosphere with a machete. In reception there is a staircase that leads up to the martial arts room. At the foot of the stairs is a pillar from floor to ceiling. Shaun came in. He's leaning against the pillar, a big fucking bloke. A lot bigger than me. I'm standing against the wall and I'm thinking, Don't look him in the eye 'cos he'll get aggressive.

It's not that I was scared; it's because I knew exactly what I'd be like. Eye contact would have been the only excuse to get me radged up. I was prepared to fight, but only as a last option. I knew who had stirred all this, remember. So he's got his tree trunk arms folded across his huge barrel of a chest. I was standing there telling him I didn't want to fight. We had nothing to fight about. He was still standing, defiant.

'Oh, what's the matter with you, Shaun?' I asked eventually. I was getting pissed off that he could be so pig-headed.

'You tell me,' he said, 'you're the one who's been swearing at my kids.'

'Who told you that? Tracey?' No answer. 'And you believe her?'

'Why shouldn't I? She was there with my kids,' he said.

It was frustrating. Frustrating that he couldn't see that she was using him in her warped little game.

I was shouting and swearing through the door – 'It wasn't at your kids, I didn't know they were in there.' There was nothing else I could say. I don't know how many times I'd told him. Tension was building and we were hurtling towards a fight. I could feel the rage taking over my mind and body as I was standing there. He started talking more shit, so I cut him dead.

'Listen. What the fuck do you want to do about it?'

He stepped away from the pillar. 'What the fuck do *you* want to do about it?'

He soon found out. No one ever speaks to me like that. He crossed the line; I stepped forward and planted him with the hardest punch he's ever felt. I hit him with pure venom. I had the speed, accuracy and was as deadly as a cobra. I had to make an example of him, to make him know what it felt like to mess with me. He had no chance at all. He was out before he knew it, thrown backwards on to the stairs with his head bouncing off the wall. His fucking eyebrow cracked and split open. There was blood up the wall and up the pillar. As he crash-landed I followed it up with two more whacks to the face … the second and third hardest he's felt. He was out cold for sure now. Goodnight, ladies and gentlemen, Elvis has left the building. Judging by the reaction from Arthur, Reggie and our Colin, Shaun wasn't getting up for a while. I knew from that first punch that the only place he was going was down. He was sparked out for a good ten minutes.

Arthur came running over from behind the counter with a cloth, wiping the blood up. 'Fucking hell, fucking hell. Just go, Ian. Please, just go.'

I told him I wouldn't. Shaun's eye was up like a cricket ball within seconds. When he came to he was moaning. He didn't know where he was or what had happened. I went back over to him; Arthur was poised with the cloth. But I wasn't going to do him again. 'Look, I've done what I had to do,' I said, 'but, if there's anyone you want to be hitting, it's Tracey 'cos she set you up. I did *not* shout at your kids, all right?'

It became personal between Shaun and me; this was just something that triggered off all the ill feeling that had built up. I can see it from his point of view, though. As far as he was concerned, I had done it. If only he knew what Tracey was like he may not have believed her, who knows. I think because we are both big men neither of us could be seen to back down; he had started the ball rolling and had to see it through. Because he still had a problem with me from Bentleys and the earlier fight, he was still after my blood and he would have seen this as the excuse he'd been waiting for. I didn't want to fight him because I knew Tracey had set it up, but at the same time I was glad to get the chance to give him a going over. I never need an excuse if I have a problem with someone, but him starting it meant I could walk in and finish it. When the last fight got split up I was gutted 'cos I hadn't had the chance to hurt him like I wanted to. We both knew we'd end up fighting in the future, though. If he were suddenly convinced of my innocence, it would look like he had had second thoughts. Tracey really played him that time. I can only blame him for not realising it in the first place. Shaun and me are on speaking terms now and all that shit's behind us. As long as I live, I'll never be on speaking terms with Tracey.

The irony is that Geordie and me were given those nametags with 'Psycho' written on them as more of a laugh than anything ... Tracey should have had it tattooed on her forehead.

Flashing lights, CCTV Cameras ... and action

***WORKING THE DOORS** on a popular bar and the biggest night-club in the town, we tended to have run-ins with the same bunches of lads week in, week out. I was still having problems with Tracey and then even more problems from another psychotic bird... my son's cockatiel.*

A lot of the fights that were kicking off all the time were because of feuds. People would have grudges against us from getting thrown out or because we'd given them a bashing. There were plenty of enemies to be made in those days. You would find that you'd clash with the same people nearly all the time. Because Sunderland is a relatively small city, it has groups of people from different places that become known to you ... the Southwick lads, for example. One night they were in Bentleys and smoking dope. We barred them. Simple as that. They were taking the piss and weren't even discreet about it. A few weeks later they returned knowing full well that they were not allowed in. Big John Cowell was on the door and we were inside, in the foyer. Big John was a bit older than us lot and, at times, took a bit of stick about it. He may have been older but he did the job one hundred per cent. People say he's too strict, but that all depends on how you look at it. If you're barred, you're barred, and this lot were barred all right. There were around fifteen of them and they had come down for one purpose – to fight. John had his arm over the door and wouldn't let them in. They started taking the piss out of him.

'Think you're 'ard, do you?' they asked. (Dodgy accent.)

'Oh yes I'm old,' was his reply. (Dodgy hearing.)

'No. Do you think you're *'ard*? A fucking *'ard* man?'

'I'm just doing my job,' John replied. He wasn't biting. He could see they were trying to wind him up. He was smiling and trying to defuse it. They took what he was saying the wrong way and one of them gave him a crack. Straight away he shuts the door and they start kicking into it. The front door was a single door and to the side there were double doors – fire doors. Down the middle of the foyer were big brass poles with rope between to separate the queues of clubbers coming and going. Once they realised that the fire doors were there, they started booting them in as well. There would be a surprise waiting for them. I knew that one of the brass poles came loose. The very end one. When they got past the fire doors I was standing waiting for them.

I had the pole poised like a baseball bat. The first one came through the door and I let loose with it, braying him in the face with full force. I ran at them. The first one was left on the floor with a gaping hole in his head. All I was thinking was to smash anything that moved. Doormen were keeping out of my way, 'cos anyone was likely to get cracked when I was in this mood. *Fucking come on!* Another bloke came in and I burst his face open as well. He went down and I continued to smash him up. Forget about it. It was a free-for-all. Anyone who came through that door was getting smashed to fuck. Simple as that. The rest of them paused. I was standing there with this dented pole shouting at them to make a move. The veins in my neck and head felt ready to burst open as I was screaming at them. The rage setting me off, I was ready to take the lot of them on with no fear. They could see that in me and I could see they were shitting themselves. This rush is the best pleasure you can possibly imagine: think your best ever sex, the best drugs, the fastest car, climbing the highest mountain, scoring a winning goal at Wembley or a touchdown at the Superbowl; mix it all together and you're only starting to get close. Anyone within three feet was waking up with either a sore head or not at all. I didn't care what happened to them. It was them or me and I'd put good odds on it being them. The doormen were fighting with them all around me and we just continued to bray the shit out of them until the police arrived.

We were left standing in the war zone. There was blood on the carpet, up the walls, shirts were ripped and there was a few headaches developing. Doormen were standing around with cut and bloody knuckles. All the action was caught on tape, so we had to take the coppers upstairs to view it. We all erupted when we saw me standing there, downing anything that moved. All of us, that is, except this WPC who had recently undergone a sense of humour transplant. Granted, it wasn't that funny – the VCR didn't have any sound, so you could make up your own dialogue – but she had a real problem with the way I had handled things. You what? There's a load of people who kick the fire doors in to get at us and you want us to talk to them when they charge at us? I was well pissed off at her. Did she want me to sit them down and put the kettle on? You cannot win with them. It was self-defence. We had to stop a bunch of blokes coming in who wanted to smash us and the club up; I was not gonna let that happen. I just wouldn't let them. I was prepared to do anything to protect my friends, the club and myself. If I didn't do what I did they would have been watching a different tape all together. Some people are fucking stupid. They let it go in the end. The tape revealed something else: one doorman was cowering in the corner. That was the end for him. As I've said before, you work there because of trust. No one wanted to work with him after that so he was sacked.

An inevitable return run-in with the Southwick lads happened a bit quicker than expected. Some people don't know when to give up. This one happened the week after the bashing with the brass pole – they'd obviously had all their sense knocked out of them. At the club, the queues have to be pushed round the corner or they end up all over town. I went out on crowd duty and saw this big skinny type, I think he's called Stevie, but I couldn't care less what his name is, to be honest. I was standing at the side of the queue when I noticed him out of the corner of my eye. He was right next to me – one of the ones I'd put out the other week, and he was standing, staring. He took a swipe; I ducked and dropped him. There was no way he could get away with such a cheap shot. I moved in but was interrupted by someone behind me so I elbowed him in the face and carried on punching the sack of shit on the deck. I only stopped when one of his stupid mates tried to be a hero. He was soon reunited with Stevie on the ground. It gets better ... over the road was three more of them shouting at me to get off their mates. That was it. I shouldn't really have left my post but I charged after them up the street until I caught up with them. I cornered them against the shutters of a closed shop front and kept hitting them until I had scientific evidence of a new shade of shit. They could have all tried to jump me and it wouldn't have mattered. They were rebounding off the shutters till I allowed them to drop and that's when the serious lesson started. That's when I turned into Dr Freeman, the cosmetic surgeon. I've rearranged more faces than a top Hollywood specialist. It was only when I got back that I found out it was Stevie Watson who I'd elbowed in the face. I'd broken his nose. When I'm tearing shit out of people, no one is safe. To me he was just something else in the way. I hadn't even had the time to see it was him. It was all happening so quickly and I needed to wreck anything that moved in front, behind, below – *anything*.

Our Colin was working security on doors and things down in London at the time. He came back up the next weekend to chill out for a bit and went out with Mark 'Can't Fight For Toffee' Howe on the Saturday night; they had a skinful and went to the Chinese takeaway at Withawack, which just happens to be right next to Southwick. And, now that I've told you these two places are so near to each other, guess who they happened to bump into in the takeaway ... The Southwick boys. One of them went over to Colin – 'You're Freeman's brother, aren't you? Tell him he's fucking dead.'

Colin replied, 'It'll take a bigger bloke than you, daft cunt,' and walked out. When him and Mark Howe were walking home, they were jumped on by three blokes and beaten to a pulp. I got a call from his girlfriend at two in the morning. I raced straight over. When I saw him I didn't even recognise him – his face was all swollen and his eyes were practically shut. He'd had a right going over and was a real mess. I was mad as fuck. This had nothing to do with Colin, but these bastards jumped him. He knew nothing about it; he was pissed and caught off guard. I was so mad I went running out of the house – but I didn't know where they lived. I was angry and wanted the bastards there and then.

A few days later I was hauled into the police station. I made sure I was in a comfortable seat as the copper, PC Aesop, told me an enjoyable fable. It was a story about a few blokes who recently got done over big style. It just happened to be the same ones who did our Colin over. Sounded like karma to me. This is how the story went. The copper started by asking if a few friends and me had paid the lads a visit. While I would have liked to, I couldn't as I didn't know where they lived, so I told them we hadn't. Apparently though, Sunday was definitely not the day of rest; it was judgement day for these lads. Their story involved a bunch of mean-looking blokes, a car, baseball bats and ski masks. The lads who got a good beating had spent most of the day drinking but then the gang ended their night with a spot of unplanned clubbing. They were smashed to fuck by the gang of bat-wielding vigilantes. One of them, Tuggsy, was put down and had his kneecaps smashed in. As Gerry and the Pacemakers would say, 'He'll ne-ver walk ... alone.' The others were also beaten with bats and fists and something was thrown through their living room window. Good on them, I thought. These lads had obviously deserved a beating. If you go around jumping on innocent blokes like my brother then it would be a safe bet that someone will want to take revenge out on you. You can't get away with beating people up for no reason and it sounded like this lot had done it to that many people they didn't know who their enemies were. The police finished their story and to me it sounded more like a parable. I couldn't help them with their enquiry. They gave me a lift home and on the way out of the car even asked me again, off the record, if I had anything to do with it. 'I'd like to help you out but I can't.' What more can be said? Those guys will never take my politeness as a weakness again.

* * * * *

The court appearances were getting beyond a joke. If I wasn't getting dragged in for Tracey making shit up, it was for doing my job or for dealing with all kinds of idiots. Geordie and me even ended up there for foiling the crime of the century. Well, it was the crime of the night, anyway. We had sussed this girl out who had been nicking purses in the club. We played it cool, following and hiding behind pillars, sniping, crawling, ducking and diving all over just like Bodie and Doyle. Soon enough, she went into the toilets to count up the loot. We tip-toed in and looked around. She was in the end cubicle; we took a sneaky peak and there she was, emptying money and credit cards from three other purses. We busted in shouting, 'You're nicked!' and we got the police in to deal with it. She may just have got away with it if it wasn't for us meddling kids ... We had to go to court as witnesses because we had foiled her evil plans, but even that turned into a farce. The only reason we went in was 'cos we were summonsed and would have been in the shit ourselves if we didn't turn up. We didn't tell them a thing. Because I've got dodgy hearing I had to keep asking everyone to repeat the questions. I wasn't doing it on purpose; the last thing we wanted was to be in there any longer than we needed to. Before long, the magistrate gadgey was getting really radged up. He came out with, 'Mr Freeman. I am not going to repeat myself again.' Well, I could barely make a word out, so I asked him if he'd say it a bit louder. He did. *Then* we saw the funny side. You could see it in people's faces – everyone was dying to laugh but we were the only ones who couldn't keep it in. It turned out that one of the girls who'd had her purse pinched said there had been ten pound fifty in it, but now there was only half a quid left. They were trying to say we had done it! What a bunch of piss-takers. They knew it wasn't us by the expressions on our faces. It couldn't have been that girl who'd had the purse nicked was trying to wrangle some money, though, could it?

Next time I was up in court was for affray, as usual. And you'll never guess who was to blame. Here's a clue: her name begins with *Tra* and ends with *cey*. I've lost count of the times I was dragged there on this charge, so I can't really remember if there was a good story behind it. Just in case you are unfamiliar with affray, I'm an expert in the field. It means breach of the peace by fighting or rioting in public – in broader terms, you can be charged with affray if someone says they are frightened for their life and blame you for it. Anyway, I was sitting waiting for my name to be called out and Stevie Watson came in. He plonked himself down next to me and was a bit pissed off that he was in there for unpaid fines of all things. He told me about the latest function that had been held in Bentleys that I had just missed. It was some kind of convention or gathering of tarot readers, mediums and psychic types. There was to be a well-respected tarot reader giving a talk to them. The place was full of hundreds of these people and time was getting on a bit. It was a non-starter; the reader phoned Stevie to say they couldn't make it. Stevie got on stage and in front of the podium with the microphone, 'Ladies and gentlemen. Due to *unforeseeable circumstances*, I'm afraid the talk will not go ahead as planned.'

I nearly fell off my seat laughing. Stevie has got the maddest laugh in the world, so once he joined in it made me laugh even harder. It must have been a good five minutes before I heard one of the ushers call my name out. I made my way in to the court but it was a waste of time. I could hardly see for the tears. I managed to stifle it until I was asked to confirm my name. Then I was off again. Absolutely out of control I was. I was told they would not carry on until I could behave myself and was made to stand outside. Even the usher leading me out had started. I'm sure she overheard Stevie telling me so, when we got out of the courtroom and he was still sitting there laughing, she just laughed along with us. She had to wait until I'd stopped crying before she could take me back in. It was mental. I'll be laughing at that one in years to come.

* * * * *

All over the place different bouncers had different gangs of people who were sworn enemies. There were running battles going on at Gillespies as well. Once a fight broke out, they would always come back mob-handed to try to settle the score. They couldn't do a thing by themselves, so they would turn up with a bunch of their mates and give us all their 'I'm hard now that I'm in a gang' tough talk. Here we were trying to hold probably a fifteen-strong crowd back at the door. No way were we going to let them in. There was fighting going on but it was just stray punches 'cos none of them had the balls to do it one on one. We were pushing them back all the time as well as trying not to get crushed against the doors. A few of them got in but Paul (another Watson boy) was waiting for them. It couldn't go on like this ... and it didn't. I reached behind the door for my 2x2 piece of wood and let loose on the bastards. They rushed the door but I had a much longer reach and started swatting them down like flies. I was like Darth fucking Maul. By the time I'd finished there were teeth stuck in it. It was cracked and splintered and covered in blood. There was a couple left standing so I dropped the 2x2 and Geordie and me ran after them. We caught one down a side street and he knew there was no escape. This was one of the lads who had started it. He was part of the group who had originally been thrown out and had brought along his army to teach us a lesson. Now, on his own, he was shit scared. He was knocked out cold. It was a one-punch fight and was all over in the time it took to hit him. When we were looking down at him, though, he looked a bit more than knocked out. His eyes were still open and the pupils were right back with just the whites showing. Not a good sign. We were so hyped up and would have carried the beating a lot further if we didn't think he was dead. We moved in to check for a pulse. You'd think we'd be dab hands at that sort of thing by now, but we couldn't find it. After feeling around for what seemed like ages, we located his pulse. We were sweating it for a bit and let out a huge sigh of relief. Geordie had just got a load of business cards printed for one of our mates, John Hogg, who runs a funeral service. He had a few in his pocket and took one out; we opened his mouth and shoved it in. That would be a warning for the next time – not that there ever was one.

* * * * *

I decided I'd get Ian Jnr a pet. It seems difficult to follow what was going on with Ian – that's because it *is* hard to follow. It was tug of war all right, constantly dragged this way and that. Tracey used to let me have him just so she could take me to court and win him back. That's all he was to her – a prize she could win by beating me. So this time I had him I got him a nice friendly good-with-children brightly coloured cockatiel called Bobby in a big cage. I thought that a pet would be good for him because of what he'd been through recently. And, because when I was younger we had the pigeons, I thought it would be a nice touch if Ian developed a similar appreciation. Only it turned out that this bird was as mad as a hatter – a *proper* fruitcake. I let it out of the cage one day and it started flying towards me. At first I was thinking it was just gonna come over and perch itself on my shoulder; it looked that way until it went for my neck! It was squawking and flapping around and actually bit me. Little winged bastard. I was a bit apprehensive of letting Ian go anywhere near it, but the thing was fine with him – then it would throw me one of its evil stares like little Damien in *The Omen*.

Things settled a bit and we would leave the cage door open in case it wanted to have a fly around. I was sitting with my feet up watching TV one day when it flew over. Oh, not again, I thought, but it seemed different this time. It landed on my foot and began to sniff at it. Hmm, this is a bit … hold on, what the …? I'm not kidding when I say it started shagging my foot! At first I didn't know if it was doing the 'Birdie Song' or what; he certainly had rhythm. Feathers were all over and it seemed to be having the time of its life. What could I do? It had my big toe in its beak while it was getting jiggy wid it. When it had finished it flew back to its cage and had this glazed and glowing look about it. I thought it was going to light up a cigarette. I was stunned. My foot felt used. I took my sock off and inspected it; there was a tiny little wet patch. Dirty bastard. Not only did I have a crazed cockatiel in the house, it was also sexually confused and seemed it wouldn't take no for an answer. I left my sock on the settee and went to wash my foot. When I came back the pervert was at it again! My poor sock. All it could do was lie there while the bird made beautiful love to it. I'll say this for it, though, it had real stamina. Luckily it had finished and flew back before Ian saw it. For him the birds and the bees would come a bit later in life but the bird and the sock would have to remain a secret.

The next time it came out of the cage I made sure there were no socks around for it to mount. It must have been well pissed off, 'cos it wouldn't go back in the cage and kept dive-bombing at me. It was biting, scratching and seemed to be going for my eyes. Ian was in the room at the same time (luckily, he was too young to remember that much about it) and it even turned on him. It was a real loony. After circling around a bit, it swooped back down for another raid. Oh no you don't. I knocked it out with a big right hander. Instead of pieces of eight I gave it a bunch of fives. It was out cold on its back with its little feet twitching and feathers falling to the ground. I put it back in its cage and decided to get rid of it. I had no choice but to tell Ian that it flew away.

I sold it on to Michael Downey as a lovely friendly family pet until he found out about its foot fetish. He complained a bit but I denied all knowledge – 'It did *what* to your foot?' He had no choice but to sell it on as a placid and tame beautiful creature.

* * * * *

Once CCTV cameras hit the streets, things calmed down a bit in town. People knew that they could no longer get away with the sort of things they had got away with in the past. The cameras meant that the tiniest bit of trouble could be zoomed in on and used as evidence. In Bentleys we now had a camera that was pointed right at the door. When we had to eject anyone through the front door, we made sure they were given a good slap and then ushered out as nice as pie. After the slapping they would come staggering out and we could say they were walking like that because of the drink. A perfect alibi. The cameras were new all over the country and sometimes it was easy to forget they were there. In the street we'd have to remind each other and it was never easy to let someone go. Things had never been so calm – but the calm never lasted. People wanted to test the water and see what these cameras would mean to the town. Do they make towns safer? I don't know. I don't really think they have brought down the number of street crimes – I'm talking muggings, rapes and knife attacks here, not just us lot fighting a gang of arseholes. It does mean that the police have top-quality video evidence if they ever catch the criminal and, looking at it like that, they are effective. The cameras are capable of reading your newspaper halfway across town, but people still commit crimes. They can be a deterrent if you believe you'll get caught.

I left Bentleys in the early '90s. I was now working for Owen Murray at the Boulevard, Ku Club and Marlowe's: a whole new set of adventures waiting to happen. I worked there for one night at first, which was the usual relief stuff to get yourself known. Les Graham was head doorman and he had taken me on. Once Owen got wind of this he told Les to give me the push. This was when I first realised that a bad reputation could be damaging for me. I needed to work but, because I was known as a psycho, no one wanted to touch me. Owen had heard that I was a nutcase and he didn't want anyone like that on his doors. In those days everyone would look at me and think, There's Ian Freeman, the psycho nutcase, and not, There's Ian Freeman, the vale tudo fighter. I was in town one night and I saw Owen so I asked him for a job. I knew there was one going but he refused to give me a start. He said he'd heard what I was like and didn't want me there. I replied that's what he'd heard, but why not give me a chance? I told him, 'I'll work your door and if I fuck up you can get rid of me. If I don't fuck up you've gained a good doorman and you know your doors are going to be safe.'

He told me he'd have a think about it and the next day I got a call from Les telling me that I started the following week. He was willing to take a chance and I proved I could do it. He didn't have to bother with me – that's the kind of bloke he is. One thing I hate is someone judging me who hasn't even met me before. 'I've heard you are like this so you *must* be ...' I can't stand that attitude. Preconceptions about someone are just a shortcut so you don't have to think.

Soon after starting there, I met up with another girl, Margie Howard. I'd been through so much grief with Tracey; now I could try to put all that behind me. We were just taking things easy at first, but then it all got a little bit more serious. I still had Ian at the time. I didn't introduce them straight away but I always got this feeling that she thought he shouldn't be there. It was like she would put up with him 'cos he was there but she didn't want him.

Tracey took me to court in an emergency hearing and, to cut a long story short, she got Ian. I'd lost my son. To me it was as if he'd died – that's how upset I was. I went round to Margie's for a shoulder to cry on ... and she was happy that he was gone. She told me how great it was now because that meant it was just her and me. At that point I didn't think I'd ever see him again properly, never mind get him back. That was a horrible feeling; a fight that I knew I couldn't win. Another massive setback that mounted up inside. It was like it was fuelling those demons; they feed off your misery and force you to react in different ways. For me it meant that I'd take it out on anyone I fought. First the skinheads and now the legal system. I fought back at them with the attitude 'Fuck 'em all. If I can't have my own son, why should I care about someone in a bar who kicks off ... why should I care about their life?'

I decided that I had to get on with things. Life goes on. I felt like I was mourning for my son, but I suppose with Margie in my life I had something to look forward to. The custody was decided, it was in the past and I now had to look to the future. After that, my relationship with Margie seemed to pick up and after a while she came to live with me.

The only weapons you need are the ones you are born with

WEAPONS WERE BEING used all over the place – guns, knives ... dogs. Even the police started using them. Fighting was beginning to change. When we needed to use something, we would. We were fighting in wars and would adapt to the situation – but, to a lot of the lads, it just didn't feel right.

When you start working the doors and are the new kid on the block, you start to hear things about people. You hear who is the top boy and all kinds of different stories, Chinese Whispers, the truth, lies, everything. The main man was Ernie Bewick. At first I'd never heard of him, but that was soon to change.

It was every boy's dream to command that much power and respect. Going on his reputation, you might expect him to be some kind of ruthless villain and a gangster; on meeting him I found him to be a genuinely nice guy. He was a true gent. I was just a doorman and the thought of running pubs or even running the town seemed a million miles away from where I was. Ernie always had time for you, no matter who you were. He would not look down at you, and he certainly looked up to no one. He would sit down for a chat and you could see in his eyes that he was interested in what you had to say. He loved to talk. Instead of hiring Bob Hoskins, BT should have gone for Ernie.

He was a very philosophical man and was well educated – self-educated. He was educated in life, in knowing people and how to treat, handle and talk to them. The knowledge he had was different to anything you could pick up in a university. This was street knowledge. He could listen and learn from experiences. He didn't earn friendship through fear or by being heavy handed. It wasn't like people were friendly towards him because they knew he could beat the shit out of them; this was real friendship. This was real respect. When I got to know him and saw the way people reacted in his presence, I knew this was what I wanted. I was probably around 21 years old when I first met him and I spoke to him many times after that. Anywhere he went he didn't have to approach anyone – they all came to him.

People assume that there was a rivalry between Ernie and Viv Graham. There wasn't. Viv was a hard man from the region who used to run Newcastle at the same time Ernie was running Sunderland. He was murdered some years ago in a gangland shooting. People think that these two hated each other – I think because there is a rivalry between Sunderland and Newcastle anyway. But the only time there was any animosity was when Ernie was fighting a guy called Billy Robinson. There were people watching and one of them was Viv. Ernie got hit from the side and thought it was Billy, so he stepped the pace up. It was after the fight that Ernie found out that it was Viv who hit him – and that was that.

One time I'd been talking to Ernie in Bourbon Street in Sunderland. On the way out he asked me where I was going and if I fancied going for a dodge around to Annabell's with him. I said yes but on one condition ... that I could drive his BMW there. This BM was the cat's ass; black and mysterious, looking très cool. He said I could drive and I was like an excited school kid – 'Can I? Can I really?' This was an honour for me. How many people do you think he let drive his pride and joy?

We walked round to the car park. What I didn't know was that there had just been a little segregation wall removed from it. In taking a wall away you are left with the foundation, so there was a kind of trench where the wall used to be. It must have been done recently, 'cos the trench still hadn't been filled in. I started by reversing out, and then pulled forward and the front two wheels went straight down the hole and the bottom of the car ground to a halt. Oh *shit*. All I could hear from Ernie was 'My car. My fucking car.'

We got out and had a look. It confirmed our worst suspicions. Oh *fuck*. Of all the cars in the world I had to choose Ernie's BMW. To get it out he lifted the front end of the chassis while I had it in reverse. On reassessment it didn't look too bad. It had me sweating for a while but he still let me drive to Annabell's in it. I asked him if it was still OK a few weeks later and he said it was fine.

Working at the Boulevard group is the bollocks. Set in the middle of Sunderland, it's a really good patch to work, with a good bunch of lads. We look after a bunch of others as well. There was Ian Brown, Les Graham, Michael Surtees – the list is endless and there were too many coming and going to remember every name. We were still doing one or two things that I'm not entirely proud of now, but it's just the way things were back then. Not that we'd ever be on our knees to repent our sins – you've gotta understand that this was still in the 'hit first' days. They were violent times and at any sign of violence we never held back. It would seem a bit harsh now but, like I say, it was going on at the time and we were all a bit young and crazy. Apart from all the violence, I also started gambling.

I know Owen would look disapprovingly at all this. Owen is one of the nicest, friendliest people you could hope to meet. He's out of that side of things now, running his own company – instructing on the best ways to restrain different forms of antisocial behaviour, including air-rage nutters, and believe me he's an expert. He's still very well respected round town. Remarkable is a word I'd use. He's even got a CBE for all the charity work he does. What's even more remarkable is that he does all this and has only got one arm. He lost it when he was twenty years old. It's his philosophy to talk to people and calm them down in those situations – but it was different for us: we weren't really into the talking side of things. I can't stress enough that I was a different person then. I was living up to my image. It was something I couldn't help. I was working with my mate Ian Brown in Boulevard at the time; we were young, we wanted to prove ourselves and were known to go a bit mental. We used to have bets with each other. That's fair enough, you might be thinking, but these bets were slightly different to the ones you may be used to; the type of bet you couldn't really place in your average high-street bookies. We used to bet each other that we could knock out the first person who kicked off with one punch. Don't get me wrong here – these were not people who were just drunk, a bit rowdy and having a laugh; these were people who would pick on and abuse others who were trying to enjoy a night out, and that's not on. I don't think they quite expected to be knocked out, but a bet's a bet. We would just steam straight over and clobber them with a big right. Once all the others saw what happened to you if you started anything, they thought twice about it. I suppose it was the challenge that drew us in to doing such a thing but we were all a bit wild at heart and didn't really think about the consequences. Not the type of thing you can do these days and get away with ... gambling, I mean. It's a terrible habit, innit? Ian was, and still is, a good mate. We've been through all kinds of crazy shit together and come out laughing. He's a great fighter and I'll always trust him with my life.

I was still going through all kinds of shit with Tracey and found out this way that I had some really genuine friends. She was still playing stupid games, but Margie was a good distraction. While it hurt me that Ian was out of the picture, the fact was that I didn't have him any more and it seemed daft to fall out over something that couldn't even become an issue.

Once she came to live with me I started to notice that a few things were going on. I could tell something was wrong. Some mornings she wasn't able to fasten her shoelaces, her hands and feet would swell up, but other mornings she was fine. This was worrying for both of us, but I think for her she could cope with not knowing. Sure, she knew that something was up, but if she didn't know what it was then it wouldn't – or couldn't – affect her. It was plain to see that it wasn't going to go away and, while ignorance may be bliss for some people, it isn't for me. The fact was that it *was* affecting her. I couldn't go on living in denial. She went to have all the necessary blood tests and examinations and, to cut a long story short, she got the results back after we'd been together for a year and a half. We were told she had Lupus.

If you have had any experience of Lupus, you will know how bad it is. It is described as a chronic inflammatory autoimmune disorder. That means it affects the skin, joints and internal organs. It affects around eight times as many women as men and can hit at any age, usually between ten and fifty years. The worst case scenario? She was told that, by the time she reaches forty years of age, she could be in a wheelchair. Imagine being told that when you are twenty ... it really got to her, as you can imagine. She was finding it hard to cope and her self-confidence started taking a battering – she'd wonder aloud why

I'd stay with her when I was fit, good looking, work the doors and all that and could get any woman I wanted. Well, I'd made my decision and I was sticking by her. I told her not to worry and that we would cope.

Of course, it's not always that easy in real life. Margie would start her day so negatively by going through her 'Why do you stay with me?' routine. Without sounding nasty, it used to bug the piss out of me. I'd made my decision and that was it. It would take me all day to persuade her that I wanted to be with her, I was happy and that's where I was staying. By the end of the night everything was fine, we'd go to bed and when we woke up it would be straight back to square one. It was starting to do my head in. It went on for weeks. Eventually, I came out with it and said that the best she could do was go back to her mother's – maybe she could make her feel more welcome. All I could do was show her love, and it clearly wasn't working. At last we agreed on something! She moved out, but we kept seeing each other. Big mistake. Because she wasn't with me all the time, she was getting more and more paranoid and jealous: where was I last night? Who was I with? All the questions would come out next time I saw her. It was a real strain because I was still trying to get on with things and treat her the way I always had. I didn't want to patronise or feel sorry for her; I needed to be strong for her and show her that she was still the same person to me. She was beginning to put me in an impossible situation. But we struggled on.

I wasn't the only one going through stress, though. Round about the same time, Owen took on a whole world of shit. It was a real eye-opener to anyone wanting to enter into this line of work, or if you had big plans for the future. There was some trouble brewing down at one of Owen's pubs and it was on the cards that something would happen. A drug dealer from a known family had moved in and was beginning to cause some problems.

This was a real sensitive one – it had to be handled properly and there were only a few options for Owen to take. The person or persons in question could have been barred from the place, but that might have had repercussions. They wouldn't have taken too kindly to it and the chances were that they would take it out on the manager. The last thing to do would be to drop the manager in it; we were there for his protection, after all. They could have been beaten up on the premises. Easily. But again, this would have put the management in danger, 'cos he probably would have been blamed for the whole thing.

As Owen would have put it, there were certain steps needed to make sure they didn't get in again and those were the steps we took. We got a team together in a car and were kitted out with ski masks, bats and iron bars. We knew there were two of them likely to turn up but didn't know what kind of hardware they would have on them. The plan was to smash them up outside the pub, or inside if it came down to it. God knows what we looked like – five gigantic blokes squeezed into a car with these masks on. It was pretty obvious we weren't planning a skiing trip. We must have been lying in wait for an hour and a half. How boring was that? Apart from being sick of waiting it was like a sauna on wheels. We had a vote and decided to take the masks off and go for a pint – so we did get to go on the piste after all. Let's just say that a confrontation between Owen and the drug dealers did take place, and things were sorted out the old-fashioned way.

Things really kicked off after that. The following day a group of people from Middlesbrough came up to the pub with shooters. For them to come up for a fight would have been pointless and they knew it. Owen was due to go and meet them but, luckily for him, the manager tipped him off saying that he'd be a lot better off if he didn't go there. If he turned up they would have killed him. Now that is one scary thought: knowing that someone was prepared to put a bullet in your head. There would have been nothing he could have done about it. The kind of trouble we'd all been involved with in the past was just fighting, in one form or another. We were good fighters and everyone knew it. We were confident of our abilities and would have taken anyone on with our fists. Guns are a different thing altogether. I'm not saying for a moment that we were out of our league here; when you're a fighter the only weapons you need are the ones you were born with. A gun is something that was manufactured with one thing in mind – to kill. Anyone can get their hands on one if they want. See what I'm saying? A fight is all about the hardest man left standing. In this situation it's the one with the gun. And any coward in the world can own one. The only weapons we'd consider using would be bats or knuckle-dusters, something that will hurt someone, immobilise them wherever you hit them. A gun has the likelihood of killing someone wherever you hit them and that's not what we were about.

Drugs were beginning to flood in from all over and we did our best to keep our patch clean. I've never been under any illusion that you can keep an entire area drug free. You can do your best to make sure it doesn't happen, but with big money involved some people's principles decide to take a back seat. When drugs are around, then so is a lot of money; and, once a lot of money is up for grabs, people are prepared to kill for it. It's a way of life for a lot of people now and in a lot of big cities around the country. People can make money from this kind of thing and are quite prepared to kill to control whichever area it happens to be. Money and greed. Owen taking the action that he did was seen as a very big brick wall in the way of a fortune.

Word on the street was that he was gonna get hit. And I don't mean a slap; I mean the kind of hit that you don't walk away from. After the threat we got a load of doormen together to surround and protect the pub and it was a real show of strength. The only way we could protect Owen and ourselves effectively against guns was to get with the programme. Obviously it was past the talking stage and, no matter how hard you are, unless you can stop bullets with your bare hands, you've gotta protect yourself the best you can.

We got all the lads together and decided that we'd need to put in a bit of shooting practice. Owen has a shotgun licence, so we headed down to his place. He had a farm down on the riverbank that was right out of the way so that we could let off a few rounds, and not be bothered about people reacting to the noise. This way we made sure that everything was above board: his licence, his land, his shotguns. We set to work by making targets out of buckets and putting them upside down over fence posts. Then it came to the crunch. I don't think any of them had ever fired a gun in their life. They were all fighters, not assassins. You don't have to be a tough guy to pull a trigger on someone; anyone can do that. No one had ever needed to pick up a gun before now. I'm not saying that it was *Gunfight at the OK Corral*, but we needed to know what we were doing, just in case.

The recoil kick was quite a weight on the wrist of whoever was shooting it. Once the first gun had been shot, nearly everyone was backing down 'cos they didn't want to damage their wrists. If you shoot with your right then you will no doubt punch with it – if you damage your wrist then you are not much use for sorting fights out and dealing with every other problem a doorman takes care of. It was a nightmare. Instead of fighting to get our hands on the shooters, we were fighting not to be next in line on the shooting range. No one fancied the prospect of being put out of commission so, seeing that they were likely to get injured, no one would volunteer. It sounds mad that all these doormen who had been in hundreds of fights each – all of Owen's hardest and most trusted – were not dying to get hold of a shotgun and live out some fantasy.

Poor Owen. I could see the life draining out of him before my eyes. He was under more stress than Dolly Parton's trainer bra. You could see what he was thinking: If my lot can't even fire at thin air, what are they going to be like if these people come? The reality was that they were prepared to do anything to bump him off. The farm is right beneath a bridge off the A19, so he was an open target for petrol bombs as well. In the end there was only me and I think two others who had a go with the shotguns. We all stayed over that night in case the farm was hit. It was a sleepless night for Owen in more ways than one.

Time moved on but the threat on Owen's life didn't. It was still known that he was a target and he wouldn't go anywhere without the necessary protection. He's a very calculated bloke and would not take any silly risks. It was like that for around ten months. There were certain precautions placed in different locations around town – the places where things were likely to go off. You want to know the real mental bit? I know that, right up until a week before all this started, he was ready to pack it all in. Seriously. Because he was a target and was in it all the way with us, he could not bow down at that point. He had to see it through because he wanted to finish on top.

One night at one of our clubs we had a tip-off that something was going to happen. All night the atmosphere in there seemed weird. Like it was the calm before the storm or something. We had an eye on *everyone*. It got to chucking-out time. Nothing had happened so far; if something was gonna go down it would be now, when we were at our most vulnerable. Getting people out of the club is always a nightmare and this night was no different. Instead of letting them all pile out down the stairs, we needed them in single file. This meant that, if a shooter came in, they couldn't use everyone as camouflage and get up close to one of us. One person going against the grain when it is a full-on crowd is very hard to spot, but not if it is against one long line. You could see by the expression on the doormen's faces that they were just waiting for it to happen. We'd taken our own steps to make sure we were in a position to counter whatever came through that door. Everyone had a vision in their mind of exactly how they would react – where they would dive, who they would cover and, more importantly, who was going to retaliate and shoot back.

Then it happened. Just as we were getting the last of them out and were about to lock the doors, a shooter suddenly appeared and let rip with four or five rounds. Everyone dived for cover. It was exactly how this sort of thing comes across in films. Why does everything slow down? We grabbed the last of the clubbers who were still hanging around and hit the deck. Instant confusion. Who had been hit? We were straight up, dragged the shooter into the foyer and locked the doors. The gun smoke was still in the air and bodies were beginning to stir. No one was injured and there didn't seem to be any bullet holes anywhere. He was scared shitless and started shouting 'Sorry!' straight away. Something was up. The gun turned out to be a fucking cap gun. He was just some kid larking about – the few clubbers who were left were his mates. He now found himself in a similar position to the one we had just been in. He was surrounded by the hardest, most pissed-off people in Sunderland; and one was brandishing a real shotgun. Keeping our faces as straight as possible, we gave him a good telling off. This was one of those situations where talking was the right thing to do – any kind of violence was unnecessary. Not even coming close to understanding what he had almost caused, the lad apologised again; we let him and his mates out and relocked the doors. The place just erupted – a mixture of laughter and I don't know what. The whole build-up to the incident and then that night of all nights to bring a cap gun to the club! We were just so relieved that it turned out to be the kind of thing we could laugh about. I think it was just the tonic we needed. OK, getting a gun pulled on you is no laughing matter but, because we had been on edge for so long, it was a great way of letting all that build-up in the system just flood out. That kid was luckier than he could ever imagine.

Owen left the job soon after that, taking early retirement from the company. Once he left, the threat left with him. The war was with him, not with us. Once in retirement, he did have a chance to settle the score with the bloke in question once and for all. They had a one on one that Ernie witnessed. Owen could easily have smashed him to pieces, but it turned out that he just slapped the other guy about about and didn't do him in because he thought there still might be repercussions. End of story.

* * * * *

Relations with Margie were not exactly a picnic for me, either. She was going through a very anxious and worrying time, but she didn't seem to grasp that I was going through it with her. I was patient with her because of all these mood swings, but I never quite knew where I was with her. On a Saturday night I'd been out with the lads and went up to see my folks on the Sunday morning. While I was there Margie phoned up. The same old questions: why was I there? Who was I out with last night? Who did I have round at the flat? Who did I have in the bed? It was unreal. I was almost bored to tears with the same routine day in, day out. I was like, 'Change the record, will you?' If anything was gonna lead me to be unfaithful it was this amount of shit. Know what I mean?

Later on that Sunday night was the Boulevard staff Christmas party. This was a few weeks before Christmas, at the beginning of December. I told Margie that we'd go to the party, have a good time and forget all this – I advised her to chill out and said I'd go and pick her up later. I should have known that it wouldn't go according to plan.

The shirt I was wearing had quite a low neckline and blokes

will know that the middle of the breastbone area is prone to getting the biggest spot in the history of the world when you least want one. I'm no different. So I put it on, and the way it hung, it just led your eyes straight to the spot. Bollocks. I put a tee-shirt on to cover it, put the shirt back on and went to pick her up. When I got there she was glaring right at me. She took me to one side and started quizzing me about wearing a tee-shirt under the shirt. This was the first time I'd worn it with something under, so that set the alarm bells off in her head. I thought nothing of it and told her the reason. We got in the car and went to the party. As we parked up she asked if she could see the spot. As if I wasn't self-conscious enough, I pulled the tee-shirt slightly and leaned forward to show her. I didn't want to pull the thing out of shape.

Now you've got to understand that Margie was practically an emotional wreck here and the slightest thing could easily have set her off. As we entered Boulevard, the slightest thing happened. Our Colin turned and shouted, 'You were jumping all over last night, weren't you?' All the lads were there and they joined in as well. That was it. Colin had handed Margie the ammo she needed. She was now convinced that I'd had such a good night out that I brought a woman back, was covered in love bites and *that's* why I was wearing the tee-shirt. She made a scene in front of everyone. I was disappointed and angry but at the same time I was tired of having to explain my every move. Now I had to explain why I'd worn a tee-shirt. I kept my cool when I could easily have lost it. I took her through to the toilets, took the shirt and tee-shirt off and showed her the spot on my chest. 'Are you fucking happy now? As I said, that's why I'm wearing a tee-shirt!' I told her.

'Oh, well, *I* thought it was love bites,' she replied. 'It's only a spot so it's all right.'

It was very fucking far from all right. I put my things back on and told her we were leaving. 'It's all right,' she told me, 'I'll get a taxi.' No way, I thought, I brought her there and I was gonna take her back. I drove her back to her mother's place in complete silence, dropped her off and haven't seen her since. It wasn't as though I found out about her illness and then told her it was over. I was willing to stay with her and, if it came down to it, I'd be there if she were confined to a wheelchair. I gave her my word and I would've stuck by it.

Things had come to a head (no pun intended) with me wearing that tee-shirt. That was when I knew she didn't trust me and all that time I had wasted in telling her how much I cared had clearly gone in one ear and out the other. I could not be with her a second longer if she could not trust me one hundred per cent. The thing that really got to me was that, in my year with her, I was completely faithful.

It didn't just stop there, though. I got a call from her saying there were bits and bobs in the flat belonging to her that she wanted back. No problem. She still had a key and I told her to take whatever it was while I was at work. When I returned at around three in the morning, I saw little strands of carpet in the corridor on the way to the flat. It was the same colour as mine and the alarm bells were set off in my head. As I opened the door, I opened it to an empty flat. She'd taken more than a few odds and ends – she'd taken *everything*: the carpets, the furniture, the pictures off the walls, literally everything but the kitchen sink. I went round to her mother's to have it out with her. It turned out she'd gone round with her brothers to clean me out and was gonna use it for her own place. She even had the police there in case I arrived midway. The police were turning to crime! It was my fucking place, not hers. I was left with nothing and had to get in second-hand stuff temporarily. She left the new bed 'cos she didn't want the bed I'd shagged some tart in – sad, isn't it? Still, it was a small price to pay for getting rid of her and we all know that hell hath no fury like a woman who nicks everything you own while you're out at work.

* * * * *

That particular Christmas was particularly memorable for those of us who happened to be working when the Sunderland Association Football Club party was in full swing. I'm not going to mention the name of the drinking establishment it was held at to protect the innocent – and the totally guilty. I doubt it's that memorable for those who were on the team at the time, 'cos they had been drinking most of the day and were completely sozzled. There were a few other faces around, including a well-known local boxing hero. The party took place upstairs in the function room and everyone had really unwound after a season of training and football. It was now time for the entertainment to arrive.

As the strippers were getting ready for action in the back room, we were also preparing for action. There is a ledge that runs right the way round the room and placed on it behind the bar was a box. Inside that box was a video camera. We'd been told that, when the phone rang on the bar, it meant we had to move whoever was in the way of the camera in the box.

The two strippers came out and did their warm-up session to get the lads in the mood. They were still on floor level, so they all formed a circle around them immediately. It was our job to keep them back at a safe distance. The girls did the usual stripper stuff and went off, keeping the lads eager for more. And it worked. They were all shouting and screaming for it; there weren't that many people but they were making the noise of a few hundred; they were really getting into the Christmas spirit. After ten minutes the girls came back out one at a time to do their own show. This one went a bit naughtier. They had baby lotion and sex toys and incorporated them into their act ... and boy could they act. The circle started closing in, as they were all dying for a closer look. We had to keep pushing them back; they would stay back for all of ten seconds then we'd have to start pushing again. After that the girls left, reappeared, did a bit more, then went off again for a break. The lads were going berserk by now, but they all had time to get another drink in before the feature presentation. This time the girls came back on together and started to lez up. They had more toys but these ones were not manufactured with the single woman in mind, if you know what I mean – like a tandem, these toys were intended for two people to ride. They both began to drink from the hairy cup. Around fifty pairs of eyes popped out on sticks. It was unbelievable. At the time I was thinking, Yes! but after it I'm like, 'I was just a few feet away from two lasses getting it on with each other!'

I don't need to tell you what the circle was like at this point; it was smaller than a Polo mint. The audience gave up pushing and just stood there, open mouthed. It was a real trouser arouser. Once they'd finished doing each other, the girls went to get cleaned up then one of them came back out. One of the spectators shouted words to the effect of having something a bit special. A pint glass got handed round and everyone was told to put in five quid each. When the girl re-entered the circle, she was going, 'Who's first. Who wants it first?'

Well, now we knew what the something special was gonna be. People were shouting, 'Me, me, me!', but for most of them it was the drink talking. The first one stepped forward and dropped his pants. The girl tried to work her magic on him but was getting no response. I doubt even those three babes from *Charmed* could do anything with him. Jeers and laughter erupted when he couldn't get a boner. He was oblivious to it all, and so was she as she tried in vain to administer the kiss of life to his knob. She was determined, though: 'Who's next?' she shouted. She could have put Frankie Dettori to shame; a real jockey she was, but couldn't find a worthy stallion amongst them. It was pitiful. Another two tried but still they couldn't get it up. In the end one of them managed for at least twenty seconds but that was the best they had to offer.

I know the video is still in circulation, but if it ever comes out it will prove what they couldn't do, not what they did do. They were useless. If it had been an audition for *Boogie Nights*, they would still be out-of-work actors. It's just as well they know how to score on the pitch because this was definitely their worst performance. She'd tried her best with them but in the end it was six-nil to her, home win.

* * * * *

The situation with my son, Ian, was on my mind constantly. I just couldn't deal with the fact that I wasn't able to be with him. One Wednesday, I was leaving to go to work when the phone rang. It was the Social Services; they asked me if I had a son called Ian Freeman. Straight away my heart missed a beat – I thought something bad had happened to him; then I found out it had.

He had been in care for three days in Washington. Tracey had taken him in there and dumped him like he was an unwanted novelty – a responsibility that she didn't have the time, energy or patience for. When she left him there, all she said was, 'This is Ian Freeman.' He was three years old. When they asked him his parents' names she told them her name was Tracey and that his dad had the same name as him. It still hurts to think of him all alone there in a strange place and having to go through all that. If you have any children, put yourself in my position. How could she do such a thing?

Once they knew my name they ran a check and found there were two Ian Freemans before locating me. The check also revealed that I was the same Ian Freeman who'd had a few run-ins with the law and had a violent reputation. We discussed this over the phone. I was told, 'Rest assured. Your police record does not make you a bad father.' They arranged a visit the following day so, instead of going to work that night, I stayed in to scrub the place from top to bottom. I didn't want anything to get in the way of being reunited with my son.

The next day, Thursday, Social Services came over and we discussed Ian's future. They discussed fostering and adoption – as far as I was concerned, these two were not an option. We also discussed what the police check had revealed. They could see I was anxious and put me at ease – I was able to collect Ian! I couldn't believe it. All kinds of things were going through my head. I was still upset that Tracey could treat her own son like that, but so pleased that he was finally mine. Going to pick him up, my head was all over the place: 'No, you can't have your son' one minute to 'Yes, you can have him' the next. I didn't believe it was happening until I could hold him; that's when I knew it was all real ... And, yes, being *upset* at Tracey is the biggest understatement in history. It's one of those things that are hard to put into words. There is definite hatred there – hatred for what she put him through and also for what she put me through; all the tug of war when she had no intention of keeping him. It's too upsetting to think what she did to him, and how scarred he must be because of it. I know now that nothing like that will ever happen to him again – or to any of my family.

Tracey still lies about this incident today so that she doesn't look like a bitch. The story she tells people is that she gave Ian to me because she knew I would look after him better and I have more money. I suppose the story is partly true, but she forgets to mention to people that she dumped him in care for three days first. Can you believe that? Selective Memory Disorder it's called – a strain of the old Selective Language Recognition Disorder that Coggy developed all those years ago. All liars are selective in what they can remember and seem to have a distorted version of reality; you should know this by now. I can rest safe in the knowledge that Ian will have no time for her as he grows up … and rest a lot better knowing that she's gonna rot in hell for what she did to him. I'd like to be able to tell my son that his mother and me simply didn't get on. The truth of it is that I can't even pretend to like someone who promises things to their son time and time again and does not deliver. It's like she goes out of her way to punish him for some reason only known to her. The actions of a spiteful and cruel bitch. In my lifetime, there will only be a few people who I will hate with a real passion; Tracey Chambers will always be top of that list, no matter what.

* * * * *

I don't care how hard you are or how fearless you may be; you can never get used to having guns pointed at you. No matter how many times you see or handle a gun, they have a certain effect on everyone when you are faced with one. The fact that whoever is behind that gun can decide the course of your life – you can live or die and the right or wrong moves on your behalf will help that person make their mind up.

We were out clubbing one night in The Venue and I was driving us home afterwards at around six a.m. on Sunday morning. There was me, Reggie and a couple of others in the car. All was going well until I saw a cop car close behind us in the mirror. I continued driving, knowing full well that they were going to pull us over. I was checking the mirror and going, 'Why doesn't he just do it? Why won't he pull us over?' They kept right on our tail. Waiting. Then another cop car came tearing up and pulled in front of us, so we were basically trapped between the two of them and from that position they were controlling our speed. It was mental. At this point there were no lights or sirens.

We didn't know what the fuck was going on, what their intentions were or what was gonna happen. We soon found out. After two or three minutes, an armed response unit positioned itself to our right and then they all made with the lights and sirens. So, with one in front, one behind and an armed response vehicle alongside us, their tactics worked and I pulled on to the side of the road. We couldn't believe what we saw – fucking storm troopers! Well, they could have been for all we knew.

They burst out of the car with their guns and ran straight for us. This was the first time that an armed response unit had ever been used in the area and it was the kind of thing that puts the shits up you. One of them had his gun ready and it looked like he was going to smash my window in with the butt of it, so I wound it down before he got the chance. He put the gun to my head and was shouting, 'Get your hands up, get your hands up!' before reaching in and turning the ignition off. It wasn't just a traffic cop asking to see your licence: we had sub-machine-guns trained on us from all directions and were told to get out of the car slowly. A perfect end to a night out. We got out and were told to put our hands up on the roof of my car. I was driving a blue F-registration Ford Sierra at the time and I remember it wasn't too clean this particular night. We didn't really want to have to touch the thing in case we caught dysentery or something from it, but with a gun up your arse what can you do?

There were around ten of them, with two on each of us. While one searched us another had a gun pointed in our face. We had no weapons, but I was praying that none of the lads had any gear on them. A five-quid wrap of speed would probably be just the excuse they were looking for to test their shiny new machine-guns out. All the time they were shouting at us: 'Where is it? What have you done with it?' Some were scrapping around in the car, obviously looking for 'it'. One of the coppers had a beard and I felt sure it was Jeremy Beadle in one of those poxy disguises he always used to wear. I must have grinned at the thought, 'cos another one shoved his gun right in my face and said, 'What the fuck do you think you're laughing at?' Deadly silence ... I stared him right in the eyes ... He had his finger on the trigger ... dying to pull it ... Then a voice on the radio saying, 'We've spotted the car.'

In less than a second they were back in their cars and away. We were still standing with our hands on the car, wondering if we'd just imagined it. We let out sighs of relief. Fucking hell, lucky I didn't try to pull Jeremy's beard off. We were standing around in disbelief giving our own accounts of the story, as you tend to do in that situation. It was quite a moment: so tense in so little time, then it was all over. It was so quick that we didn't have time to react – not that you could with the firing squad in your face. The one thing I couldn't believe was that there was another car in a similar state actually in existence. We didn't even get an apology or an offer to pay the dry cleaning bill for our trousers or anything. No manners, some people. I suppose if you're brought up the wrong way, you're bound to become a copper though.

* * * * *

The Venue was a good place to let your hair down after work. We used to go there quite a bit, even if we weren't working. That's where I met the love of my life – Angie. I was in the club with a bunch of mates when I first spotted her. I was gobsmacked; she stopped me in my tracks. Know that whole butterflies feeling? It was all that and more; I was under her spell. Later on that night I saw her standing on the balcony so I went up with Ian Brown. I stood on one side of her and him on the other. She could tell I was looking at her but was playing it cool. I'd seen her a week or so before but hadn't had the chance to see her up close like this. She went back to her mates and I saw her again later on the dance floor. I had to speak to her but didn't know what to say – probably the first time I'd ever been lost for words. I went over and asked if she wanted a drink of my water. OK, so it wasn't the best line in the world, but I ended up dancing with her. The closer I got to her the more beautiful she became. I knew she was the one. Right then. She was dressed really smart, as well; me, I was wearing a prison shirt that one of my pals had given me – appropriate, eh?

We started going out and during that first month I didn't tell her what I did for a living. Not that I thought it would scare her off – I knew she wasn't that shallow. I just wanted to see if things would develop the way I'd hoped they would first; I knew it would definitely be a lot to take in. I just didn't want to risk spoiling anything. Remember that feeling when you first start courting someone ... You take it slowly and cautiously at first and you're itching to see them more often and want to spend every second with that person. You want to know everything about them and are fascinated by the little dimples that form when they smile or the look in their eyes when they laugh ... That build-up and anticipation before you next see them and the kiss goodnight that you never want to end. It was all there and I loved it. We spent loads of time together and before long it was like I'd known her for years. After being out on a Saturday night I'd stay over at her place and then we'd be together all day Sunday. Then, one Sunday, I told her that I had to go to work. Because this seemed a bit unusual she asked me what I did for a living and I told her I was a doorman. At first she didn't believe me! I couldn't tell if it was a compliment or not. (If only the police were like that ...) Another thing I didn't tell her at first was that I had a son. After Margie having no interest in him, I didn't know how Angie would react. If working as a doorman was a lot to take in, then a son would be the icing on the cake. I didn't want to scare her off so I had to wait to see what happened and if there was a right moment to tell her. This was my biggest worry of the lot.

It felt great to be with such a woman because Angie was everything Tracey wasn't – beautiful, caring, loving and understanding. Speaking of which, Tracey was still on the scene and trying to sabotage any chance of happiness I could have with Angie. She used to go to the same club as well and would always be in the background somewhere, still trying to bring me down – but Angie brought me back up again and made me feel like a man.

I started to borrow Kim's car to get over to see Angie. By now, the Sierra was on its last legs, so it was good of her to let me use it. At the same time, there were times when she needed it and I couldn't get over. It was time to get my own set of wheels. I was getting desperate; I needed another car. I saved up and got myself one – an orange Manta for three hundred quid. It wasn't exactly *Knight Rider*, but it got me from A to B, and got me over to see Angie. With a car that colour I couldn't take any chances – I had to keep Colin well away from it. After the Manta I moved on to an Orion a little while later. Colin hadn't made any vengeful attacks on the Manta, but the Orion went through one or two courtesy of Tracey. She'd deny it every time but it was even caught on camera and, as we all know, the camera never lies. The amount of times I'd finish work to find the wing mirrors smashed was a joke. It could have been innocent enough – she may have just looked in it and cracked it – but the video footage told a different story. Reggie Conlin had a similar car and once she even smashed his up by mistake! Now that was funny.

* * * * *

Guns seemed to be all over the place back in the '90s. I had a mate called Kevin Nightingale – 'Nighter' – who worked on the doors of Boulevard over in South Shields. Obviously, working with people all over the area you get close to them, and Nighter was no different. He was a good mate. We'd go out clubbing with other doormen for people's birthdays and what have you. Nighter was a good lad, always up for a laugh. He got a lift from work one night from Oz nightclub, where he used to work after Boulevard closed for the night. He was dropped off at home and while he was putting the key in the door someone came up behind him and shot him three times in the back of the head. He died instantly. His wife came down to find him with his brains splattered all over the place. Can you imagine the shock of that? He had kids as well. It must have happened at around three in the morning and I got a call from Jarra (Jarrow) Kev – a top geezer and real good pal of mine – just before nine telling me what happened. It put the shits up a lot of people. He worked for me and was nowhere near as high profile as some of the rest of us. For him to be followed and get shot at point-blank range really hit home for a lot of us. No one knows what he'd got involved with. There are so many stories about what happened, but that's all they are. When the police started asking questions, some lads went into hiding. People thought it would be them next. His best mates were running away instead of trying to hunt down who it was. The known facts so far are that three people who were all questioned without charge gave him a lift home. Someone was accused of the murder, but the charges against him were later dropped. In a recent newspaper report, it said that three people, along with a fourth person serving eleven years for other offences, are to be charged with the murder. Again, no one knows the truth except those who did it. I hope they get everything coming to them.

* * * * *

I don't think there has been a time when working in Sunderland hasn't been like a huge madhouse. I know I've said it before but you've gotta believe me: the whole town centre being the nuthouse and all the bars and clubs are the different blocks where all the punters are on day release and we were the wardens who had to keep them in check each night. It's starting to mellow out a bit now, but there are some places that will never let up. A Block: arseholes and arsonists; B Block: they were all real bastards; C Block is obvious and D Block was full of drunks and dickheads. Which leads us nicely back to Tracey. Things with her only went from bad to a whole lot worse, while things with Angie were going from great to fucking brilliant. Angie and me moved in together in Sunderland and got ourselves a house. We moved quickly, 'cos we didn't see the point in hanging around. No more travelling over to see her every night; we were together and were really happy. It felt like I had real stability. I hadn't felt this good for a while. Life with Angie was perfect; she was everything I wanted and more. She had taken the news of Ian brilliantly and they got on well with each other. I don't know why I'd panicked so much in the first place. Ian was not even an issue, having him only enhanced the relationship. Things were looking good for us.

Our Colin turned up at the house one day but it was no social visit ... not so good. His girlfriend's car had been stolen and something had to be done about it. As if there wasn't enough to do at work ... but having your car nicked is a real piss-take and if they thought they could get away with it they were very wrong. One thing I couldn't understand was why he was so bothered about the car. He moved from one girl to another in as many weeks, so surely she was on borrowed time anyway. He told me he had seen the blokes responsible for it and had given one of them a slap. They came from a known family in the area. They only lived a few streets away from us so we decided we would pay them a little visit to sort things out. In the meantime, two of them came to my door. The fucking cheek of it. They asked Angie where I was and she told them she wasn't my keeper and that it may be good for their health if they didn't talk to her in such a tone of voice. Next they told her to tell me that I was gonna wish I'd never hit their nephew and she told them to tell me themselves. Not only were they thieving bastards, they also thought it was big for the both of them to intimidate a woman in such a way (not that she was scared of them). Shortly after that we returned to the house and Angie got me up to speed with what was going on. I was getting angrier by the second and was about to explode. Next thing we heard was the sound of screeching tyres and five of these guys got out of the car with iron bars and bats: time for a scrap, methinks.

We confronted them and the scuffle only lasted a few seconds. It was hardly a fight. I was grabbed from behind in what was basically a bearhug while one of them laid into my face. It was one of them beatings that looked a lot worse than it actually was. I knew that Angie would be watching and thinking I was getting the hiding of my life, so I couldn't let it go any further. It's quite hard to get the upper hand in that position but I did. I broke free by backward headbutting the guy who had hold of me, got loose and tore straight into them. They made for the car and took off down the street. Spineless bastards. It wasn't going to be a five-on-one hit-and-run. I was off down the street after them shouting, '*Come on! Fucking come on!*' and chased them all the way to their door. If you try something like that you've got to be prepared to take it all the way to the end. You cannot start it and then run away if things don't go your way. Colin was nowhere in sight, so Angie phoned anyone she could think of for back-up.

I'm now at their place and they've locked themselves in. I was shouting for them to come out and face me. I was mad as hell. Having one of them hit me like that only got me pumped up even more, and then running after them got me to the point of wanting to rip their heads off. My whole body was heaving with the adrenaline rush. I gave them one chance to show themselves before going in. The only thing that stood between those cowards and me was the front door. Not for long. I charged at it and it caved in under me. Inside I headed straight for them. Two had legged it out the back door, leaving the others to bear the brunt of my aggression. I smashed through two of them to get to the eldest one. He was going to pay big time. I made it last by dragging him around and giving him the odd slap along the way. I wanted him outside so I'd have room to really do some work on him. I heard a dog barking but couldn't see where it was coming from, so out into the front garden we went. We were standing toe to toe. My lads had arrived and were parked up. They could see I was in control so they watched me get on with it; they stood nearby in case the other three returned with back-up.

I moved in with a crack to the jaw. This was a big right-hander and it took the wind right out of his sails. He was trying to remain standing, but you could see he'd lost his legs. I could have just watched him stagger around for a few minutes and then blown him over, but I wanted to hurt him – really fucking hurt him. Instead of hitting him with a few light jabs, I lunged in and hit him with everything; I watched him drop like the bag of shit he was. No one stays standing after that – no one.

As he hit the deck my head was throbbing with rage. I was ready to burst. I wanted more of them. I needed to do more of them in. Any fucker would do, I didn't want it to stop. I know there's people out there who know exactly what I'm describing. I'd lost all sensation and could feel the hate and the venom running wild through my entire body. Breathing heavily through the drying blood in my nose, I turned to the lads who'd come to back me up. They should have been as ecstatic as I was, but they had looks of complete horror on their faces. I followed their gaze and looked down.

The fucking dog! Because I was so pumped up I hadn't even noticed the dog, but now I knew why it had stopped barking. It was now hanging off my dick with its jaws firmly locked round it. It was a Staffordshire terrier. A right vicious bastard. It had jumped up at me when I was decking its owner (I bet they were best friends). The lads were shouting at me to get it off, as if I hadn't thought of that myself. The pain was beginning to set in and it was just staring up at me snarling, growling and pulling at it as it hung on. I didn't know what the fuck to do, but I knew I had to do something. There was no way I was gonna put my hands anywhere near them jaws. Fuck this ... I punched it right between the eyes and knocked it out cold. Its head was as hard as a rock! As soon as I hit it, it dropped to the floor. It was sparked out on its back – just like its master. I was looking down at the blood and thinking the worst. I booted the fucking thing into the next garden.

I got to my feet and assessed the damage: two knocked out inside, one knocked out in the garden, the door broken off its hinges and a dog lying in the next garden completely sparked ... all that was missing was a partridge in a pear tree. We all went back up to the house so that I could have a proper look at what the hound from hell had done. My nose was broken, the teeth marks in my hip were pretty deep, and of course there were the other teeth marks in a place that still hurts to mention it. Talk about give a dog a bone. I put an ice pack on my nose and I could feel the bruises forming around my eyes to complete the look. I needed a trip to the hospital. I wanted Angie to go and stay with a friend while I was away in case anything else happened but she was determined to stay put. The doctors were used to patching me up after a fight, but they weren't prepared for the teeth marks. I needed a tetanus jab. That was when the lads told me to show them the full extent of the battle with Jaws. I thought I could have got away with just showing them my hip but, seeing as though they were not bitten off altogether, the lads thought it would be a laugh to tell the nurse about the dog's attempt to steal the family jewels. She took a look and told me they were really big and you know what I was thinking; I was assured it was the bite marks she meant.

The next day Angie drove to pick her friend up around ten miles away while I had a gentle stroll down to the shops. The shops being a lookout position where I could see any activity going on at the house from yesterday; then I saw some movement. Seeing this lad come out of the house I went over to him – 'You!' Kerr-fuck! I was in no mood to beat around the bush and landed him on his arse in the street. I wanted the guy who'd broken my nose and now I had my prime suspect. I grabbed him by the scruff of the neck and dragged him to my place. He was kicking and screaming, saying it wasn't him. He was frantic with panic 'cos I was gonna tear him apart when we got to mine. He even took out his club card to prove he wasn't who I insisted he was. Of course, he would say that, wouldn't he – anyone can have fake identification. There was no reasoning with me. I wanted blood and I wanted his.

I got him to the door and shouted Angie to come out. 'Is this the bastard who hit me?' I asked. I still had a tight hold on him. 'No,' came the reply. *Shit* ... I turned to this frightened lad with blood running down his face and dusted him down rather sheepishly. He was on his way to the Working Man's Club just down the road, so I even gave him a lift there in way of an apology. He still thought it was part of my evil plan, I think. He'd come out of the house next door but because of the angle I was at it had looked like the other house. Everybody makes mistakes – I never said I was perfect! What more did he want? He got a lift out of it.

A few days later I had to go back to the hospital to get injections in my nose and to have it set properly. I was convinced they'd start charging me rent if I ever went back.

* * * * *

When Owen left the job he instantly transformed himself into a legend. There were stories about him that were going to last and get passed on to other doormen. That's what happens, always has, always will. Another one of those men of that time who were, and still are, legends was Geoff Oughton. Ronnie Besford, 'The Beast', introduced me to Geoff. Geoff and Ronnie were very well known in certain circles and were both judo men. Geoff is a fourth dan black belt. He went to Japan many years ago to train and is well ranked in the profession. He was a friend of Owen Murray, but knew Ronnie better and we got together one time at a meeting. He had an unbelievably confident manner and huge stature; on meeting Geoff I thought, This boy knows exactly what he's talking about. He stands at around six foot tall and has an awesome physique. What's even more striking about him is his mental attitude – he knows he cannot be beaten and, with such positivity, he never will be. Covered in tattoos as well, he could so easily have auditioned for *Cape Fear* and been given the role of Max Cady.

I'll always remember this story about Geoff. I had just met Angie and I took her through to South Shields one night. Geoff has got a lot of pull in Shields; I was in one of his nightclubs sitting with Angie when I felt a tap on my shoulder. I turned round and there he was. He was a proper gent, shook my hand and welcomed us to the club. Once we'd had a chat and he was walking away, I said to Angie, 'That is a man that I'd like to be like, I've heard he can fight.' This was at least six years before I even knew any ground moves (martial arts), but even then I definitely knew exactly what I wanted to be.

So, once Owen stepped down, Les Graham took over. This was still the same three doors that Owen originally had. It turned out that Les wasn't there all that long but there was still plenty of action along the way.

Wednesday was rave night at one of the clubs. They were

always real hectic, with hundreds of people off their tits every week. There was nearly always a good vibe in the place; you know what the rave kids are like. This particular time, though, there had been a bad atmosphere in the club all night; it certainly wasn't the same vibe we were used to. Once it finished, the music came off and the lights went on. It was the only way of getting them out but even then they would still be dancing with the music off.

There's a kitchen towards the back of the club and we heard a noise there. Les and me went to check it out while the others carried on getting the punters out in as orderly a manner as possible. When we got to the kitchen we saw a kid I recognised from school, Dennis Jackson. Obviously he still hadn't had the letter of membership from MENSA; he was letting off the fire extinguisher and spraying foam everywhere. I took it off him and said, 'What y'doing, you idiot?' Once I had hold of it Les just banged him one and sent him flying across the floor. Everything went up. It was suddenly fight night. We were dragging punters out the back and front and it went on for ages. There were clubbers fighting, shouting, kicking ... and a huge percentage of them were on something so they were that bit trickier to handle or reason with. The front doors were locked and a pick-axe handle was inserted through the door handles to keep them secure. It was like thunder with the noise of kicking and bins being thrown. In the street outside there was a fucking huge crowd; they had bins from lampposts and were throwing them up at the office windows above as well.

When it got to the stage that things were being hurled at the windows – missiles if this was a news report – drastic action was called for. I heard later that a bottle of ammonia was squirted out the window on to the crowd below. A girl's eyes were burned in the process, but I wasn't upstairs at the time so I can't comment. The idea was that this would disperse them, but it only made things ten times worse. I was out the back and Michael Downey, the manager, came down. It was as near to insane as you can imagine. The back yard was wall to wall with fighting. We were right in the middle, fighting as many as we could at the same time. A good friend of mine, Peter Kirkwood, waded in to lend a hand (and a fist, knee and both feet). He wasn't even working the doors that night, but he stood with us regardless. I saw someone give him a sly dig so I ran over to help him. It was like trying to run in the sea – impossible. It was a kid called Stuie who'd hit him. He came at me and I dropped him with one punch; he's a real bag of shit this bloke. Next thing I know he's grabbed hold of my trouser leg and ripped them wide open. I'd turned my attention to someone else by now and only knew what he was up to when I heard Michael shout, 'Ian, he's got a knife!'

Michael was over in a second and grabbed hold of him by the hair; Stuie was still on the ground and trying to get up. What a fucking spineless bastard he was pulling a knife out on *me*. There wasn't the time to take any kind of run-up; I just booted him in the face. It nearly took his head clean off and Michael was left standing there with a handful of hair. Stuie was out cold.

Now the only question was: how do we get back in? People were everywhere, taking pot shots and laying into us at any opportunity. In turn we were lashing out at anyone who got in our way. I shoved and punched my way through. It was one of those situations where one-on-ones were out the window. All you could do was strike out at anyone and everyone and make it count. Anything more than one punch was leaving you open to hits. You had to finish whoever you hit. The two doormen inside the club had shut the doors on us. Peter, Michael and me were left outside to fend for ourselves. Talk about an angry mob ... you could not put your guard down or stop punching for a second, or they would be all over you like a swarm. Then, out the corner of my eye, I saw Les Graham. He had a metal bar and was swinging at and hitting everyone in sight to clear a path. People were going down all over the place; he was breaking anything that moved. He was just like an angel! (Well, if you can imagine one in disguise and hitting people with an iron bar, that is.) Or, more accurately, he was like a snowplough clearing the way. We made it to the door and started banging on it. No reply. 'It's fucking *us* man. Open it.' We piled in and locked the doors behind us. The police arrived and dispersed the clubbers. We'd had no idea when – or if – it was going to stop, until Les turned up to even things out a bit.

At six in the morning, Stuie turned up at Reggie's looking even more pig ugly than usual. Once he managed to convince him that he hadn't just been scalped by a load of Red Indians and then been pushed off Marsden Rock, he told him what had happened a few hours earlier. (Marsden Rock is a cliff face in Tynemouth overlooking the North Sea, by the way.) Now things made sense. He told him that it was the hardest he'd been hit in his life. I'm inclined to agree with him. Dr Freeman strikes again … should have sent him an invoice for that one.

Knives are for losers and cowards. You see kids going in to town for a night out these days and they take a knife with them. Why would they take it if not to cut or stab someone once they're pissed? Then of course they'll start a fight and straight away the knife comes out. That's the mark of a coward. I'd rather fight a brave man with a knife than a coward with a knife. A brave man would fight first and go for the knife as a last resort, if he isn't knocked out by that point. A coward will go for the knife first 'cos he's scared to fight; I know because I've seen it happen and because I have fought cowards with knives.

There was one such occasion at the After Dark rave club in South Shields. Two lads went outside for a fight and, as they squared up to each other, one of them put his hand in his pocket.

Sensing something was up, the other lad started asking what he was doing and got the reply of 'I'll show you.' He started fumbling around, but the other lad didn't hang around to find out what he was going to pull out. He came back to the club – we only let him in 'cos he was a friend of a friend. Then the one with the knife tried to get back in and I stopped him; it was obvious what was in his pocket and I asked to search him. After refusing, he backed off, pulled the knife out and said, 'Come on!' pointing it right at me. I just saw red. He didn't know what the fuck he had just started. I was surging towards him, there was no way I was gonna let some piece of shit point a knife at me like that. It could only be finished now when one of us was fucked. He was backing off as I approached and when it seemed his bottle had left I moved back to the door and he came at me saying, 'I'm gonna fucking stick you.'

I couldn't let this one go. He was in far too deep and he still hadn't realised. I had my padded jacket inside and went in to put it on. My plan was to come out like I was a punter with the jacket zipped right up and destroy him on the spot. I came out but he was walking too far to the left to launch a surprise attack, so I went round the back to meet him round the other side. As I got there I remembered something – I had a metal bar in the car for things like this. If he wanted to fight with weapons, he was messing with the wrong bloke. I got the bar out, hid it up my sleeve and noticed he was at the door talking to the manager so I called one of the doormen over. I asked him if the lad had the knife out and he said no. Perfect. No weapons needed. He copped hold of the bar for me; I steamed over to the lad and dropped him with a massive sidewinder blow to the head. He was in mid-sentence as I caught him. I kicked him from arsehole to breakfast for ten minutes. I'm surprised I didn't cripple him, 'cos I booted his legs, his body, his back and his fucking bollocks ... each time he started going for the knife I was booting him with lefts and rights – never giving him the chance to reach it. He was fucked. I left him half-unconscious in the road and after a while he got up and staggered off. Just like that prick in Bentleys before him.

In years to come, when, I started working with Graham Potts, we even had a syringe pulled on us. It had blood in it and the bloke holding it said, 'I'm HIV positive. Come anywhere near me and this is going in you.' What do you do? A knife can cut you and worst case you can be stabbed. The slightest pinprick from this thing and you are a dead man walking. He may not be HIV, but do you take the chance?

It's weird how you can deal with so much grief on the streets or at work and still maintain a great life at home. I know millions of people everywhere deal with stressful jobs and come home and do their best to unwind. I'm not saying I'm the only one, or trying to take anything away from you. I was used to fighting in my personal as well as my professional life. This feeling of domestic peace was new and I loved it. My personal and home life was perfect with Angie and the point naturally came when we decided we wanted to do things properly. We decided to get engaged and had a party to celebrate. It wasn't long since Tracey had fabricated another story that I'd assaulted her, to get me locked up or charged. Once she heard about the engagement she came out of the woodwork to make up another story that I'd done it again. This was a day before the party. I'm not usually one to say, 'That's some coincidence, that', but I did this time. Can you believe it? She was riddled with so much jealousy and anger that she couldn't stand to see us happy. Sad old cow. When the assault charge went to court she didn't even turn up. She had to be dragged there and for some strange reason it turned out that I was innocent. She just couldn't stop lying to get herself out of things and dug herself into an even deeper hole. They say you need to have a good memory to be a liar ... a brain would be a good starting point, then. Most of the time they always get found out. The judge commented that the court cases had gone on longer than our marriage. Best one-liner I've heard in years, your honour. Take my ex-wife ... please. It was good to see that the courts and the authorities were almost as sick of her wilfully disruptive pranks and antics as I was.

* * * * *

I got friendly with a new lad on the doors and we went on to become really good mates. Carl Simpson got a job on the doors at Ku Club from Michael Downey. He was young then and won't mind me saying that he was a bit immature. He sees life very differently now and is definitely a force to be reckoned with. I got to know Carl when he came to me for help. In those days he would hit anybody without really thinking about the consequences. It could be that subconsciously I saw a bit of the old me in him, but I agreed to help. It wasn't that long prior to meeting Carl that I was a new kid myself. Carl and Michael had bashed some well-known hard men in one of the bars. They were real gangsters and had vowed revenge. When that happens, revenge is quite inevitable but you never know when. Carl was getting paranoid that he was being followed, and wanted it sorted out.

Jarra Kev knew one of them so we went to the bloke's house and had a meeting. We sat down and got it sorted. Carl was grateful for it; I think he realised that he was a bit out of his depth. It shows he had the bottle even then to take anyone on but I don't think he quite knew what he was stirring. After that I got him a job at a club called Marlowe's and we became good mates. Carl is the one who sorted Des Ball out at the golf club, and another one of the lads who would stand by me through anything. He's definitely grown up a lot since then and is learning all the time. A solid bloke now, Carl is gonna go a long way. In the years to follow, we would become good buddies. He's a valued member of the group, as well as the whole town over.

Don't take my politeness as a weakness

I CAN ALMOST guarantee that if you show people kindness when they are not expecting it they will assume they can get away with things. They will take liberties until you show them that your politeness does not mean you are a soft touch. It happens in all professions, mine is no different.

Les wasn't running things for very long. No more than six months went by before he was sent to prison for dealing drugs. He was given a five-year sentence. That's one of the other reasons I wouldn't allow drugs into my bars: the years you serve when you get caught are too much. Five years away from my family would seem like a life sentence to me.

When Les got put away was when I first came to power. I took over the three doors and with it the responsibility of looking after the punters, taking care of the daft ones. And I suppose the same must be said of my doormen as well; I looked after them and they looked after me. All the blokes I've mentioned along the way were now becoming part of something special. It always comes down to teamwork: you're only as strong as your team. If I had any ideas that I was bigger than the team behind me then I wouldn't deserve to have them.

This was a huge leap for me, and it was excellent. I'm not some power-hungry maniac, but to suddenly find myself in that position was as close to the dog's as you could possibly get. I didn't really answer to people I'd worked for in the past, but now it officially meant that people had to answer to me. As you can imagine, with my higher profile there were always more risks involved. I'd still get locked up, but the police began to treat me very differently. My position meant that I had quite a bit of influence over people and could stop a few things before they got out of hand. In other words, they had finally grasped that I wasn't just there to tear heads off people and could actually make their job that bit easier. It's not like they suddenly wanted to be friends or invite me to tea; they were giving me some degree of respect or an acknowledgement, but we will always be sworn enemies, I reckon. I think that secretly there are a few of them who would like to be able to handle situations the way I do. What they don't like is that I sometimes break a few rules. The bobby on the beat likes me 'cos I'm doing what I can to keep the drugs out of town and I keep the shitbags out of town. I know I can't keep everything out, but they do know I'm trying to and in that respect I know I'll never be up for any drug charges.

One thing I had to do now was learn the rules before diving in headfirst. This meant I had to unlearn the other ones – I could no longer just hit first and not bother to ask any questions later. I had to start using my loaf a bit. Eyes were on me and I couldn't afford to mess up. The police would certainly keep more of an eye on me, but more importantly the bigger boys on the street always have a keen interest. These were the people who mattered more. I had to show I could do the job well and do it properly.

Back at home we received some excellent news ... Angie was pregnant! This was the best news I'd had in so many years. To me it signalled complete closure from Tracey and all the mess she'd put Ian and me through. It also signalled the start of a completely new life for us as a couple and a new little life to look forward to enjoying. We were over the moon. It also meant that it was the first time I could show my true feelings about fatherhood. As much as I love my two other kids, I simply could not enjoy the whole excitement of the pregnancy and the excitement of the togetherness that it brings. We were on the way – a real family.

Here's me saying that the pregnancy was exciting, but I doubt whether Angie would quite have described it as that. She didn't enjoy it half as much as I did. Women complain of how bad being pregnant is when all they do is sit around watching *Richard and Judy* and eat all day. I'm kidding ... I'm *kidding!* I know it's one of those things men will never understand. I was constipated for a few days once, if that's any help.

We had plenty of ups and downs along the way, and we both know it was down to all the strains of the pregnancy. Not so funny at the time, but something we can laugh about now (I hope). Angie felt too closed in to start with. Living in Sunderland when all her friends and family were miles away couldn't have been that enjoyable either. It was time to compromise. She went back to live with her parents for a few weeks until we got a house near them and then I came over. She knows I'd do anything for her and moving out of the area was not the end of the world for me. If anything it was better for me because I could separate my work from my private life. At first I was worried that if I left Sunderland it wouldn't be my town any more. I was wrong. It was definitely a smart move.

Having these three doors to start with, I began to get offers of more doors along the way. Because I was new to all this, I didn't want to start off on the wrong foot and go upsetting the wrong people. I had moved up a tier but was now the new kid on a different block. And being new I couldn't go around stepping on toes.

I went to see Ernie, approaching him as the friend he is. We were more acquaintances than best mates. He didn't know me well enough to trust me one hundred per cent – you have to earn trust and it would take him time before he could trust me to that level. What's more important is that we had a mutual respect for one another. I told him I'd been offered a bar and, at such an early stage, I wasn't sure how things worked because he ran the town. He could see I was genuine and could appreciate my honesty. I asked if it would be him running it or if I would be running it for him; he told me, 'Ian, if it's offered just take it.'

That was the green light I was looking for. I took the bar and was offered another and then a few more as time went on. Apart from the added responsibility, to be offered doors is a good sign that people believe in you. For me to get those doors meant that I had made my mark and people wanted me to help them. That, again, is another satisfaction about my job: the recognition and the fact that I am making a difference in some way is a real plus. The offer of doors means people have faith in my ability. Ernie had a lot more of them than I did, but it was important for me that I also had them. It marked another big turning point in my life. We were the only people running doors in the town.

When I take doors, as with every job I do, I tell the owners, managers or whoever the points of my job that they need to know. They do not need to know the finer details and I don't want to know their job inside out either. If I take a door, I tell them that I can offer them a guarantee of 24-hour help and security. People know who I am and that they cannot come in to one of my bars and cause any trouble. They know what happens if they do. I'm firstly a gentleman and secondly a businessman. Any myths that you get doors by brute force and threats are exactly that: myths.

As much as people would love to hear that it goes on, it doesn't. What usually happens is that pubs or clubs will get gangs or a family taking liberties. When the owner stands in their way they get threatened or beaten up. That's when they can approach me and I can assure them that one way or another it won't happen again. To put it simply, I'm helping them and giving them peace of mind from those bullies. If they think the trouble has passed and the bullies have moved on, they are under no further obligations to me. So there's another myth destroyed. If you ask me for help, you are not selling your soul – you can back out at any time. I tell people that from the start. They don't have to pay for a service they don't think they need. They have my number if they want me back. But, of course, as soon as the bullies or bully sees that I'm not connected to the place any more, most of them go back and make people's lives hell again. It's a sad fact.

You have to remember that, in some pubs, the owner or managers live in the accommodation above the place with their families. So straight away these thugs are causing them grief at home as well as at work. No one wants shit on their own doorstep. The problem the police have is that it is sorted out in a way that they cannot use. For example, a bloke is causing a lot of trouble in a bar and threatens the owner. The owner is losing money having a thug in his bar. If he goes to the police he will be told it's a civil matter and all the police can do is warn him. To get the thug stopped from entering the place he could take out an injunction, which may take a few months. The only way the police can intervene is if the thug actually does go ahead and punch the owner's face in. What use is that to him? Why wait until the damage is done? I can go round and tell them they are not wanted there. I don't threaten people for a living. I make it clear I am connected to it and they are not welcome.

That bloke I mentioned earlier at the golf club – Des: once I'd told him, he knew who he was dealing with. He waited till things had died down before going back. That's being stupid. I could have gone to see him the first time and gave him a major kicking – it would not have been a problem. I was polite and made my point clear. When you are dealing with people like that they are not used to politeness. They think something is wrong if you don't rush in shouting and swearing with a full army behind you after their blood. They take your politeness as a weakness and think they can get away with things or do it again because of the delivery. This really fucks me off, because they will never get away with it. Don't take my politeness as a weakness ... simple as that. It grates on me more than anything.

There was this other bloke, Nick. He started drinking with our Colin and because he knew him I ended up giving him a chance. I gave him a job on the doors as a favour. He was basically a two-bit nobody. I got to know him from working for me and I was putting a wage in his pocket. One day he told me he needed money for his family, the whole sob story. I gave him a loan and told him to pay me every week. He agreed and began paying me back each week. The manager didn't like him and he didn't want him working there. Once he told me, 'I knew I was gonna have to finish him 'cos, as I said earlier, you can't work with someone you don't like, trust and respect.' This gave me a problem; if I let him go there was no way he could pay me back and I wanted my money. I asked the manager to do me a favour by putting up with Nick until he finished paying me and said that I'd get rid of him then. Again, I was helping him out by leaving him with money instead of taking it all.

I told him the score and soon enough he started missing his repayments. What a fucking balloon, a real dork. I was beginning to lose my patience with him and had no choice but to take the money from his wages before it went to him. It was eventually paid off and he was told to go. Instead of thanking me for the money and for giving him a job – giving him a break instead of a *break* – he went to friends of mine saying, 'Ian Freeman? I don't work for that dickhead any more.'

One day I was at the garage in Millfield getting my car fixed. A car pulled up and Nick got out. He saw me and nearly shit a brick. It was one of those situations where he knew he'd been bad-mouthing me but didn't know if I knew. He hesitated for that fraction of a second that gave him away. I knew he was just that bit too far away for me to run after him and catch him, 'cos he'd have a head start. Best thing to do was play it cool and speak to him as though things were fine between us.

'All right, Nick. How's it going, mate?' I asked. I greeted him with a big smile, 'cos I was genuinely pleased to see him. Pleased to see him 'cos it meant I could fill the bastard in, but he didn't know that. Now he thought he was in the clear and replied with a 'Fine, thanks.'

Not any fucking more. He got within two feet and I turned and whacked him in the face. Dropped him straight to the floor. Punched the living crap out of him. He was absolutely shitting it. He scrambled to his feet and had nowhere to go. I chased him round like a scene from *Benny Hill*. A grown man running away, I don't know ... one of his shoes even fell off but he didn't stop for it. What a pathetic sight. I caught up with him and smashed him into the car doors headfirst – every surface got dented to fuck as I rammed him into it. By the time I'd finished the car was a virtual write-off and he wasn't too far behind it. I was going to choke him unconscious but he was covered in so much blood I didn't bother. I flung him to the ground and looked up to see our Colin's car pull up; he came over to see what was going on. As I was telling him the story I turned round to Nick on the ground. He'd only scrambled to his feet again and was legging it up the road! He was so petrified I don't think he realised what a state he was in. He still had only one shoe on.

It turned out that he'd used the money from me to get his car resprayed and didn't spend it on his family as he'd said. He knew that if he told me he wanted the money to spend on his car I'd tell him to save up like the rest of us. If it was for his family, then I could sympathise. He'd lied to me and taken things too far. I don't know how he expected to get away with it. Once I'd told our kid all about it, he picked up a wrench from inside the garage and continued to smash Nick's car up. That's just one example. Once me and Colin get together, no one takes our politeness as a weakness, that's for sure.

A lot of people have mistaken our Colin for me. If you don't really know me and saw him in the street you might make the mistake – I mean, he's well built, can handle himself and is almost as handsome. He's played on it a few times, which I'll tell you about later. Along with sorting Nick the Prick out, we've done quite a few other little jobs together. When we were kids we were always dropping each other in it, fighting and messing around, but as you get older you become good mates as well as being brothers. Now we are there to help each other out any time it's called for.

While I'm on the subject of cars, we got up to a bit of road rage ourselves once. Another team effort. Well, seeing our dad practically invented it we have a tradition to keep up! Joking aside, I am terrible for road rage. I'll be the first to tell you (and plenty others will back me up) that I've got a very short temper, and so has our Col.

We were in my car on the slip road to pull on to the A19. Me driving, Colin in the passenger seat. (I had a red Escort 16V at this point – new shape, of course.) As we were pulling on to it a car shot out from nowhere and pulled in front of us. I had to slam my brakes on and we were calling them every bastard under the sun. Two little boy racers in some shitty XR2 lookalike thing and they gave us the finger as they put the foot down. Bastards. I shifted the gears and went after them, flashing the lights for them to pull over. Would they fuck pull over. I got alongside them and we were shouting at them and they were shouting back. They probably felt safe shouting things back at us from a moving car, but Colin was about to prove them wrong on that point. We're blasting along at around ninety and he takes out the steering lock, leans out the window and smashes their window and doorpost in. We carried on past them after that and watched as they screeched to a stop. I doubt that they'll be doing that again.

Road rage – I think everyone has at least a little bit of that inside them. When you're the driver being cut up on a road or whatever it is, it's basically having the piss taken out of you and no one likes that. You read about it all the time in newspapers now – people take it too far and even kill. I suppose any argument or confrontation is likely to get out of hand; it all depends who you are dealing with. It really sends people mental. I'd urge everyone not to get out of their cars. I've seen some of the tools people carry in their cars and to get beaten to fuck or killed because someone tooted their horn at you is not worth it, is it? I'm not talking about cowards here. I'm talking about mean and crazy people who could tear your head off or smash you up with a weapon. Their reason? They don't need one, won't have one and will not care.

This other tosser cut in front of me once and when I blasted the horn at him he just ignored me. I pulled up to him and started yelling. He was one of those right snobbish fuckers and was looking down his nose at me. He was in a Jag and thought he was the bollocks. Talk about a red rag to a bull ... I shouted at him to pull over and he did. I got out and went over to him. His window came down and before I could speak he said, 'I'm a solicitor. I'm on my way to court.' Like I fucking cared what excuse he thought he had ... you're fucking not now; I reached in, grabbed the keys from the ignition and threw them over a wall, but this wall happened to be around fifteen feet high. He'd have a better chance of finding George Michael in bed with a woman than finding his keys.

While I'm getting things I hate out in the open, here's another one high on the list: people using my name for whatever reason. It bugs the shit out of me. Another example ... Gary in town. I say hello to him every week 'cos I know him through a friend who got me a deal on some furniture once. I was in Marlowe's one night and his girlfriend came running over saying that Gary was in trouble and could I go over to help him out. Sure. I'd help out any mate who was in trouble and he knew that. I got to the scene and Gary was scared shitless of this bloke who was having a go at him. He was so pale I could nearly see through him. 'All right, Gary?' I said and turned to the gadgey and told him to leave it out. At that he apologised to me and that should have been the end of it. Oh no. Gary turned to him and started going, 'Tell you what, don't you ever fucking ... *blah blah* ... I'll tell you what it is, you fucking ...'

I had to jump in. He turned from shaking like a leaf one minute into William fucking Wallace the next. And Braveheart he was not. I was telling him to leave it, 'Whoa, Gary. It's sorted. I've sorted it. Let it go, OK,' but he didn't know when to quit. If he thought I'd stick up for him after that he was stupider than he looked. I grabbed him by the scruff of the neck and threw him down the stairs. He was suddenly this big hard man when I was there but a scared little kid on his own. He knew the bloke (who could have easily wrecked him) would not have laid a finger on him with me around. I don't condone that kind of shit and I don't have to put up with it.

When I say don't take my politeness as a weakness, it's quite hard to fully explain. People who are friends will know I'm a bit more lenient when it comes to them. Others can see a gentlemanly and respectful nature as a weakness. They think you should be running around bashing everyone in sight to get respect, to rule by fear. I don't think that's as true as I used to. If I still acted like that now I doubt I'd have any friends. Fear can get you so far, but friendship and loyalty last a lot longer. Friends who are scared of you are not loyal. Manners get you everywhere but, to the so-called hard cases who don't know any better, if you don't go on like an animal all the time then you can't be what your reputation says you are. The fact is that I am everything my reputation says I am. I am tolerant to an extent. Do not push things any further once you ignite that short fuse because I will explode and there will be only one person who gets hurt in the blast. If people assume a weakness then it is out of their own stupidity and they deserve everything they get. Assumption is the mother of all fuck-ups.

* * * * *

There's been an association between football, drinking and violence for quite a few years now. As you know, I don't drink or like football, so I must be one of the exceptions to the rule. According to a recent survey, Sunderland has got the most violent supporters in the country. I don't know how true that is, but from my experience some of them are not too clever with it. Before you start, I'm not making a sweeping statement that all the fans are like that at all. There are daft people everywhere that spoil things for the likes of real supporters who can have a laugh, a few drinks and watch the match in peace. Most football fans can be the best punters in the world, because first off they are there for a good day out and at times there's a real carnival atmosphere. But, for those few who spoil it, you can politely ask them to keep it down out of respect for the other drinkers and you get it thrown back in your face. That's when the carnival turns into carnage. I hate this kind of shit. If I never had to have another street fight it would be too soon. People think I, or we, are a bunch of animals who get worked up all day eating raw meat and can't wait to get to work and kick people all over for the hell of it. Couldn't be further from the truth. You ask them a few times to cool their boots a bit and the next thing you know they are starting on you. You try persuading a group of drunks they are being too rowdy, swearing and what have you, and the management no longer wants them on the premises. See what happens.

Ian Brown, Pat Pearson and me were covering the doors at Boulevard on a match day. We love the supporters, 'cos we like it when they are in high spirits and we can have a bit of banter with them as they come in. There'll always be times when they kick off but they are just earning themselves a different kind of reputation. They get themselves labelled. The usual drunk in town might just get thrown out for being drunk and falling asleep. Then there's the drunk who causes fights and next up you've got the drunken football fans that start fights. A lot of them can't see that they are bringing the sport down and the team they love so much. There was a big group of fans who were singing football songs at the top of their voices. We didn't have a problem with that – it was the fact that they were getting a bit overexcited, and scaring a lot of the customers who were there for an afternoon drink and had no interest in football, that we didn't care for. The idea of a pub, a public house, is that all members of the public should feel welcome and not feel threatened in any way. Some people can't understand the meaning of a social drink. We'd asked them to keep it down twice and wanted things to remain calm. We don't go in thinking, There's a huge group of lads having a laugh. Let's spoil their fun. Let's start a fight. On the third time I told them to shut up completely. They are always as hard as nails in a group and one of them got a bit lippy. The lad behind him was pulling stupid faces and directing insults at me, but hiding behind the rest of them. I told him to shut the fuck up. There is only so much politeness and restraint you can show someone when they are not interested in taking notice, giving you lip and laughing behind your back.

They kicked off ... There were a lot of them and we couldn't let them get the edge over us. We were well outnumbered but had to steam in. I whacked a few of them and Ian joined in. Pat helped us drag them out. He didn't hit any of them, as he was also calming things down for the other people in the bar, who were looking a bit more scared now. We dished out a fair few slaps that afternoon. In fact, they were getting carted off to hospital when the police arrived to arrest us. To arrest *us*! A lot of them needed stitches, so it probably looked as though we had just jumped them for no reason. I'm sure the police could have taken a few seconds to think about what had gone on, but as far as they were concerned they had just collared The Three Musketeers.

Next we were up in Crown Court on a joint charge of affray. Mr Halliday got on the case and told me the score. On his advice, Ian and me pleaded guilty. Pat pleaded not guilty. Why? Because he was *not* guilty. The only part he had was dragging people out, and that was not affray.

We were found guilty, Pat included. The judge said he wanted to send us to jail but because he knew Pat had a small part in it he passed a sentence that was the highest possible without doing bird. We got 240 hours of community service along with costs and compensation totalling eight hundred quid. We escaped by the skin of our teeth. Doing time when Angie was expecting is not even worth thinking about; I would have hated myself for putting her in that position.

The community service was spent cleaning graveyards, doing the grass, all that kind of mundane stuff that no one wants to do for a living. On community service I had to go to the town centre, sign myself in, pick the tools up and then go and do the job; then it was back with the tools, back to sign out, with certain times for lunch breaks. After serving time on community service I was put on a placement, which is a lot more relaxed. This is to see your time out hassle free because they know you can be trusted. My placement was at Thorney Close Youth Centre. It was fine. Sure it was a punishment, but it really was easy street. I could go there myself, do my work, take my own breaks and then go home. There were no supervisors to breathe down my neck and it was good to be on it by myself and have no distractions. I got on with things and even did a good job. Our Colin was also on community service for non-payment of fines. None of us likes paying fines, but when you are given community service as a consequence you have to do it. That's why it is called a 'punishment' and not called 'getting let off with it'. Getting let off with it was Colin's interpretation of the charge. He didn't want to do it and so he refused point blank.

The gadgey who handled my placement turned round to me and said, 'I know you've got a bit of influence on your brother ... Can you tell him to do his community service or he's going to jail. He can't just not do it. It's a punishment instead of jail.'

Crisis talks or what? He was so fucking stubborn that he probably would have gone to jail all for the sake of an unpaid fine. So I said, 'Why doesn't he come on placement with me and I'll pick him up in the mornings and make sure he does it.' So I'd got our boy on a placement ... This wasn't usual, but it was a good way of keeping us all happy. Even the law can compromise in some situations. Colin was like a dog with three cocks. I even get to babysit him when he gets in trouble.

On the subject of crisis ... Angie went into labour. The crisis was that I'd had trouble with the car and disconnected the battery earlier on. Her waters broke at midnight and it was a mad rush to get to the hospital. Once we got there, *apparently* I was a right pain in the arse. I was giving running commentaries on her contractions and following them on the monitor. They had a reclining chair in the corner so I could have a sleep. How was I to know it was a squeaky chair? I was asleep. In the morning when Angie woke after a terrible sleep, our daughter was on her way and I was busy having breakfast in the canteen. I got there for the birth. Just. To witness childbirth, you'll know it's almost impossible to put into words. It's the best thing in the world ... Angie was brilliant. We named our daughter Kennedy. She was born on 26 November 1996. If there is any weakness in my life, it's got to be Kennedy. She's absolutely spoiled rotten. My other two are just the same, but you always have a soft spot for the youngest and this is the first one that I have been able to father properly from day one. I remember holding her and wondering what she would sound like when she began to speak; once she started, she's never shut up! Little Legs, we call her; a real character. When they are that young and always on the move it's like they're constantly on drugs. I'm sure she is, judging by some of the things she comes out with. She talks and talks and talks ... As long as I live she will always be my little girl.

The way you play with fun and glee
And you never walk, you always run to me
Your giggles, your smile makes me warm inside
Why cover your eyes as you try to hide?

The way you brush the hair from your face
And you try to fasten your own shoelace
You collect everything that you seem to find
I wonder what goes on in your little mind

I would do anything for my little girl
I would take the stars from out of the sky
I would do anything for my little girl
I know that you are the apple of my eye

The way you jump up and down on the bed
And never miss a thing that's been said
You're always performing; you should be on stage
How can we tell from this early age?

The way you rock yourself to sleep
And all my change you want to keep
Your kisses, your cuddles you give me at night
Now I know why I squeeze you so tight

I would do anything for my little girl
I would take the stars from out of the sky
I would do anything for my little girl
I know that you are the apple of my eye

'The Apple of My Eye', Ian Freeman

I'm a very protective father. Kids – all kids – are a weakness to me; I worry for them all. There are some real nasty and sick bastards out there. I feel for people like the Payne family who had their daughter taken from them, and in such a way. My heart goes out to them. I'd love to see every bastard hang for those crimes; better still, I'd take great pleasure in kicking the shit out of them every day for the rest of their lives. If I see things like child abuse, murders and things on TV, I try not to watch 'cos it gets to me. It makes my blood boil and I explode inside. There is nothing bad in any child, they are completely innocent and full of adventure and yet these perverts prey on them. They wreck their lives or end them. Nothing sickens me more than paedophiles. Same with rapists – they are the scum of the earth. If I am reading a newspaper and there is a story about child abuse, I won't read it. On TV, by the time I've reached for the controls I've heard most of it. In a newspaper I can stop reading. Each and every night when I phone Angie my priorities are that she and the kids are safe and the doors are locked. I've always said I fear no man, but, where my family is concerned, I fear every man. When Angie is alone in the house or if the kids are out playing, that's when I feel fear 'cos I am not there to protect them. If I could, I would probably wrap them in cotton wool. I'm overprotective in that sense, but you have to be vigilant. It's sad that you can't let your kids play in the street unsupervised and that you have to scrutinise everyone who comes into contact with them. A very sad thing, but it's something you have to do these days. It's a worry for parents all over the world.

Top Boy

IT HAD TO happen, but it wasn't without its risks. People won't know the dangers I put myself in to protect my friends and my town. I became top boy and had to prove it with every fight. I was getting challenges left, right and centre and could not afford to get beaten.

Ernie was put away in '97 for an incident down at the Eastender pub in the East End of Sunderland. A man was killed and Ernie and Graham Potts were remanded for it. Graham was released 'cos there wasn't enough evidence to connect him – it was alleged that he was there when it happened but they couldn't prove it. He had to lie low because there was a £20,000 hit taken out on him. As you can imagine, he didn't want to be seen out in public. The bloke who was killed was Tony Waters, a big gangster who had done time for drugs. Ernie and he had been friends at one time but Ernie went clean, Tony didn't and they fell out. Ernie was given seven years for manslaughter. It was a fight that had gone too far accidentally. I took over Ernie's bars on a mutual agreement – I look after them until he gets out, and I'm still doing that to this day. It's a business thing, an arrangement between two gentlemen whose word is their bond. When he comes out then we'll sort something else out; until then, that's the way it's staying. I'm still getting other bars on top of that so I'm running a nice little empire. I hate people saying it as though I'm keeping his seat warm. It's a temporary arrangement to be looked at when he gets out. People on the outside assume I work *for* him. I don't; I'm nobody's lad. I'm my own man. People pay me a wage 'cos I look after their pub but I work for no one other than for myself and my family.

When Ernie got put away everyone was scared. The town was a weird place to be at that point in time. There was a kind of eerie silence on the streets. Nerves were starting to show and no one quite knew what would happen. The guy who was killed was a well-respected man within the criminal community in this country, as well as others. Basically, no one wanted to go anywhere near the lads who were connected to Ernie. No one wanted any association with them because, as a result of the death, they were on borrowed time. There was talk of gangs coming up from all over the country to even the score. Big Richey Laws phoned me up. He told me straight, 'Ian, everyone's shitting themselves. Ernie's doors need looking after. I'm working at the After Dark, we think it's going to be hit this weekend, will you come and watch my back?'

I answered, 'Yes.' No hesitation; I didn't need to think. A mate of mine was in trouble and I couldn't sit back and do nothing. Richey and me go back years, at least fifteen. He was on the scene when I was at Greens. Richey is an absolute giant and was a good fighter when on active duty. He's off the door scene now but he's what you'd call an entrepreneur – if there's money to be made you can bet he'll be there.

Ernie was locked up on Sunday, 7 December (Ian Jnr's birthday, as it happens), and the next day I stepped in to help. There was no time to hang around. I went in and stood by them. There was no mention of money and I didn't receive a penny in the six months of doing it. So, if you thought my motivation was cash, forget it. I asked what was happening with the other bars. No one wanted anything to do with them, so I said I'd look after them. At this point, Ernie didn't really know me that well and thought I might do the dirty on him. When he was in that position, you can understand that anything could have been going through his head. Here I was on the outside going through the possibilities of hits on me – anything could have happened. I took on a whole heap of shit. *Everyone* was scared for their lives. Every time my phone rang about some trouble in a bar, I'd go over thinking I was walking into an ambush. That's how bad it was and there would be around six calls a week like that. I get calls now and I'm still cautious, but back then it was, 'What the *fuck* am I going into?' I even had sit-down meetings with different gangs from the big cities of Britain to sort things out. That's how far I was prepared to go. I was risking my own life for others. These people were after blood; they wanted revenge and there was a war threatening to go off. Out of respect I'll not mention who they were, where they were from or what was said other than it is all sorted now and there was no bloodshed.

Driving home one night I was aware that I was being followed. This was a few months into the takeover and things were still unsettled. There is always the possibility of this happening. Same as when I go in a club, you never know what may or may not happen, so you have to be prepared at all times. If I think I'm being followed I take a diversion and see what happens. If the tail is still there I have a few more routes I take. After dodging around, this one was still with me. I put my foot down and parked up behind some garages so I was facing them as they came round the corner. I switched the full beam of the headlights on and ran at the driver's side. I rived the door open and was about to knock him out when he flashed his badge and shouted that they were the police. It turned out that it was an unmarked police car. I was well pissed off ... angry as fuck. This was one of the most tense times and here they were playing hide and seek with me ... Jesus fucking Christ. I told them to turn round and fuck off. They were lucky. It was one of those times where I wouldn't usually have asked questions first. Since then, security has been stepped up quite a bit. I'll never take any risks any more; there's too much at stake. I've always got to be alert, whether it means keeping my back to the wall in a club and never letting my guard down or keeping an eye open for things out of the ordinary when I go home on a night. Remember, there are people who are nowhere near as high profile as me getting shot outside their own front door; any mistake could easily be my last. If it looks as though my garage door has been tampered with in any way, then it is a potential threat ... it means that a shooter could be lying in wait, an ambush, a gang – anything. In my position, you can never be overcautious. You've got to be fit to survive – and there's not a lot of people fitter than me.

Ernie got Joe Freeman (no relation) to run around with me. Joe is from a gypsy family of fighters. I got friendly with them, would go to the gypsy campsite and even took my dad there 'cos he knew Joe's dad, Sconny. We were getting on well till things turned to shit. Joe saw an opening for money and tried to do to me what Ernie thought I was gonna to do to him. He was scamming for everything. I was putting a lot of money in his pocket: he was getting money for Ernie's doors as well as mine. He saw a big opening and tried to take the empire for himself. He started bad-mouthing people, bad-mouthing me behind my back and making a lot of trouble for himself. He got greedy. The scheming started but he wasn't bright enough to do the job correctly.

One of the people he was bad-mouthing was my mate Colin Sexton, who worked at Annabell's, one of Ernie's doors at the time. This was where Joe started to fuck things up for himself. Colin lives in South Shields and Joe was saying that, because he lives in South Shields, he shouldn't be working in Sunderland. Shields is practically *in* Sunderland. This coming from a traveller who lived in Durham (a lot further away), so what right did he have?

Joe kept on mouthing off to Colin and the inevitable happened – Colin came down to the After Dark for a one-on-one and beat the shit out of Joe. Colin is a really hard geezer. Not just a street fighter, he is a skilled fighter in the ring. He was all over Joe and gave him a serious bashing. At the club there is a corridor with two sets of fire doors at intervals. Joe was waiting down there in the dark and, when Colin got through one set of doors, he tripped on a chair and fell on to his side. The fight kicked off and Colin could barely move the right side of his body. It was fucked, but he fought on and beat Joe to a pulp with one hand. It wasn't till afterwards he went to hospital and found that he had dislocated his shoulder; it had popped out when he fell. Because he is a fit bloke he didn't know what was going on – all he knew was his right arm wouldn't move and he couldn't manoeuvre very well. But he couldn't exactly stop the fight. It only lasted a few minutes, but if he'd had both his hands it would have been over in seconds. Colin was in hospital for a few days after to get his shoulder put right. That's the kind of bloke he is – he could not back down. If he was as good on the floor then as he is now, he could have finished Joe off permanently.

So now Joe felt that he had to save face. He was embarrassed at getting such a kicking and not being able to do anything about it, and he looked for someone to blame – me. Me! He accused me of setting him up!

I told him I didn't know Colin was coming, and that was the truth. The reason Colin didn't tell me was 'cos I was working with Joe and would have warned him not to go to work. He didn't want to involve anyone; it had to be sorted out and it was a fair fight.

After Colin did a number on Joe Freeman, it left an opening. He did us all a favour, to be honest. That's when Graham Potts came back on the scene. He'd been keeping a low profile for the previous six months and things had blown over. What can I say about Graham ... he's the politest bloke you could ever meet. I honestly thought he was false at first – no one is that polite. I thought he was too good to be true, or over the top. I was wrong. He's like that all the time. If you're a friend he's double, *double* pally. He's politeness and no apparent weakness. Another bloke who loves to fight, Graham has plenty of friends in all the right places. Well liked and well respected and another true gent ... also cool as fuck – he'd make Steve McQueen look like Mr Bean.

When we first met it was under very different circumstances. My daughter Kayleigh's new stepdad was accused of nicking a car that belonged to Lee Stoker, one of Graham Potts's boys. I didn't know them, but they threatened Kayleigh's stepdad. The next night they went round and put the house windows out. Kayleigh was in the house at the time, so in doing that they were bringing me into it. Her stepdad told me he thought it was Lee, so I went round to his house for compensation. He said something like: 'You can't prove it.'

'Fair enough,' I said, 'But if I can you are fucking dead 'cos my daughter was in the house ... The best thing you can do is give me a hundred quid for the windows.'

He told me he'd have it the next day. When I turned up, he told me, 'I've got to see Graham Potts.' I'd heard of Graham, but that was about it. You hear about someone new almost every week; people come and go and I didn't know if Graham knew who I was.

'I'm seeing nobody,' I said, 'Get the money by this afternoon or there'll be hell on.'

He kept telling me that Graham was sorting it out. I didn't care; I wanted the money. I went back there later on with our Colin; there were three of them at the door. 'Have you got something for me?' I asked, and got the same answer. That was it. I fucking decked him. The other two saw this, tried to get away and got stuck in the doorframe side by side. We stood and watched them fighting to escape and tried our best not to laugh.

At home I received a phone call from Graham. He said he knew I'd just hit one of his lads and could I go down to see him. I wanted to say, 'You come and see me', but I didn't want to sound like I was bothered. He lived near a pub called the Slipway, so I made my way down there and, to be honest, didn't know what to expect. I knocked at his door and was ready to throw the first punch. He opened it and caught me off guard ... because he was so friendly. I couldn't believe it. We shook hands and went in for coffee. We got things sorted out right away – Graham saying I could have gone to see him in the first place and me saying I didn't know who he was and, because my daughter was involved, I just wanted it sorted. That's how we met and that's what got our friendship started. So Graham and me were now working together. We went round to all the pubs and clubs to collect the wages, just as Joe and me used to, and became good friends in no time at all.

Back to Joe. He still had it in his tiny mind that I had set him up and wouldn't drop his vendetta against me. Because he knew the round, he turned up at the first pub on our round to make me pay. There was Graham, the manager and me standing outside having a chat when this car pulled up. Three of them got out: Joe, Lee and Shaun Freeman and there were two others in the car. Joe was shouting his mouth off and the only way to sort it out was to have a one-on-one right there. He still blamed me for setting him up – a right conspiracy theorist we had on our hands. I'd soon knock that out of him. I threw my cell phone down and we squared up to each other. Instantly, I could see his bottle going. He was shaking like a leaf and hesitating too much. Lee stepped forward, the hardest of them, a man who fights for money all the time, a six-foot bloke wearing his vest. Graham made sure the other two didn't interfere. It was a dodgy time for Graham; he'd just got back on the scene and probably reckoned that people were still after him. Then this bunch of arse-wipes jumps out in the middle of the street. He must have been thinking all kinds of shit was gonna happen.

This was a real grudge match, but it was over before they could say, 'We look like a right set of idiots.' Lee was the hardest they had to offer. And, in all fairness, he *is* their hardest ... but that night I bet he'd wished he wasn't. As far as they were concerned, they were gonna do me over and let everyone know they were in charge. When Lee was cut to bits and unable to do fuck all about me bashing him all over the place, they knew who was boss. Joe and Shaun turned white. Lee was whiter. He was visibly shaking and backing off. He knew that any more punches and I'd finish him. He couldn't stop me. One side of his face was completely smashed in. I really took him apart. He has me to thank for being able to walk and talk. Graham could hardly contain himself; his face was a picture and so was Lee's ... only his was more like a Picasso. Once it was over, I went to get cleaned up ... I wasn't prepared to end it like that. I wanted them all.

The next day I got a team together and went down to the campsite. I sent someone down with £1000 to put down to fight any or all of them. They told him they didn't want to. Fair play to them ... as far as I'm concerned, then that's it. End of story – it's in the past; over. I still have respect for their parents and I have respect for travellers everywhere, excluding the three not-so-wise men.

* * * * *

It was once I'd taken over things that I decided to take up martial arts. I'd been out clubbing all weekend, was feeling ill and was then back on the doors on the Wednesday. It had all caught up with me and I was worn out. I really didn't feel in any fit state to be working – if I was honest with myself, I should have taken the night off. This wasn't the best time to be doing what I was expected to do. That night a fight broke out. Nothing unusual there, but I was directly challenged by one of the biggest-looking bruisers I've ever seen. It was a put-up-or-shut-up situation. All the lads knew that I was having an off day, but they couldn't let on. I couldn't let him know I had a weakness that night. He wanted me right there and there was no way I could say, 'Listen, I've barely slept for three days. Can you come back after I've had a decent sleep and I'll fight you then?'

This was a public challenge and instantly I could feel the hatred and venom rushing through my veins. I knew I'd have to set an example. We started braying the crap out of each other in the middle of the street. I wasn't used to people going the distance; I just couldn't knock him out. It was usually one or two punches and it was over. Now it was a full-on scrap and I was probably at fifty per cent strength. I'm too self-critical to tell you that I landed punches here and there and went for this move and that. I didn't feel positive enough within myself to make any of my punches count. There were quite a few people gathered round and they must have thought this guy was invincible for taking such a beating. The fact was that he was as high as a kite, was jumping up and down – all the classic symptoms. If these had been my usual punches I would have knocked him into the next century. He was hitting back and still I was countering his every move with what would normally have been lethal combinations. This could have gone on forever, but I couldn't let it go on much longer. I still knew he couldn't beat me. If I'd gone into the fight with the wrong attitude, he would have finished me. This was the first time in my life that my mind couldn't focus on the job. It was like it was someone else fighting and I was watching. I knew it wasn't my best performance but, if he couldn't take advantage, there was no way he could win. That was it. I wasn't taking any more. I was losing strength and energy. I moved in close. I grabbed his head, stuck both thumbs into his eyes and dragged it towards me. I headbutted him as hard as I could in the nose and shattered it. It cracked open and he reeled back as I caught my breath. Anything counted. There were no rules. Fucking game over, player one. He was out of it. Once the realisation sunk in that his nose was smashed he went into a state of shock. There are no rules in a street fight. Just seeing the expressions on people's faces told me what I'd done. Every time he looked in the mirror he would think of Ian Freeman. I went to the back room of the club and got myself cleaned up. Fuck or be fucked.

After that fight I decided to look into other fighting techniques. Up till then I was a boxer. All my fights were punching and blocking. What if I came up against someone who could kick? What if we ended up on the ground? I knew there was so much more to fighting than just using your fists, there is a whole philosophy and spirituality about the discipline of fighting that boxing doesn't teach. There is more to a fight than just punching. I wanted to learn groundwork. Challenges were coming my way all the time and now I had to master fighting. I took up jiu jitsu, which is a Brazilian fighting art of submissions and grappling. From there, I moved on to vale tudo – Portuguese for 'anything goes'. In the UK, it's commonly known as Total Fighting, in other places like the USA it's known as Ultimate Fighting. Stand-up fighting is fine, but here's the way I look at it: a boxer against a vale tudo fighter will lose most of the time. They can trade punches and no doubt the boxer may get the upper hand. The vale tudo fighter just needs to take it to the ground and the boxer is like a fish out of water. Sure, it depends on the skill of both fighters; if it were a fight where they could use their own technique against each other, a good boxer against a mediocre vale tudo fighter would stand a better chance. A vale tudo fighter who knows what they are doing can counter just about anything. If the vale tudo fighter could not out-box them, it would be taken to the ground in seconds.

There are still certain rules – biting, eye-gouging or hitting in the bollocks will all get you disqualified. It depends who is holding the tournament; people enforce a few new rules to protect the fighters. I think that sort of thing is important for the UK scene. It still has a reputation for being over-the-top violent and a fatality at this stage would ruin it. It must be said, though, that it has a far better safety record than boxing – that's a fact that I've used in the past to defend the sport and I always stand by it. Having certain rules does limit the anything-goes factor for some fighters, but safety and control must be the priority of all promoters, organisers and fighters. The whole fight scene is known now as MMA – Mixed Martial Arts. That defines it as kick boxing, boxing, vale tudo, jiu jitsu, karate – basically, any and every fighting discipline.

I took up jiu jitsu not just because of that street fight, though that was the one that ultimately convinced me to. I took it up because of my nature. I always take things as far as I can. If I excel at one thing then I like to try something else. I trained with weights, became a bodybuilder and went on to win competitions; I started boxing and rose to the top of the class and earned a reputation; I started working the doors at twenty and ended up being the main figure in the town. I was a fighter and wanted to become the ultimate fighter. I've said it before; it's not a compulsion where I need to win everything. It is an interest to see how far I go. You cannot do what I do and be a bad loser or you'd be finished if things didn't always go your way. I suppose I felt I needed to do it for my lads as well. I protect them as much as they protect me. To compare vale tudo to boxing is like comparing Formula One racing to go-karting. They are that different.

As the man Dirty Harry said: 'You've got to know your limitations.' As a good boxer I still felt limited. I still felt that there was further for me to go as a fighter. There was a whole new fighting art out there and I wanted to be one of the best. Vale tudo knows no limits.

Going all the way

Once my career as a fighter kicked off, I took it as far as possible. No one has ever done this much in such a short time. I was turning heads in the ring and still breaking them on the streets. You know what I'm like when I start something – no matter what happens along the way, I can't give up. I don't know how to.

Those of you who know about my fighting career will know of my quick progression. I started training under Sensei Peter McQueen (third dan black belt), who runs the Goshin Ryu Jiu Jitsu Kia at the YMCA in Herrington Burn. In the early days, classes were held upstairs in Arthur's Gym. I went there with Jarra Kev. Kev is another one of the lads who would put anything on the line to help a friend out. Once he was over at my place and was taking some boxes out to his car and was fiddling around trying to get the keys into the boot. The next-door neighbour came out and was watching him suspiciously. Just as I got out, Kev lost his rag with the bloke staring at him and went over to have a word with him. Oh, Christ. Not the neighbours, I thought. I went over and stopped Kev wrecking the bloke and Kev said he only went for him 'cos he was staring at him. Fine. 'Why were you staring at him?' I asked the neighbour. In a shaky voice he told us that it was his car. Kev had only gone over to the *wrong car* and the geezer thought he was trying to nick it. The poor gadgey was absolutely bricking it. That's the sort of thing that Kev can get himself into. He's a real funny bloke.

Anyway. Jiu jitsu ... we went training there together and didn't know what to expect at first. I didn't really know what jiu jitsu was. We used to train twice a week and when I found out what some of the exercises were I felt a right prat. Jumping up and down to warm up was not really one of my favourite things, but now I know it is all part of the martial art. I think starting anything new you are always a bit sceptical and self-conscious, but once you get going you seem to lose your inhibitions. Another one for me to get used to was practising groundwork and having someone on top of me. That feeling of being smothered when you are used to being on your feet and being free to move used to drive me mad. I picked it up quick enough, though, and now I'm just as dangerous on the floor as I am on my feet.

Just as in boxing I mastered jiu jitsu almost immediately. It was pure determination that helped me and got me where I am today. It came naturally to me and I could put my opponents in all kinds of submission moves without thinking. I was at the point where I needed to test myself. I went to other clubs in the region to fight the best people they had to offer. One was Sensei Cliff Pollard's gym in Guisborough – he's also a third dan black belt. I fought his top students and beat them all. There was no stopping me. I'm not taking anything away from the people I beat or being disrespectful, it's just that, when I'm good at something, I excel in it and pursue it as far as I can.

I definitely think I was a born champion. Fighting is something you can be taught, but to be a champion, I think, is something you are born with. It's an innate ability to succeed. Don't get me wrong here, I'm not saying that if you don't go all the way it is pointless doing it. It's a love for the sport that drives me. It doesn't matter what level you are at; it's the fact that you are doing it that counts. There are people out there who may have more skill in this than me, but you will be hard pushed to find anyone with more determination and more drive. I'm learning all the time and getting stronger and quicker with it. I'm now putting vale tudo on the map for people and, if it even encourages one more person to take it up, then that is a good thing. The doors are beginning to open for the rest of the country now and it would be great to finally see the rest of our fighters get the recognition they deserve.

To get this far your personal life has to be perfect. To go all the way you need to have the kind of strength behind you that I know I have. You cannot give one hundred and ten per cent in a fight if you have all kinds of things on your mind. Now when I go into a fight I know that everything at work will be fine. I trust everyone and I know they are an excellent team. I have faith in them and so I don't need to worry about anything. And I know everything at home is exactly how it should be; it's a team effort between my friends, workmates and family. I don't think I could have done all this if it wasn't for Angie. She is my rock. To have that perfect kind of home life for me is more than meals on the table or a tidy house. Every last detail has to be spot on. She understands everything. She knows at work that I'm not Saint Ian of Sunderland; she knows I'll tell her anything and everything I can; she knows there are times when I may have to ask for a quick change of clothing and that I may come home with the odd bruised knuckle. If I kept things from her there would be no point in going on. To keep things from someone is like admitting you don't trust them or that you know they'd disapprove. Knowing that I may be home in bed and get a call to be somewhere is quite a bit to live with. I'm on call 24/7 and she is behind me: another reason why I will never drink. It's not just because of what happened with the skinheads and drinking while I was depressed. I need to be in control all the time. I wouldn't be able to help anyone if I was drunk.

She also understands my level of commitment when it comes to training. Angie was a gymnast herself and is also my training partner. She makes sure I eat right and makes sure I relax at the right times. Every little detail builds up to create the picture of perfection. The last piece of that picture came when I had to make another court appearance. Yes, you did hear right … it was an *enjoyable* court appearance – and it does look strange to see those few words in the same sentence. This was the time when I was finally awarded sole custody of my son. The hammer came down and signalled he was officially mine. Tracey didn't even turn up for the hearing. That's how much she cared. It was brilliant news for Angie and me. We were definitely a family now – by law. It meant so much more to us that it was decided in court. Yes, he *was* mine and, yes, I'd *had* him ever since she dumped him in care; but this was the stamp of approval by the authorities I'd been waiting for. The fact that Tracey wasn't there spoke volumes. Angie is more of a mother to Ian than Tracey ever was.

Angie's even prepared to stand by me in a fight. One time we were driving in Holmside, Sunderland, and these five geezers jumped in front of the car. I slammed the brakes on and shouted something at them. They shouted back and that was my cue to jump out. I told Angie to wait in the car as I went out and battered them. I had a little something for them to even the score up a bit, and while they were rubbing at their eyes I knocked the shit out of them. It was another frenzy. I looked up when I knew they were all finished and there was Angie with the steering lock in her hands smashing one of them up on the ground. Knowing that she is even prepared to fight with me shows her commitment. There were plenty of blokes out there who wouldn't have done what Angie did.

Angel, like a blossom in the summer
Like the early morning dew
Like the flower needs the raindrops
I need to be with you

Like the winning of a race
And addictive like a drug
Like the sunset at the daybreak
You're a blessing from above

Oh, oh, Angel, Angel you're my sunshine
Like the sunflower needs the sunshine
You're the sunshine of my life
Like the sunflower needs the sunshine
You're the sunshine of my life

Angel, you're the reason for my living
You're the laughter in my heart
You're the teardrops in my sadness
Whenever we're apart

Like the wind beneath my wings
Like a walk along the sand
Sound of waves inside a seashell
Together hand in hand

Oh, oh, Angel, Angel you're my sunshine
Like the sunflower needs the sunshine
You're the sunshine of my life
Like the sunflower needs the sunshine
You're the sunshine of my life

'Angel', Ian Freeman

When she was pregnant with Kennedy I used to sing and play 'Angel' for Angie on acoustic guitar. I wrote it especially for her and, each time I sang it, she would feel Kennedy kick. I'd lie next to her and feel the movement and kicking as she drifted off to sleep. Kennedy still listens to that song today.

* * * * *

I was really building up a reputation now. If I thought I was big before, then now I was about to go through the roof. There was a whole new reputation to build up and live up to. I'd come a very long way since the days of working relief on doors a few nights a week. I wasn't just Ian Freeman who runs the doors and is known as a fighter. I was now Ian Freeman the professional vale tudo fighter. Being known as that carries a lot more weight. Peter was amazed at how quickly I was moving up the ranks. I was an amateur fighter with the dedication of a professional and the heart of a champ. It seemed inevitable that I'd go far. I was determined to make the sacrifices that many weren't. Nothing was going to stand in my way. On the streets I'd say that my martial arts have helped me, but not as much as you may think. Being a martial artist doesn't mean that every fight you have is like something from a Bruce Lee movie. If I am faced with a few people in that kind of situation I am always a good few steps ahead of them. If it seems like a fight is brewing and there are four or five of them, I know they are not just being sociable by stepping into my personal space. In my mind I have already worked out who is getting hit with what. And when it happens it is a quick, fluid motion. They won't know it's happened 'cos I'll be that fast. Every punch I land will be the punch to end the fight. I'll never waste it by giving a couple of jabs then a strong right. Every punch will destroy them. If anything, I have used my knees more in street fights. A few knees to the head and they are finished. A street fight is over in seconds and that is usually the way it happens – punches and/or knees and goodnight, but sometimes it doesn't even go that far.

One time there was this gadgey in the toilets who had been mouthing off to his mate. Get this: he was standing there in one of my clubs saying he was going to do me over. I was standing with Jarra Kev when the DJ came out and told me what he'd just overheard while having a piss. We were at the DJ stand, which is a bit higher up from ground level, and scanning around for this bloke. Then we clocked him at the bar. 'Is that him there?' I asked. It was. They tried to stop me from going over to him, but no one was gonna threaten me in my own place and get away with it. I got to him just as he was taking a drink from his pint and punched the glass right into his face. I didn't do it deliberately; it was more bad luck and very bad timing on his part. The shock alone nearly killed him. He bolted, but he ran into the club instead of out of it so I waited for him to come back through. A few seconds later he ran past and I started punching and kneeing him to help him on his way. One of the lads passed him while making his dramatic exit and said, 'What the fuck was that running down the stairs?' so I told him: 'That was the bloke who was mouthing off about being able to take me.'

As long as people like him continue coming to town then I don't think things like that will ever stop. It certainly is not an isolated incident. It really makes me wonder why people go around saying such shit, 'cos you'd think that deep down they must realise what will happen to them.

Another example: there was this big bloke in town called John. Big fucking charva, over six foot six and 280lb. Apparently he was quite a tough guy, but he used to go on like a proper dickhead. He used to say to people, 'See this hand? It's like Paul McKenna. Why? 'Cos it'll put you to sleep just like that.' Now that may work for Bruce Willis in his next blockbuster but it won't get you very far in my town. His mates kicked off in one of the clubs and the doorman ran over and grabbed a hold of them to tell them to calm down. John grabbed hold of the doorman to start on him and I grabbed hold of John to tell him to leave it out. I knew he didn't like me but I wasn't exactly gonna lose any sleep over it. I had him against the wall and he started giving it some: 'Take your fucking hands off me ... Who the fuck do you think you are?' The usual shit. He had a reputation as well and from his point of view there wasn't enough room for the both of us. He was shouting his mouth off and I was calm. I let go of him and he started back up with, 'What the fuck do you think you're doing?'

'Look,' I said, 'you grabbed hold of one of my lads. I'm not doing anything. You've let go and I've let go. That's it. End of story.'

So now, according to him, I was talking to him like he was shite. I told him I wasn't and that I was giving him respect. But he just kept up with the bullshit. I cut him dead: 'Now you're the one who's talking to *me* like shite.' As I was talking he raised his hands, so I steamed into him and hammered him to the ground. If his hands were like Paul McKenna, then my right fist was Morpheus. He's never been back to town since. I know he's phoned a friend of mine to see if he can come back. Another case where someone took my politeness as a weakness. He was a big bloke with a big rep. I knew that, but it didn't mean I would talk to him any differently. I talk to everyone the same way, no matter who they are. If he thought that I was polite to him because of who he was then he was dafter than he looked. I was polite to him 'cos I was talking to him. If it goes from conversation to argument, then I ain't gonna be nice any more. You can't push everyone around just because of your size and this guy had tried it once too often. People didn't like him. If he found himself in the middle of Sunderland one night and he spontaneously combusted, there would not be one single person in the entire city's population who would piss on him to put the flames out.

* * * * *

The first test of my new skills came at the British Rings Rule Grand Prix on 29 June 1999. This was still at an early stage in my fighting career. It was an amateur event with the promise of a trip to Japan for the winners to compete over there. Peter McQueen came through for me at this event – the association he was affiliated to was not going to let me fight under their insurance, so he changed the affiliation and I was able to fight. Nice one, Peter. When I got the opportunity to fight in the British Rings Rule Championships, I got in touch with Geoff Oughton to train me for the groundwork. There were only three weeks to go, but Geoff agreed and he really helped me out ... and it paid off. Not long after that, Geoff and me went off to train with Marco Ruas, a vale tudo fighter from Brazil – my first taste of 'ground 'n' pound'.

My first fight was against Scott Smith and I won by TKO in nine seconds. Nine fucking seconds! I just went in there and started beating straight into him. He backed off the mat and refused to come back on. I don't blame him. To win my title I had to fight three times on the same night. I beat Tony Bailey in one minute twenty-nine seconds when he tapped out to a guillotine choke, and then beat Kamal Lock after nearly four minutes with an Achilles leg lock. It was the best buzz in the world. This was amazing. People were cheering for me and it was a massive step up from having to sort some drunk out in a bar. It was skill against skill. I knew I was capable of doing it; I would not have been at the event if I wasn't confident. My first event and my first title. A big difference is not having a team in there with me as back-up. It's an individual effort. If I make a mistake there is no one to help me out; I'm the only one who can do it. It's still very much a team thing up until getting in the ring, on the mats or in The Octagon. I have Carl, my corner man, Angie, all my family, friends and supporters. I'm now training with people all over the world. My team is huge. This was the one my mate Geoff Oughton helped me train for ... another world-class fighter to add to the list.

The offer of going to Japan? A load of bull's knackers ... it was just some ploy to entice people to enter. The winners of each weight division were promised the same but none of them have been to Japan on the strength of that event. This event seems a long time ago now but, because my career rocketed, it isn't really that far back at all. It's my progress that's distanced it. Respect to my opponents in that event. All good fighters who will continue to do well.

Round about this time, I'd arranged a charity raffle and needed to pick up some prizes in town. There was this fairly new place, which sold all kinds of electrical goods that were new but ex-display. All we needed was a portable TV, so it wouldn't be too much hassle to find one. Carl and me were standing looking when the bloke asked us if he could help.

'Are these all the TVs you have?' I asked. They were. I pointed out the one I wanted and asked if he could put it in a box. This is when the complications set in. I'm pretty sure I'd said it in English but he was standing there with this puzzled look on his face. I turned to Carl just to make sure I wasn't in *The Twilight Zone*. He was thinking the same.

The bloke goes, 'A *box*? What do you want it in a box for?'

Was this bloke really so stupid? I told him I was the one who was buying it and I wanted it in a box. I may be wrong here, but every time I've bought anything in my life, it comes boxed, bagged or at least packaged in some way. You'll never believe what he came out with next.

'Well, why do you want it in a box? You're not going to sit and watch a box,' he said.

I could not be-fucking-lieve it. Here was some ten-stone scrawny little jerk-off talking to me like that. On the street no one would dare talk like that and here he was thinking he could get away with it 'cos he was in a shop. He had this patronising look on his face like a box was the weirdest thing he'd heard of.

'Who the *fuck* do you think you're talking to?' Mr Nice Guy had just left the shop. Now he knew he'd pushed me too far. I started off with the intention of giving him a slap, but the way he ran round the fridge freezer display and the vacuum cleaners I couldn't keep my laugh in any more. I was shouting, 'Come here! I'll put *you* in a fucking box!' as I ran after him.

I may have been laughing but if I'd caught hold of him I would have made it clear that the customer is always right. He ran out the back and locked the doors. 'Time to go,' suggested Carl. Some people have no idea.

The next fighting event was a month later: 28 August, The Complete Vale Tudo Fighting Challenge. You'll never guess who won this one. I was unstoppable here as well. To me these fights were minor hurdles along the way. I'd been fighting all my life and now to do it in the ring was a dream come true. The people I was up against didn't have a clue what I'd been through. I'd demolished people on the street with no rules at all. I'd taken on gangs, families, a bull terrier, everything. I knew there was nothing that could be thrown at me that would cause the slightest bit of damage. Nerves didn't even enter the picture; I was looking forward to getting out there and showing everyone what I was made of. I finished Keith Dace in fourty-six seconds with a guillotine choke. And then Mark Lambourn tapped out after fifty-five seconds to a rear naked choke. I was just getting warmed up and barely broke a sweat. Another title to The Machine: Professional CFC Vale Tudo Champion, and, again, big respect to the other fighters.

Back at home the local press was going wild about it. We all know the sport has bad press, but I'd say the coverage was pretty much down the middle. This was when I started to become quite the local celebrity. People were, and still are, really supportive, especially those in the village. I was appearing in the local papers on a regular basis and putting the North-east on the map. Alan Turner's gym, Cutz 'n' Curves in Leadgate, also got good coverage 'cos he was named British Powerlifting Champ at around about the same time as my first pro win. I got into the national press and all the major martial arts magazines like *Combat* and *MAI*. Being in the papers and things is fine. It's never gone to my head, 'cos I'm not the type of person to let it. I wasn't getting overexcited and took it all in my stride. People would say to me, 'So, you're famous now', and I'd reply with, 'I've always been famous, I'm just letting people know about it now.'

The lads on the doors and my family were behind me all the way. To have them come and support me makes it all worthwhile. Every fight video you can hear our Sue shouting over the top of everyone else! (So that's nearly as loud as I screamed when she pounded that brush handle into my head.) On 3 October – still 1999 – I became the Professional Rings Rule Champion. A professional title and I sailed through it in two minutes and two seconds by another TKO. That one was against Dave Short, in front of the biggest crowd I'd seen back then – two thousand people. The atmosphere was electric. The buzz was getting better. People couldn't believe what I was doing in so little time. My first amateur fight was only four months previously, and now I was establishing myself as a pro. As with every fight I went in there calm and collected. I don't go in with strategies because every fight is different. I'll always go for the first strike though, goes without saying. Back then I wasn't half the technician I am now but I still dominated every opponent. I was as comfortable on the ground as I was on my feet – you have got to be an all-round fighter.

I love the recognition that comes with fighting in the ring, but I still have a job to do. I need to be seen around town and to protect my interests. Keeping Sunderland safe and sorting trouble is my priority and I will never back down from whatever duties need to be taken care of. After turning heads in the fighting fraternity by disposing of Dave Short, I started getting all kinds of phone calls and fight offers. One in particular was The Millennium Brawl at The Pavilion, Hemel Hempstead, in December against American Travis 'Iron Man' Fulton. This was the big league. Travis is an excellent and respected fighter who has fought and beaten some of the toughest men in the world, as well as fighting in the biggest competitions. I jumped at the chance to fight him and stepped up the pace to train for it. I train five days a week, twice a day anyway, so in preparing for a fight I make sure I put in my usual routines and then some more. This one for me was gonna be my biggest fight and I was hungry for it. For a relatively new bloke on the scene this was a big chance to show not just fans or sceptics, but the world. Travis is a name fighter and it was the first time an American had come over to the UK to fight. A lot of people would be watching this one closely.

Six weeks before the fight I ended up with seven stitches in my knuckles from a fight at work – another challenge. Three lads came into the pub to start a fight. It wasn't just a spur-of-the-moment thing – they came there to do me. The place was pretty empty, 'cos it was early on in the night. I'd been outside and needed to take a leak. As I made my way to the toilets at the back, there were three kids playing on the fruit machine, which was right next to the toilet door. I got a bit closer and they moved on purpose to block my way through. 'Excuse me,' I said. They just ignored me so I pushed one of them out of the way and walked into the toilets. Nobody goes on like that unless they are about to kick off. Any normal bloke would have moved – don't you just hate bad manners? Inside I was standing focused on the door waiting for them. I stood psyching myself up but nothing happened. Being kick boxers, they didn't follow me in 'cos they wouldn't have been able to kick in such a small area, but I didn't know this at the time. Still none the wiser, I came out and there's the three of them standing just outside the bogs waiting for me. If I'd known they weren't coming in I would have had time for a piss at least. The one who wanted me was the one I'd pushed, 'cos he came out with 'Think you're fucking clever pushing me? Let's you and me step outside.' As soon as he said outside I fucking turned and cracked him square on the jaw. Who the fuck did he think he was coming into *my* pub and asking *me* outside? Right then it was as though all the lights turned to red, 'cos that was all I could see. I hit him so hard that I knocked him over the table on to his back. His legs were still on the table pointing upwards, a chair had fallen on him and he was covered in their drinks. I turned round to take the others on but they had legged it out of the place before their mate had even hit the deck. That was when I looked down at my fist and saw that my knuckle was cracked open and bleeding. One of the doormen came over to help pick him up and we saw the two halves of the kid's front teeth lying on the floor. This lad had won competitions and wanted to prove himself by beating me. He used to work the doors on some bar, but not after that little incident. I wasn't bothered about having to fight; it was the fact that I'd damaged my fist by knocking some fucking loser out that annoyed me.

Round about this time I was having a documentary shot on me and my career, and the build-up to the fight. It was while they were filming me training one day that I aggravated an old rib injury. It hurt like hell. I'd warmed up then had four fights in a row with my training partners when disaster struck. I was doubled up in pain on the mats and could hardly breathe. At that stage it threw the whole fight into doubt. I needed to go into the fight one hundred per cent fit and so I went to see a specialist in this sort of thing. In the back of my mind, though, I knew I would fight regardless of what they said. I couldn't let something like that hold me back and on 5 December 1999 we got it on. I travelled down there a few days before the fight with a bunch of friends and the documentary crew to prepare for it. I went into the fight with the utmost respect for Travis, though after it he was a little less respectful towards me ...

As we squared up to each other he moved in to shoot my legs to take me down and I kneed him in the ribs. After a clinch we went to the ground and he ended up on top of me. He was in my guard right up to the ropes and I was hitting the side of his face. I didn't feel under any pressure. I forced him up and he got into the side mount and just hung on; the referee called us up on to our feet and we restarted. Travis kept grabbing hold of me and leaning in so we were against the ropes. From here I was able to throw punches to his body, that was when the ref pulled on the ropes and I lost my balance as we crashed to the canvas. Travis is known as a 'ground 'n' pound' man and when it went to the ground that's exactly what he got. This is his territory, where he usually dominates, but not this time. I didn't feel in any danger on the floor and I felt sure I'd quelled his imagination. He couldn't get anything on me and couldn't overpower me. Back to our feet and I was urging him forward, knowing I can slug it out with anyone. Remember – I'm a trained boxer and a lethal streetfighter ... I love the challenge of somebody standing in my way. Back to the ground and I was in his guard for the first time – this is how you do it … I started pounding into him and boy could he feel it. His head was rocking from each punch. Right after left was connecting, his face now beginning to show the tell-tale signs of a Freeman bashing. End of the first round and I knew what the outcome was gonna be. I went to my corner and watched him drag himself to his feet and make his way over to his.

The second round started with him going in for the clinch, taking us to the ropes, leaning into me and holding on. Again the ref pulled on the top rope and literally catapulted us to the floor in the centre of the ring … and again I'd lost my balance and Travis ended up on top of me in a half guard. He couldn't take advantage of it, so back to our feet. This was my opening. We exchanged a few punches, then I took him to the ground. He was hanging on to me 'cos he knew as soon as I had a clear shot he'd be mine. I cracked him with some big punches, loosened his grip and held him down on the canvas. A quick adjustment of my gloves and I let loose with the big guns. I whacked into his face and he found out first-hand about my punching power. He was trying to grab my wrists, desperate to stop the bombardment. He couldn't match my strength. I went for a body shot; he tried to block it and fell into the trap. I used the body shot as a smokescreen, and followed through with a massive right full in the face. More lefts and rights and his head was bouncing off the canvas again. These were really rocking him. We ended up practically in my corner and I could hear Carl shouting encouragement. I was really going for it now. He was struggling but couldn't shake me off. The ref brought us to our feet to restart and I knew I could finish him. That was when Travis conceded. He didn't want to subject himself to more of those punches. I knew I was doing real damage and he knew he couldn't stand any more of the punishment I was dishing out.

Then, after the fight and he was back home, of course, he

started with the cry-baby routine. The old sympathy vote? Surely not! He said I had eye-gouged, bitten him, kneed him in the bollocks, everything to take the heat off being beaten in the second round. Calling someone a dirty fighter just 'cos they have beaten you is not the way forward. Maybe if there was some truth in it, then fair enough ... but come on. He couldn't do a thing against me. I was all over him and he could not control the fight like he usually does. He usually dominates; I made him look bad and I pounded his head in. After the fight he said he'd never been punched that hard in his life. I couldn't agree more. I can trade punches with any man on this planet and once I got in his guard and let loose with the big guns, it was good night, Mr Fulton. He had no other choice but to give in and I picked up the title of Intercontinental Vale Tudo Champion. At that stage in my career I would have been happy if it had gone the distance and I had got beaten on points. I knew I was a good fighter, but Travis was an established professional with around eighty fights and I wasn't. I just didn't want to get beaten within the time limit and anything else would have been a bonus. For him to give up because I had pounded him and him being well known as a big hitter – I was thinking, I've just beaten you at your own game. He beats people by getting them down and beating the fuck out of them and that's exactly what I did to him.

I knew it would open doors for my career. It wasn't Travis that got me where I am, it was me. If the fight wasn't against him then it may have taken a little bit longer, but I know I would have made it. I think of that fight as a short cut to international fighting – I know I still would have beaten everyone in the UK and got the recognition, but definitely a while later. I didn't like the fact that he said what he did, but you find that with some people. The only one crying that the fight was unfair was the one who got beaten. Shouting matches or arguing over it are not what I'm about – I let my fighting speak for itself.

Earlier on that night I was sitting in the crowd with the lads when I noticed someone walk in. He was a well-built bloke with a shaved head, dark shirt and white trousers, dripping with gold and had a huge cigar in his hand. An impressive team of heavies surrounded him. When I clocked him I thought he was obviously one of the lads. Jarra Kev realised who he was: Dave Courtney. Me being me, I didn't want to go over to him and introduce myself there and then. It was after my win against Travis that we got talking. He came and congratulated me and we got on really well. I remember him asking me what I was thinking during the fight and I replied, 'I just wanted to get in there and kill him.'

Remember earlier I mentioned that our Colin looks a bit like me? This was where he milked it like a cow. On the way out of The Pavilion that night he'd gone round to bring my car out front. I drive a white BMW with personal registration – it is the absolute dog's bollocks. (I must have got a taste for BMs after driving Ernie's that time.) When Angie and me came out, we witnessed him thanking his fans and them wishing him all the best. (I bet he was hoping I'd forgotten about that one.)

Following the fight I had even more press coverage – along with all the backlash about this barbaric sport I was pioneering. Well-known website SFUK had named me 'The Iron Ambassador' for all the positive things I was doing to promote the sport. I also defended it on a BBC Television programme, *Close up North* – some of the questions and comments from the sexually deprived woman I talked to were bordering on the fucking ridiculous.

The documentary was shot, edited and looks good. It's called *Ultimate Fighter*, by Apocalypse Productions. Also after that fight, a good mate of mine called John Hogg came through with a gesture of his friendship. He knew I wasn't earning the best of money from fights like the Travis one, but saw great potential at the same time. He gave me a few hundred quid so I could buy new gloves and kick pads – something I'm still grateful for.

Remember the undertakers' business card that Geordie put in that sparked-out gadgey's mouth all those years ago? That's him ... we're always putting business each other's way, even now.

Things started moving quickly. I decided to set up Total Martial Arts (TMA) with my good friend Julian Woodridge in the New Year. I'm not gonna big him up too much, 'cos he knows he's excellent at what he does. My aim behind this was to get together with the British Medical Association and work out a set of rules for the sport – a compromise so we can get rid of the word 'barbaric' every time it's mentioned. I also want to get fighters a decent purse for their fights. When I fought Travis Fulton the money I got was a veiled insult. Due to my travelling and accommodation expenses, I actually ended up losing money. In the UK there just isn't money in the sport at the moment. If we can make a difference to what fighters earn, then it can't be bad. I know of fighters turning up to watch tournaments as spectators, then ending up as a competitor because one of the fighters hasn't turned up. This one fighter-spectator stepped in at the last minute to make sure a fight took place – he got beaten and didn't even receive payment for it. That's fucking ridiculous. We now have some of the best fighters in the country signed up and things are going from strength to strength. We've got so many projects lined up for the future ... *Machine Media* ... step aside, Richard Branson, or your time is up, mate. Just after setting up TMA I became friends with another name you may be familiar with: Charles Bronson. There is talk of a film being made about Charlie and I was asked to get involved with the project. The papers loved that one. I also tried out Charlie's *Solitary Fitness* regime, which he uses in his cell. I'm still in touch with him now, and I'm sure he needs no introduction ... a top geezer.

Because of all the coverage I received in newspapers, I was becoming well known in the region. In Sunderland I'm well known anyway, but now the average man on the street was getting to hear about me ... and also the not-so-average man on the street. I received a call from Sir John Hall's chief security guard. John Hall is a very well-known man in the North-east. A businessman who was once chairman at Newcastle United Football Club, he has done some great things for the region and is well respected and liked. The call was to see if I would be interested in some work – to teach John Hall's grandchildren a few basic moves and fighting techniques. After a few further calls I agreed to do it and we set a date. I went over to their place – Winyard Hall, a fucking huge mansion in the North-east. You drive through a private estate first of all where Alan Shearer and other football stars live, drive through all kinds of security gates, cameras, everything. It was like *Indiana Jones* ... the only thing missing was a tribe of savages blowing poisoned darts at my car!

A bit of background information. A few years ago, Sir John had retired from football and, I think, was concentrating his efforts more on Newcastle Falcons – the new rugby venture with Rob Andrew on board. Left at Newcastle Football Club was his son Douglas and businessman Freddie Shepherd, who were the better-known people on the board of directors. They became even higher profile when they fucked up on such a large scale. Apparently they would travel all over the world mixing with prostitutes and getting pissed, spending shitloads of money and doing whatever else people in that position do and get away with. Their downfall came when they were video-taped by a journalist when they were really pissed up and started bad-mouthing Alan Shearer and calling the women of the North-east ugly and dogs – not really the best of moves if they wanted to win any popularity poll. Needless to say, they didn't. Even today they are about as popular as ... let's just say they are as popular as Douglas Hall and Freddie Shepherd. Two things that any Newcastle supporter loves are Alan Shearer and women, and probably in that order – even beer comes in at third place. Hall and Shepherd were exposed in nearly every newspaper in the country and the shit really hit the fan. All hell broke loose, and they were lucky they weren't lynched. The scandal continued for well over a week and parts of the video were even shown on the national news. What a fucking embarrassment. Sir John threatened to come out of retirement to rebuild the damage but it was already done. We've all disappointed our parents at some time, but no one deserves this amount of shit on their own doorstep.

It turned out that John Hall's grandchildren were Douglas's kids. Their bodyguard stayed with us the whole time and I taught them basic self-defence moves. It was a bit weird at first, but it was easy money so I soon got used to it. Douglas used to watch for the first ten minutes of each session before leaving. He enjoyed watching and said he wanted to get involved a little bit more, which was fine with me. This particular session I was talking about kicks. Douglas joined in: 'Do kicks really work?' he asked. So I told him they do and said that, with his permission, I could show him. I said I'd not kick him hard, but it's a lot easier to demonstrate something along with an explanation. I was telling him that you have nerves in your thigh and if kicked there it will deaden the leg. Then he asked if it would hurt your foot by kicking the person's leg. You don't kick with your foot, you kick with your shin against the side of the thigh ... again, easier with a demonstration.

I'd said that I wouldn't kick him hard but, after he'd rambled on about being trained in karate, I thought, Fuck it. You're gonna find out what it feels like to be kicked by The Machine. So he stood there bracing himself and all that was going through my mind was those comments about North-east women being dogs. Let's not forget that Angie is from the North-east and she definitely ain't no dog. I could imagine how many Newcastle fans would have loved to have been in my shoes right then. I felt duty bound. I gave him a decent kick. Knocked him to the floor and he went down like a stinking sack of shit ... oh yeah, and I proved how effective the move was. The people of Sunderland and Newcastle have always been at each other's throats for as long as I can remember – whether it's down to football I don't think anyone knows any more. When I dropped Douglas Hall it was like I was rebuilding the bridges, like I was the Special Peace Envoy for Geordies and Makems. So next time you want to bad-mouth the Makems, just remember that one of them did you the best favour you're ever gonna get! I can only apologise for not finishing him off. The next time I taught the kids, Douglas didn't turn up. Pretending to be concerned, I asked if he was OK. They said he could barely walk – it was so bad that when they were paint-balling the day after the demonstration, everyone else was running around while he was driven round in a golf cart to shoot at people. I don't know if that thigh kick had anything to do with it, but I'm still waiting for payment for the last session I took them for. There's no bad feeling from me, though; it was worth it – I'm sure there's loads of people who'd love to get paid *by* Douglas Hall to *kick* Douglas Hall.

* * * * *

While my professional career was taking off, I still had to contend with every degenerate you care to mention at work. I couldn't expect things at work to suddenly change. Things will never change but, at the same time, you'd like it if people did. Remember that bloke I booted down the stairs at Gillespies? Well, he showed his face again with something else to prove. What point he wanted to make, only he knows. I turned up at Ku Club with Carl one night; Jarra Kev was on the doors and Michael Downey was with him. 'Lucky you weren't here two minutes ago,' Kev said, 'some bloke has just been here calling you a rapist.' I couldn't believe it. A fucking rapist?

You know me by now ... They told me where he had gone – just up the street to the phone box. I headed up there, though Carl was trying to stop me. First of all, I wanted to see who it was and secondly I wanted to cripple him. No one is gonna call me something like that. I went up and saw who it was. Sure enough it was that bloke I'd kicked down the stairs that time and he obviously thought he'd settled the score. He was on the phone with his back to me. I was nearly exploding with anticipation 'cos in my mind I'd already seen what was gonna happen and it didn't look good. As I ran up, I was just going to smack him on the back of the head but he might have time to grass to whoever he was talking to, so I held back. I was standing behind him ready. I'm surprised he didn't hear me breathing. On the phone he was giving it, 'Oh yeah, I've just been up there and told him. Said he was a rapist ... *blah blah blah* ... see you later.' As soon as he put the receiver down I cracked him across the side of the face. He bounced off the phone box wall and hit the floor like a sack of shit. I picked the receiver up and started smacking him in the head with it – 'Who's *a fucking rapist*?' I cracked his head open with it then just left him in there with it dangling on the wire. BT will understand, I'm sure – it had to be done. I left him a ten pence piece to call an ambulance and walked back down to Carl like nothing had happened.

As part of TMA, I now have Julian acting as my UK manager and Stu handles all the arty-farty media stuff. Then we've got sponsorship from clothing company Choke Athletic and JTD Sports Nutrition, who produce protein drinks and supplements. There's also our Internet designers. All in all, we've got a good team together and I see big things happening for us. To settle Travis's bitching about our fight, Julian and me sent tapes over to a few influential people in America – a top manager called Phyllis Lee, John Perretti the UFC match maker, radio presenter Eddie Goldman, among others – to let them all judge for themselves. They got to see that none of what Travis had said was true; it was good to wipe the tarnish of my brand-spanking-new belt. Not too long after that Fulton was scheduled to fight Tim Lajcik in the UFC – the Ultimate Fighting Challenge. This is one of the biggest fighting events in the world and not everything went to plan for him. Tim popped his shoulder during training and was unable to fight and Scott Adams was brought in as his replacement. Not long after that, Travis Fulton broke his hand while training so they decided to bring in the bloke who had just beaten him: me.

By now Phyllis had become my USA manager and she helped arrange things. She's been brilliant, pushing me forward when there are so many other fighters she could be pushing. I got a phone call on the Tuesday, flew on the Wednesday, arrived on Thursday and fought on the Friday. First off I travelled to Manchester and caught the plane to Chicago, Illinois, then on to Dallas, Texas and from Dallas to Lake Charles in Louisiana. Up until then I'd never been on a plane in my life. I got there at one o'clock in the morning, signed in and went straight to bed. I was jet-lagged, tired, exhausted, you name it. What affected me most was that I was alone; it didn't feel right. I didn't take anything in as I made my way to my room. Just before nine in the morning I was woken up and taken to hospital for an HIV test and then off to fighters' meetings. All that was on my mind all day was the results of that test. It was weird, 'cos it was something I'd never thought about in my life; I wouldn't have thought of having a test if I were at home, but this was a fight prerequisite. Suddenly I was thinking I might have HIV and not be able to fight. What if I had it? What then? I'd never be able to fight and never be able to get where I want to be and only then could I begin to take in actually having it and dealing with it. My head was buzzing; all I could think about was how this test was gonna change my life.

The results came back fine. Panic over. The next day was the day of my fight and I was an absolute wreck. It was like a temporary breakdown or something. One minute I was at home with my family then the next I was here and walking down the runway into The Octagon at UFC 24. It felt that quick. It *was* that quick. I was walking down there like a fucking zombie. I couldn't even take any of it in. To be honest I was expecting the crowd to be hostile towards me because of all the ill feeling or controversy after the Travis Fulton fight, so I felt I was fighting everyone from the start. The fight itself was like an out-of-body experience. I didn't function as a fighter; I can't remember what happened 'cos in reality my mind was still somewhere over the Atlantic Ocean on its way to Chicago. Jet-lag, the fuck-up of international fighters.

The fight started and we touched gloves before getting into it. This is where I would usually move in and strike first. Scott took me to the ground and straight away went for a series of knee bars. It was only when we were on the ground that I realised he'd shot for my legs. Everything was so delayed it was a while before I knew I'd been taken down. I had no reactions whatsoever. I rolled out of his moves and had him in my guard. Even then my reactions were slow, I wasn't thinking with the fighter's instinct that's driven me all my life. I was a distant spectator. He hit me with a few body shots, but they didn't have much power; then we rolled out and he put me in a heel hook. As soon as he applied pressure to the move the ligaments in my ankle snapped. We could both hear it. I felt the pain all right and my energy level left my body completely. It wasn't exhaustion cardio-wise, it was a heavy, tired feeling and I just wanted to give up. He was going for the submission move from the very start and had damaged my left leg. His entire gameplan now would be to work on my leg; mine would be to try and roll out, but he'd got in there early. Scott is a leglock specialist. Everyone has their most comfortable positions and most polished moves and set pieces. Scott's is finishing off exactly what he'd just started. He was trying for the knee bar or the heel hook all the time. We were rolling constantly, with me trying to break his hold. I felt my ankle snap again but I managed to get out of it. Scott knew he'd snapped it again and I saw him look at his corner as if to say, 'What the fuck do I do now? I've snapped his ankle twice, he's not giving in and I'm running out of ideas. What should I do?' I then grabbed his ankle and put him in a heel hook. He leaned forward and pulled at my gloves, which is an illegal move. I shouted to Dan Severn, who was the referee; Dan told him to let go and immediately Scott grabbed my ankle, got a better hold on me and snapped the ligaments for the third time. I had to give in. It was unbearable pain. Throughout the fight I didn't even punch Scott once, and anyone who knows me will know that there was no way on this earth that would have happened. The fight lasted just over three minutes.

I'd spoken to Angie not long before the fight and it just messed my head up even more. To hear her voice she sounded so close but she was six thousand miles away. Right then I just wanted to be back home. I was in no state to fight; I even told her, 'I don't care whether I win or lose, I just want to come back home.' Once we'd finished the call she knew I would get beaten – she told me so when I returned. She had never heard me talk like that. I was lonely. I'm used to having people around me and here I was going into a massive fight without even my corner man (Carl) with me. When I go into the ring I always have my mouthpiece, or gum shield as we Brits call it, but here I had two corner men I'd never used and one of them had my gum shield. It sounds daft but I was worrying about it. Did he really have it? Where was it? The tiniest detail like that can make all the difference to you when your head is already mashed. All these things had mounted up till I didn't know what I was doing. I couldn't talk to people 'cos they couldn't understand me, couldn't really order things from menus – not that I had that much time. Cultural differences like ordering chips (instead of 'French Fries') and getting a packet of crisps just added to the frustration. I met up with Phyllis Lee and, although she took on the sort of mother role, it wasn't the same as having your pals there 'cos you're always on your best behaviour when you meet someone new. The whole situation contradicted everything I'd stood for: going into the ring with a positive mind. Being mentally as well as physically prepared, or at the very least expecting serious injury ... and that's what happened. It wasn't that serious, but still needed a cast to stop it setting at an angle. I spoke to Scott after the fight and he was full of respect for me. He said he couldn't believe I didn't tap out earlier 'cos he could hear my tendons snapping in the three ankle locks he put me in. Friends have said they didn't know whether it was stupidity or bravery. I don't know either. It was probably a bit of both, but I think most of all it was a stubborn fighting spirit – I couldn't admit it to myself until the very last second. It hurt like fuck each time he snapped it, but I didn't even have the energy or sense to react. It's too hard to predict what would have or could have happened; it's just an experience I want to put behind me now so I can get on with things. At the fighters' party afterwards I just didn't want to be there. I didn't go around sulking, 'cos it was still a great opportunity to meet all the fighters I'd only seen on tapes, and I ended up meeting a few people who are now turning into good friends.

I was on crutches and left the States two days after that. It was a shame, 'cos I was invited deep-sea fishing by Andy Anderson, UFC 5 fighter and all-round stand-up guy. He's real generous, polite and approachable. He didn't even know me then but I'm sure one day soon we'll go on that fishing trip.

The thing that hurt most of all in the Scott Adams fight was that I'd got beaten. I knew I was walking into defeat but I couldn't not do it. This was the UFC and there was no way I could turn the opportunity down. Even in defeat I was still the first ever Briton to fight there and that meant everything to me. Having my leg in a cast was so fucking frustrating. I'm always on the move and it was just getting in the way. Saying that, my mates couldn't believe the speed that it heeled up. It seemed like no time at all to them, but to me each day was like a year. It was in a cast for a week, then after two weeks I was back in training again. This was my first ever defeat in a fight. It was a real bastard to come to terms with. I think once I'd got home I could have gone either way: if it turned out that I was a bad loser I could have just given up everything right then. I didn't even know if I was a bad loser or not at this point. But being a sportsman, it's something you need to be prepared for and something you need to be able to deal with. Apart from anything else, there are a lot of fighters who look up to me and I couldn't let people like that down. There was no way I could let my family down. This is my job and you can't just quit if everything doesn't go smoothly. If it were too easy I wouldn't be doing it; there would be no challenge. Too much was at stake here. All I was interested in was getting back into training and getting straight back into fighting. People would be watching to see how I coped, critics dying to get stuck in, but I had good friends and family ready to support me. You always hear people say how they learned from their mistakes and now I know it's true. I would never go into a fight with that kind of preparation ever again and it was foolish to do it, but at the same time opportunity had knocked and I had to let it in. If I hadn't fought I might have regretted it forever.

Men of respect

***NOT LONG AFTER** the Scott Adams fight, I met up with Dodgy Dave again. It wasn't exactly how we'd planned it a few weeks previously, though. Let's say on this particular meeting it was 'No Bedding and a Funeral'.*

I coped well with the defeat. It didn't mean that much to me because of the circumstances it happened in – though I'm not taking anything away from Scott. I needed to get back on my feet as soon as I could and look positively towards my next fight. After it, I still got press publicity, which was nice, but it wasn't long before the backlash. I've got good relationships with newspapers but in the months that followed there were a few that soon started to paint a different picture. When I beat Travis or was the first man in Britain to enter The Octagon, that was news. But I had a charge for common assault looming overhead and they all picked up on it.

Common assault is no more than pushing someone. There was a big fight in town and we went in to stop it; in doing so I had to push someone out of the way. It is my job to sort fights out. People were getting glassed in the face ... should I just stand there and watch? Others were charged with more serious assaults, but because of who I am, I made a few front pages with my picture alongside. I didn't even get that kind of coverage for beating a world champ, but I touch someone in the street and I'm front-page news. Make of that what you want. I know what I make of it.

A few weeks after returning I met up with Dave Courtney again. He was up in Newcastle to sign copies of his book, *Stop the Ride I Want to Get Off* (more commission ... cheers) and I went along with Carl and Stu. Dave was there with his wife Jennifer; Stevie Wraith, Big Graham and John handled security; Kenny 'Panda' Anderson was there and there was even this huge Jaws lookalike (from the Bond films), Gary Tiplady. Knowing Dave, I was half expecting Elvis, Sir Lancelot and Che Guevara to abseil through the windows just for a laugh. It was good to meet up with him and later on Carl and me went back into Newcastle for a get-together at *Geordiemission* in the Planet Earth nightclub. It was an excellent night and Dave was on top form, with his trademark cigar in hand at all times. As soon as he clocked me walk in he left whoever he was talking to and came over for a handshake and a hug. 'I knew you'd come,' he said. 'We're gonna be great mates.' He had no argument from me. We talked all about our different interests and business, family, friends – everything. You just cannot dislike Dave; he's a real goodfella. At the end of the night we said all our goodbyes and exchanged phone numbers. He even welcomed Angie and me down to stay with him and Jenny any time we wanted. A lot of new friends were made that day; well worth it. It could have just been one of those things where you say you'll keep in touch and that's all that happens, but sure enough things progressed. I later heard all about Dave from other people who had read about him. It turned out that Dave was an inspiration behind the character of Big Chris in Guy Ritchie's *Lock, Stock and Two Smoking Barrels,* and in watching the spin-off TV Series *Lock, Stock*, I could see a certain resemblance in Ralf Brown's character, Miami Vice. He's a real card.

Probably a month after meeting Dave in Newcastle, I was down in London for a visit but it was under slightly different circumstances to those we originally had in mind. I was there to attend Charlie Kray's funeral as Dave's guest. Charlie was the elder brother of Ronnie and Reggie, the infamous Kray twins. The Krays' notoriety spread not just all over London in the '60s, but all over the world. Charlie had been locked up not too many moons ago for his involvement in a drug conspiracy of some sort. He had not been well and he'd died on 4 April 2000. I'd seen all the pictures of Reg being transferred to Parkhurst Prison on the Isle of Wight to be near him. As far as I could see, that was as compassionate as the authorities were gonna be. I think it's wrong that Reggie was kept in prison and considered a threat after all those years. After numerous calls for his release they finally let him out after a national newspaper printed pictures of him in hospital and raised the profile of his plight. An old man dying of cancer is not a danger to the public and his debt to society has been paid in full – threefold. Rapists, child abusers and child murderers, all kinds of sick and twisted paedophiles and wife beaters – three-year sentence, serve two, slap on the wrist, don't do it again. Know what I mean? If Jack Straw can explain that one I'd love to be there when he does. It was all politics. They released him far too late and he only had weeks left to live. Reg had a book only to be released after his death; he had the last laugh on all those people who wanted to crush his soul.

Charlie was in his seventies when he was sent down for a twelve-year stretch. I didn't know him personally but I know that sentence would have been enough to finish any man. I got a call from Stevie Wraith with an invite to travel down with them lot: Big Graham Borthwick driving, Ray Cann the tattoo artist in the back with me. Steve has been a family friend of the Krays for years and got to know them through hundreds of letters.

It was a sign of respect for all the known faces around the country to show up and I now had the recognition to hold my own amongst them. The funeral was on 19 April, which also just happened to be the day I was due in court for my relentlessly vicious, savage and barbaric common assault charge. It would have to wait, I'm afraid. Something more important had turned up. Steve sorted a wreath out: a 3-D diamond with the word 'Geezer' underneath and we made our way down to London the night before. The journey down didn't take too long for me, 'cos I was out like a light as soon as I sat down. We got to Dave's place at around half-five in the morning. This was the first time I'd set eyes on his house and they nearly popped out. Picture Will Smith's face in *Independence Day* when he clocks the UFO for the first time. Now you're getting close. He always told Jennifer he'd build her a castle, so guess what he went and did ... he went and built her a castle! The whole theme centres on Camelot; it's amazing. Outside there is a huge painting of Dave wearing a suit of armour on horseback and the words 'dog's' and 'bollocks' instantly sprang to mind. Dave had left the door open for us, so we made our way in to find people asleep all over the place. Dozens of the biggest blokes you've ever seen; it was a case of every man for himself and find an empty spot somewhere for a few more hours' sleep. Here I was, Britain's top heavyweight vale tudo fighter, flying the flag around the world, special guest of Dave and having to find somewhere to rest up without so much as a blanket. I was expecting five-star treatment!

I was woken up from my one-hour snooze when I got that feeling of being watched; I opened my eyes and there was Dave in his dressing gown. 'Awight, my son!' We had coffee and breakfast and talked over what we'd been up to since our last meeting, then got ourselves ready for the long day ahead. By around 8.30 a.m., the house was packed wall to wall with massive doormen sporting shaved heads and crombies. There were blokes who hadn't seen each other for years, from all different parts of the country, but they all greeted one another as if those years were yesterday. You don't need to see mates all the time; friendship lasts. Some of them hadn't met since Ronnie's funeral five years previous. It was like *The Wanderers*, but anyone who saw us would definitely not fuck with the baldies.

A brand new Daimler arrived for Dave and then Stevie, Ray, Graham, Mad Pete and me made our way in Dave's Rolls. A chapter of The Outcasts arrived to lead the convoy of expensive cars (a chapter is a bike gang in a certain part of the country – different chapters to different gangs). There were around ten of them on their gleaming bikes. Dave had arranged for them to guide us – much as the police would guide a presidential entourage – through the morning rush-hour traffic of London. Each time we came to a roundabout or a junction they would stop the cars in a military-style operation. No one on the roads would dare say anything. Phil, leader of The Outcasts, is an awesome sight; he had this bowler-type hat on with a feather in the side, and a big long leather trench coat with their name on the back. He was basically a cowboy on a motorbike. They did an excellent job, 'cos in that kind of traffic it would have taken hours; with The Outcasts it took minutes. What a sight it was; even the police didn't dare stop us. Road signs meant nothing to us lot, we had right of way and no one wanted to argue about it.

As we reached Bethnal Green the traffic was at a standstill. The crowds that had built up outside English's Funeral Parlour spilled out from behind the barriers and out on to the road. Once again, our escorts made sure that we arrived right outside the door. Mad Pete parked up and we climbed out of the car to the blinding flashes of the photographers' cameras ... now where did I put that ammonia? It was mayhem. A who's who of British crime: there were all these people you only knew as legendary underworld figures or had read about or seen on TV or in films. In no particular order I met: Tony Lambrianou, Freddie 'Brown Bread Fred' Foreman, his son Jamie Foreman the actor, Frankie Fraser, Joe Pyle and son, actor Ray Winstone – fucking excellent in *Nil by Mouth* – Bruce Reynolds and New Zealander Christian Simpson. 'Course, there was dozens and dozens more, but too many to remember in a short space of time. We headed for a pub over the other side of the road, where most of the faces I'd seen earlier at Dave's place were. I went to the back room of the pub with Dave and he took on all comers at pool ... with one hand. He was beating everyone as well and I must say he was good at it. It was my turn. We started playing and I was beating him with both hands, so I suggested I use one hand to even things up. Dave was going, 'No, you just carry on as you were. Just play normal', but I still played with one hand for a laugh. I realise now that playing with one hand is Dave's thing and I shouldn't have tried to take his glory away. He's never been beaten. Sure enough, he cleared up and racked 'em up for another game. He said, 'I'll let you pot four balls first before I even start.' So here was my chance; I potted four, Dave entered the game and still wiped the floor with me. All credit to him.

I turned to him and said, 'You're one flash bastard, aren't you?'

He replied, 'Takes one to know one' – and I take that as a compliment from him.

We finished our drinks and made our way back to the cars. The police told us it would be quicker to walk to the church; there was a suspected gas leak further down the road. It would make more sense for us to arrive before the hearse, so our army made its way to St Matthews Church, Bethnal Green, only about half a mile away. You can imagine what we all looked like: about thirty massive blokes – doormen, villains and celebrities – marching down the road in dark suits, crombies and dark shades. No one was gonna give us any grief – or so we thought. As we turned the corner to the final stretch, Ray Cann was attacked ... by a Jack Russell terrier. It grabbed hold of his trouser leg and kept trying for the double-leg take-down. *Everyone* burst out laughing, Ray included. Lucky it went for the skinniest bloke – Big John was there, one of Dave's mates, an enormous bloke weighing in at around 300lb. Basically the size of an elephant, he is rock solid and scary as fuck. If it had picked a fight with John I'm sure he would just have scooped it up and eaten it.

At the church gates we were greeted by lads with CKS (Charlie Kray Security) badges on (I thought they were Calvin Klein Snides at first). Whoever handled security, I was told they hadn't done the job that Dave had done with Ronnie's funeral, but they had a lot to live up to. They weren't gonna let us in till they saw Dave with us. There were more familiar faces from TV and the film world and then the hearse arrived, with nineteen limousines in tow. As soon as Reggie stepped from the car, the thousands of well-wishers began to shout and scream for him and for his release. We formed a double line of honour inside the church gates on either side of the coffin as it was carried inside. We followed it in and stood at the back for the hour-long service, which Reg himself had compiled. There was also an emotional reading from Jamie Foreman. Reggie was clearly moved by the whole thing. I didn't think it was very respectful to film a man while he was grieving for his brother, whoever it is; they should be given privacy. Yes, the funeral was news, but to watch a man's reaction as the last member of his family is buried is just an invasion of his privacy. I don't think it is news. It was just another added weight on the bloke's back.

Outside, the service was relayed back to those who couldn't get in the church, via a tannoy system. I'm not sure what the exact head count was but the streets and roads were jam-packed. Everyone had turned up to show their respects, to cheer for Reg or even just to catch a glimpse of him. There were dozens of photographers and camera crews to catch all the action. They were even on stepladders to make sure they didn't miss a thing. The huge turnout just proves the kind of support he still had after all those years.

After the service we went back to the cars and made our way to Chingford Mount Cemetery in Essex. This is where the Kray family plot is. The Outcasts did us proud again. They guided us through the traffic – to the amusement of the motorists and bemusement of the police. Mad Pete wasn't doing too badly keeping up with Dave's new set of wheels either. After parking up again, there was a short pathway to the graveside. There was complete silence, unbelievable quiet. With us in long coats marching forward it was like a posse of outlaws descending on to a town ... straight out of a Western. All you could hear was our footsteps and then the clicking of the cameras as we passed. Our army outnumbered the mourners as we took our place on a small mound overlooking the plot. We kept a respectful distance as the coffin arrived. Reggie now had the chance to say a more dignified and final farewell to his brother.

To look at him, I couldn't help but feel for his plight. Reggie had been given a recommended sentence of thirty years and was now into his thirty-fourth. He was frail, a crushed soul and still he remained locked up.

Mourners and friends said their goodbyes to each other, which seemed to take forever with the endless handshakes and hugs. We made our way back to Dave's house. We didn't have The Outcasts with us on the way back, so it took a lot longer. What a day. I'm sure Charlie would have been pleased with the turnout, because

I'm certain Reggie was. Steve and the lads had a piss-up organised for later that night. Dave turned to me and told me we had different plans for the night – we were going to a private boxing function: Dave, Jen and me.

Many of you may know all about Dave's Rolls-Royce. He lost the keys a while back so he hot-wired it and now uses a dumpy little screwdriver to start it. We arrived at the boxing do at this really posh hotel in London and it was valet parking. We got out of the car and up the stairs to the doors. The valet parking attendant came up to Dave and said, 'Yes, sir?'

Dave just looked at him, handed him this screwdriver and said, 'Just park that up for me, please.'

It was a classic! The attendant is looking down at the screwdriver and back at the car wondering if it's stolen and not knowing what to do. Dave just held his arm out for Jenny to link and we made our way in. To this day I still can't work out whether he plans these sorts of things or they just happen. Either way he is a proper entertainer.

Inside all the names and faces were there. All the ones I mentioned before and then some; all people from TV programmes such as *The Bill*, *EastEnders* and *London's Burning*. They have this guest of honour list that gets read out before the fights kick off. The bloke stood up to announce people like Ray Winstone – fucking amazing in *Scum* – and Roy 'Pretty Boy' Shaw ... and then the no-holds-barred British Champion, Ian Freeman. I had no idea that was gonna happen. I stood up to receive a round of applause and caught Dave's eye. He winked and gave me the thumbs up. He knew I appreciated it.

As the night progressed I met up with Roy Shaw. What a bloke – one of *the* original hard men. He said he'd heard about me and admired what I was doing. When the likes of Roy Shaw say such words it really hits home. We had a good chat and I found that he was a real knowledgeable bloke. I also met up with Kenny

'Panda' Anderson. I first met him at Dave's book signing but didn't really have much time for talking then. Panda is a legend in the North-east. He is known as a hard man and a proper gent. No one in this country will tell you otherwise. We talked a lot about life back home and what we had been up to; he offered advice and we talked about some of my fights.

Considering the reputations these men have, they know exactly how to conduct themselves and talk with the utmost respect and politeness at all times. A great bunch, and accepted me with open arms; they all made me feel welcome and were comfortable with me. I respect every man for what he does, every gangster for what they do, but I'm not the type who gets awe-struck by the whole thing. Not that I wasn't moved by it, 'cos this was a big thing, but I like to think that I'm just as good at what I do as they are at what they do. People are all at different levels; what level I'm at I don't know. If people want to look at me as some kind of superstar or whatever, then let them; if they want to look at me as just a normal person, then let them. It was a privilege to meet up with Roy but I spoke to him exactly the way I would speak to anyone and that's how he spoke; with respect. May be hard to imagine, but these are real people and they prefer you talk to them like that instead of any hero worship.

Once we'd left and were on our way back, Dave made a wrong turning, pulled across the lane without indicating and his back end clipped a taxi. He just kept on driving and Jen turned to him: 'I think you've hit a taxi, love.'

Dave replied, 'I know, dear. Let's see if he tries to stop us.' So we drove a bit further and the taxi started flashing its lights at us. 'I think I'd better pull over,' said Dave.

We stopped and he got out to meet the taxi driver behind the car. I was having all kinds of déja vu from the Gateshead incident, so I got out in case things got a bit nasty … nasty meaning in case I had to drag Dave off him. I heard the taxi driver say, 'Look what you've done to my fucking cab ...' Then he realised who he was talking to. '... Oh, Dave Courtney. Well, it's not that bad, it'll be all right, mate.'

Dave just went, 'OK then', flicked the ash off his cigar, we got back in and drove off. The taxi driver didn't say shit.

I went down to visit Dave again, not long after the funeral. I was in London for a business meeting about getting some fights screened on satellite TV and the bloke I was supposed to be meeting up with didn't show. What a fucking piss-taker. I'd gone all that way for nothing and was absolutely foaming. We went round to this bloke's office and I booted the door down to leave a note on his desk. He owes me big time. I went over to Dave's to spend the rest of the day with him before he gave me a lift to the train station on his bike. No ordinary bike, as you can imagine. A Harley. So many things in common ... even Dave loves blasting around like Dennis Hopper, only he drives more like Barry Sheen. So it turned out that I got the five-star treatment after all. He really knows how to look after a mate.

A Maximum High: skills to pay the bills

***THERE'S NO OTHER** way to describe it. I was training in America and got offered another chance to fight in the UFC. It was my last chance to prove what I could do and nothing was gonna stop me. Even if it had taken me ten years, I knew I would return. I had to exorcise those demons and put the past behind me. I was thinking of this as the most important fight of my career. Everything rested on it and success in the UFC would probably change my entire future.*

I was invited back over to America to train for a couple of weeks and jumped at the chance. I trained with Jason Godsey and stayed with Gary Meyers. Two more world-renowned fighters to add to the list of friends and training partners. I've already trained with the likes of Marco Ruas (vale tudo – training with him was awesome), Renzo Gracie (classed as the best in Brazilian jiu jitsu), Carley Gracie, Mauricio Gomez (the Gracies' uncle – he trained them), John Machado (Brazilian jiu jitsu – very technical), Steve Barnett (seventh dan jiu jitsu), Brian Morris (ninth dan jiu jitsu), Brian Cheek (seventh dan jiu jitsu and judo). All known and well-respected fighters.

Carl came over with me this time. Straight away I felt more confident having a mate with me. It was good of Carl to take time out like that and I was itching to get back to America to overcome and chase away any doubts in my own mind about my previous visit. Having plenty of time to play with this time, the first thing I worked on was my accent and the way I speak. People were thinking I was from Scotland – I had to slow it all down a bit or no one would ever understand me. It was hard, 'cos Carl and me would be speaking, then we'd have to remember to change back to our cut-glass, silver-spoon-up-our-arses accent in front of others. I used to get up early and go through a good training session; then the afternoons were free before grappling and wrestling on a night. We had weekends free and even went shooting over at Jason's place one day. He's got every kind of shotgun, rifle and pistol you can think of – I'm just glad he doesn't work for the postal service, if you know what I mean. Up until then I'd only ever shot an air rifle at our Colin's tractor and a shotgun at Owen Murray's that time. These were a bit different, but I was well into it. If I'm good at something, then forget about it. Jason couldn't believe I hadn't secretly been a hitman; I was a natural – like a SWAT Team sniper with the rifles. We had placed sticks some distance away and I kept picking them off and Jason was convinced I'd been shooting all my life. Then we went on to a different range for the clay pigeon shooting and Jason showed me how to aim with the shotgun. With shorter types of shotgun, you have to keep it down at hip level, but with these things you actually have to aim. The first clay pigeon that came past I smashed to pieces. It was hellish. Carl was excellent at shooting as well – I mean, he could pull the trigger well; he couldn't hit the side of a bus if his life depended on it, though. The odd time he hit one he was jumping all over the place like Jennifer Lopez had just asked him out. It was mental.

The training was going excellently. I knew how to grapple and I knew how to do submission and when we got there it wasn't really learning how to do submissions as such, it was learning how to do 'ground 'n' pound', and how to keep moving all the time. Before, if I was on my back with the fighter between my legs I would defend and wait till they'd done a false move and then try and counter them; if I was between someone's legs in their guard I would just punch fuck out of them. Now I'm constantly moving, no matter what position I'm in. I'll never give an opponent an opportunity to hit and now I know I'm lethal with my elbows and knees. I feel I became a constant, flowing fighter instead of sitting back and waiting for the fight to come my way or seeing what my opponent would do next. If I'm moving all the time then I am impossible to hit and the longer I go on in a fight the stronger I get. I recently grappled with Colin Sexton, the bloke who annihilated Gypsie Joe, and after an hour I still felt fresh. He said he couldn't hit me 'cos I was all over the place.

It was while I was training in America that my managers swung into action and John Perretti gave me my second crack at the UFC. This was the one I'd been hoping for. I knew I was ready this time and I couldn't wait to get it on. Everything was perfect. I'd been in touch with Angie every day and she knew I missed her like crazy but that the fight would mean me staying over longer. In the end, we arranged for Angie to come over for it, and once I knew it was arranged I felt invincible. It's like I feed from support. I had my best mate and corner man with me and now Angie was going to be there too. We were preparing to move house just before I left, so while I was over there she had been moving everything by herself and had her parents, Mac and Pauline, helping with things. Not exactly a stress-free break for her, but a break all the same. I couldn't wait to see her. And Carl was proving his friendship as well, 'cos it was his kid's birthday while we were over – he would have been back in time but for the fight. Because he'd come over with me and stayed on he'd missed the birthday, but he didn't complain once.

We used to train at Bally Total Fitness Centre in Indianapolis. It was a real smart place and we were made very welcome. The people there were excellent ... well, most of them. When we went along Gary Myers introduced us to the manager, Kent, and said I was fighting in the UFC so he offered us four weeks' free training as a gesture. It was great. Every time I was in he'd introduce me to friends, customers, members of staff, as 'Ian Freeman, here from England to train for the UFC ... blah, blah, blah ... a top bloke.' Down to earth and really likeable, Kent was. I'd also been introduced to the resident fitness instructor, who was a pro wrestler too. He was one of those types who enjoyed attention. He was the star as far as he was concerned, the dried-up has-been clinging on to the very last thread of recognition. You know the type. He couldn't stand the fact that I was there and he was just a figure in the background.

When Carl and me turned up at the gym we weren't deadly serious all the time – we never are. We'd train, have a laugh and a joke. But this bloke, Charlie I think he was called, didn't really appreciate our brand of comedy. His head was that far up his arse I'm surprised he wasn't bumping into things.

The beginning of a new week: Monday. The fight was on Friday. I started winding my training down a bit; my anxiety was building up and I started gearing myself up for the fight. I walked into the gym and there was the manager in the office with Charlie the wrestler and another member of staff. I went in to say good morning and the manager turned to me: 'I hear you're having a worked fight.' (For those who don't know, a worked fight is one where you already know who is gonna win before the fight even starts. A bit like the WWF type of fights. A fixed fight.) Because he said it with a smile on his face, I thought he was just having a laugh. Smiling back, I said something like, 'Yeah. wouldn't it be nice …' I'd never do a worked fight but, because he didn't really know me and I was kinda laughing, he must have thought I was all right about it.

'Oh, it's just what I've been told,' he said.

Hold on a sec, he's serious here. 'What do you mean, it's what you've been told?' I asked him.

Charlie joined in: 'Some of the guys I wrestle with have fought in the UFC and said they were worked fights.'

So I went, 'Like who? Give me some names.' He started stuttering and finding stupid excuses 'cos he was caught off guard and didn't have a clue what he was talking about. 'I'll tell you what it is, pal,' I said, 'you ever insinuate that I'm doing a fucking worked fight, I'll knock your head clean off your shoulders. I've been away from my family for nearly five weeks. Why didn't I just come here two days before the fight if we know who's going to win? Why would I come here to train?' Angry would be an understatement. Carl was behind me trying to drag me away, so I just left it at that.

The manager came out, apologised and made me a protein drink before my workout. I explained the situation to him, telling him it wasn't a worked fight and how I felt about the whole thing. The fight was four days away and the last thing I needed was some jealous fool like that stirring things up 'cos he wasn't flavour of the month any more. I finished my drink and went round the corner to find the bin. Charlie the wrestler was there; I should have guessed he'd be hanging out at the bin.

'Ian, Ian …' he started.

I stopped him: 'The best thing you can do is fuck off.' I may be wrong but that seemed to me like a big enough hint. He didn't see it. He came right up to me, so I shoved him back: '*Fuck off.*'

'I only wanted to know if you did worked fights or not,' he said. Now he was really beginning to test the patience of Saint Ian. He just didn't know when to give up.

'What the fuck do *you* think?' I asked.

'I don't know. You tell me,' he replied.

I'd taken his shit for long enough. I slapped him – yes, slapped, a punch would be too good for him – across the face and dropped him on to his arse. It was that quick he didn't even see it and he was lying there dazed. I walked back round to Carl and said he'd better get himself round there. He ran round the corner and saw Charlie on the floor. 'What happened?' he asked.

Charlie looked up at him and went (assume American accent here): 'He put me on my ass!'

From where I was standing I couldn't see Carl, but we both burst out laughing as soon as we heard him. I slapped him like the bitch he is. I wasn't gonna put up with the likes of him saying that when I'd been separated from my family all that time. He left work that day and never returned.

Friday came – 9 June 2000 and UFC 26 … my fight against Nate Schroeder in front of his home crowd. I felt invincible going into this fight. I was completely confident and focused. I had Carl, Jason and Tony Ross with me and Angie was in the crowd for support, so in a sense I also felt at home. This was the first time where I could actually take in the whole atmosphere. I knew exactly what was going on, aware of everything. Nate's home crowd were excellent and I found their cheers encouraging. Walking down towards The Octagon is an awesome feeling and an awesome sight. I knew there were a few ghosts I needed to put to rest. Every dog has its day – today was gonna be dog day: my day.

Inside The Octagon, I was staying calm and focused as our names were read out, and signalled my appreciation to the cheers I received. I went into this fight weighing 221lb. The fight started and we touched gloves in the centre as a sign of respect. In the first round I was just sussing him out. From my point of view, a lot was resting on this fight. The UFC don't want losers and I knew if I lost this one then the chances of getting a third invite were slim to say the least; in fact, they were skinnier than Kate Moss on a diet.

Nate started off throwing a few kicks to my legs – not really connecting, though. I was pressing forward ready to punch, always focussed on him. He shot in and we locked up against the side fencing. In the clinch we exchanged knees and punches until I took him down to the floor. I was in his guard for a second or two and then I passed it and went for the choke. I hadn't applied it the way I wanted to and he reversed me and got into my side mount. He went for the full mount but I threw him off with ease. A few seconds later and we were on our feet up against the perimeter again. Nate was pushing me against it and I was able to connect with a few more punches – not really with the opportunity to hit with my full force, but I knew I'd get the chance. Again we went to the floor and Nate got in my side mount with my head pressed to the wired fence. He gained the mount again and landed a few blows and one big right before I dismounted him, forced my way up and back to my feet and laid into him with some knees to the body. We started really going for it right on the buzzer for the end of the round.

I remember saying to Jason at the end of the first round that I was gonna finish it in the next. From my point of view, I had to. In that first round we were pretty evenly matched and now I had to step up a few gears. We touched gloves leading into the round, Nate going for those kicks again and me using my fists. I caught Nate with a big right cross, making him try for the shoot. I sprawled and drove him to his back. I got into his guard and let rip with some nasty elbows to the face – if there were any doubts about my ground 'n' pound abilities, there wouldn't be any more.

I hit him with a few good punches, before passing into the side mount. I was doing some damage with those elbows – I knew they were connecting big style. A few massive punches to the face and he was hurt … I moved in … cracked him on the side of the head with my knee and finished him off with another. He was out of it on the floor and the referee had to jump in to stop the fight … UFC victory to The Machine!

It was my chance to shine and I was fucking blinding. I was a different fighter altogether, but more importantly, I knew it. My performance proved that the last defeat was a one-off and a distant memory. I knew I'd rocked him with that first punch to the chin; once the elbows took it further, I knew those knees from the side mount position would put an end to it. He was battered. People who have seen that fight know how focused I was, but many don't know the half of it. While I was over in Indianapolis preparing for what I saw as the fight of my career, my dad had been taken to hospital. He was very ill with a blood clot on his brain. Angie didn't know whether to tell me or not; she knew it would knock me for six and it did. It was a lot to cope with, but I had to go on and be strong for him and the rest of my family. It was great to see him when I got back home. My mam told me that he'd been up to his old tricks. He'd had one of the doctors up against the wall by the neck! Can't think who I take after …

It's always a blow to you to deal with any illness in the family – more so if it is one of your parents. I've mentioned that I knew my dad wasn't the invincible superhuman bloke who was always around when I was a kid. But you still have this notion that your parents are untouchable by anything. The worst feeling in the world is when you realise they aren't untouchable and are vulnerable to illness and accidents just like everyone else. It's hard to take but it's something you have to help them through. It's the first time you think of your parents as people. You think about what one of them is going through and then the helplessness and the anxiety of the other. I worried a lot for my mam. All kinds of things were flying round in my head ... remember that time when your grandmother or grandfather died and the effect it had. Seeing your grandparent for the first time as a widow or a widower hurts. They are so lost and empty and alone, no matter how many people they are around. Completely different people, like they were this team and cannot function properly when it's incomplete. That was hard enough for your own parents to go through, all those thoughts they had, and then you can find yourself in that position. They worry about you when you are younger, and you worry about them as they get older. We are a very close family and we were all very worried for both of them. My mam took quite a bit on at the time, coping with everyday life and dealing with my dad being ill at the same time. It was a big strain for her and we all felt for her. Mother is the name for God in the hearts and in the minds of all children. It's true.

In your mother's arms, as a little child
Growing up you're always, always on her mind
She gives you, you the best, the best she can give
She'll always be there: Mother

Make your meals, lets you go out to play
Fastens your coat, on a winter's day
Helped you tell, tell the time, when you were young
She'll lend a hand: Mother

Mother oh mother, she's always there for you
When you're alone, when you're feeling blue
Mother, she's your mother

Mother

When, when you fall and hurt yourself
Who do you run to, but no, no one else
In her arms, feeling so safe, safe and warm
She makes you happy: Mother

She worries about you, when you go out late
Watches out the window, as you close the garden gate
Wondering what time, time you'll be, be returning home
She cares about you: Mother

Mother oh mother, she's always there for you
When you're alone, when you're feeling blue
Mother, she's your mother

Mother Mother

'Mother', Ian Freeman

It wasn't until after the fight, when I'd got changed to watch the rest of the fights, that I realised just how much the people had taken to me. I went to use the phone and people were coming to congratulate me; and then, when Angie and me went for a drink, I was getting more well dones and handshakes. A woman and her young kid came over. I was wearing a *Tapout* tee-shirt and she asked where she could get one for him. I told her I didn't think they were available at the show and they turned to leave. As they were walking off I saw the little kid's face … 'Do you want this shirt?' I asked him. His face lit up. I took it off and gave him it. It was great to do something like that. It's something that would live with me for the rest of my life and I hope it does for him. If I had thousands of tee-shirts I'd do the same for thousands of kids.

The UFC was the biggest buzz. Like I said at the start, it's a lot better to fight in the ring and get the recognition than to fight some drunk on the street who thinks he's a tough guy. And to fight in The Octagon is one step higher than any other fight I'd had. You can never put into words that feeling you get walking towards it and then the adrenaline rush you get when you hear the cage door close behind you. From then on you are on your own; you can either walk back out victorious or be carried out. To fight a skilled man like that is the ultimate test. Any fight is a test, but these people have earned the right to fight there. On the street, anyone with enough beer in them thinks they've earned the right.

When I returned from the UFC, I decided to get a tattoo done on my back. To say it's the bollocks is a bit of an understatement ... it really is a work of art. 'The Machine' in huge lettering across my back. Ray Cann, who I met at the Charlie Kray funeral, did it for me. It took ten and a half hours, but as the saying goes, 'No pain, no fucking brilliant tattoo.' I'd wanted it for quite a while but up until winning in the UFC I didn't think I'd earned it. It felt like I'd earned my stripes, earned the right to wear my name after that win. I'd probably have felt like a hypocrite in getting it done too early. This way it came at the right time.

* * * * *

Even though my fight career has kicked off now and I'm fighting the best in the world, my main job is looking after the city. It's a big job, if not bigger than fighting around the world. All the little jobs that have to be done, all the things that others wouldn't want to take on – I'm still doing them. I'm a lot wiser now and know I don't need to do everything myself. I know that I can trust all my men when I delegate. I can now sort problems out with the use of a phone. Last time I was in hospital to have an operation on my nose, Angie asked the nurse to remove the cell phone from my ear. I don't think she quite got the joke – 'You can't use a mobile phone in here, Mr Freeman.' Obviously she was still waiting for the operation to have the stick removed from outta her arse ... bloody NHS.

Joking aside, though, I'm constantly in touch with all my lads – every kid who works for me has my number and me theirs. We need the reassurance in order to make things work. You have to make sure all your employees are looked after; it's the same in every business. If you forget about your staff then things just go down the pan. I always make sure I get together with my main doormen on a regular basis. Our strength is contact – their families know the numbers of everyone connected and know they are safe all the time. I think there has only been one time I've been without my mobile phone *ever*. And this one will be stuck in quite a few other people's memories as well: the Chambers incident.

We were standing on the doors at Boulevard and these lads came along who had been barred – and they were in big numbers. I had my phone in my hand and turned round to see them approaching, so I handed this punter my phone to keep. I didn't know his name but I knew his face and knew him as a regular; to save it getting smashed I asked him to hold it and he said he would. The group of lads didn't really kick off. There was a little bit of bother; they went. I turned round and the lad with my phone was nowhere in sight. I asked the bar staff and the DJ if he'd left it with them. He hadn't. I knew their next stop would be Chambers, so I drove down there after them. I told the lads on the door what was going on and went up to find my phone. I got upstairs and found the lad. There was a group of around fifteen others with him. Once I'd asked him where my phone was I knew something was up. He started shouting John Kelsy over. I know John well and this lad was getting him over to square things out with me; the lad said it was left with the DJ ... bollocks. I knew it wasn't.

'Where's my fucking phone? I asked him.

He started bottling. 'I want nothing to do with this,' he said.

'Nothing to do with this?' I could feel my temper rising when this other lad came over to say the group of lads had taken it off him and smashed it on the floor. Two different stories in as many minutes – that meant ultimatum time: make or break. Make with the phone or get smashed to fuck. I told him he had three seconds to give me my phone or I'd punch his head in. That was when another lad chipped in with a different story and that's when I kicked off with the lot of them. The one who had my phone was the first to get dropped. Anyone or anything within my reach got hit. I was a madman. Another mistake they made was thinking they could take me 'cos I was outnumbered. Wrong. In that mood not even a tank could stop me. As I was laying into one of them, I felt someone jump on my back. In true Western style I chucked him over the bar and into the optics. The doormen came up and knew it wouldn't be a good idea to step in my way, even though they were pals of mine. When it calmed down, Eddie Gillespie told me to get out before I did any more damage. I only left after I told them I'd be back for my phone.

Back at Boulevard, I had another look round and even walked around outside in case it had been smashed. Nothing. At the end of the night I was at Marlowe's and the doormen were exploding with the rumours they'd been hearing all night: that Ian Freeman's a complete madman and he's just trashed Chambers and around fifteen kids. Yep. All true, but not without reason. A while after the whole thing had blown over, the kid came and apologised to me. Then I got the full story … It was the boys that we'd had the scuffle with at the doors when he had hold of my phone. While this was going on, his mates were leaving and he didn't know whether to leave or not and told them he had my phone. One of the troublemakers overheard him, took it off him and smashed it. That was the story – but whether it's true or not,

I don't know. About a month after the incident, he was at the bar one night. I went up to him with my new phone and said, 'Can you keep hold of this for a second, mate?' He nearly shit a brick at the thought of it. It's good that, even though shit happens, it can still result in a laugh, friendship and no hard feelings. It doesn't always happen like that, as you know, but we all love a happy ending. That's just another side to what goes on as part of my job. It's funny to think that I can be fighting in one of the biggest tournaments in the world one week, then the next having to bust up a nightclub and sort out a gang of wankers who smashed my phone up.

* * * * *

There was still a buzz from the Nate Schroeder fight and I was asked back to fight in UFC 27. I said earlier that I needed to win that fight as they only ask you back if you win and entertain the crowd; now I knew I'd really made it. I was matched up against Tedd 'The Gladiator' Williams, a fucking big bloke of six feet one, and just under 260lb, with an impressive record.

I stepped up my training over here and went over to America to carry on training two weeks before the fight. This time I went over with Leigh Remedios, a TMA fighter who is named as Britain's best Lightweight fighter, and Paul Corkery from Choke Athletic. I've met Leigh a few times before and Paul really came up trumps while over there. Leigh's still got a lot to learn, but I see big things for him in the future. We chopped and changed between the houses of Tony Ross and Jeremy Bolt, so we wouldn't outstay our welcome anywhere. While I'm there to train hard, I still feel it's as important to relax, and so minimal tension is the name of the game. Through the days I trained back at Bally's (still no sign of Charlie), doing cardio work and weight training and on a night I'd concentrate on grappling. Tom

Erikson (290lb, six foot four) came over to train as well. He's a great guy, one of the top five fighters in the world, as well as the guys I trained with last time – Jason, Gary and Eddie Moore. Yuki Kondo, Yoshiki Takahashi and Daisuke Ishii came over from Japan and stayed at Jason's mum's house. Yuki is the best fighter the Pancrase organisation in Japan has; he was fighting on the same bill as well. All was going perfectly up to this point … then – disaster.

I'd borrowed a car from a friend and on the way back from the gym around a week before the fight disaster struck. In my defence, I'll say that road markings in America are shit. They really are: no lines down the centre, no give way markings at junctions, nothing … apart from the stop sign I didn't see 'cos we were talking. We were hit by a van and spun round 180º, facing the opposite direction and crawling along backwards. The car was completely written off – totally wrecked. And the force of the impact threw my body sideways and tore through my oblique muscles. I was sitting there out of breath, unable to breathe properly and doubled up in pain. Leigh and the other driver were OK but obviously shaken by the accident.

The police arrived and were eager to prove that they are the same over there as they are over here – power hungry and unable to comprehend logic. Within minutes I was convinced. I had to show this cop my driver's licence on the spot or face a court appearance – the snag being that it was at my friend's house and I wasn't allowed to leave the scene of the crash. I phoned Kev at Bally's who came over to help and then went to get my driver's licence. While I was waiting for him to return the cop asked us why we were over there. I told him I was a UFC fighter and at first he didn't believe me (this wasn't the time or the place for a Douglas Hall-style demonstration), but once I'd told him my name he said his son was a fan. I had my training bag with me and took out a few pictures and signed them for him. At that point Kev returned and looked gobsmacked. He'd seen the transformation of unreasonable cop to good cop and could hardly believe it. We got things sorted out with Officer Schizophrenia and were on our way.

For the next few days my side was absolutely fucked. My breathing was laboured, I could barely move and Jason told me to rest and strap it up. After resting for two days I trained on the third and did a bit of grappling with Leigh. Leigh is only 155lb, but I could hardly move with him on top of me. How could I expect to fight someone twice his weight? People were telling me not to fight and deep down I knew they were probably right. *Probably*. But the fight with my conscience would be a lot harder than any physical fight, so I knew I would never drop out. The most important part of grappling and groundwork is being able to move your hips and I couldn't do that at all with my side being torn. I could move slightly better on one side than the other, but being barely able to move a little guy in training was a bad sign. The pain was unbelievable and I didn't know what to do.

With the fight only three days away, I didn't know what to tell John Perretti. I couldn't just drop out – how would that look? I was over there training for it, he'd given me the opportunity; it was too late in the day as far as I was concerned. I was supposed to appear on Eyada.com – Eddie Goldman's *No Holds Barred* radio show – but I didn't turn up for it. In talking to him he would have easily picked up the fact that I was injured and no way did I want to tell the world about it – no way, mate. If Tedd knew I had a weakness, I'd be fucked. My plan was to stick with it. I was sure that, once the adrenaline kicked in, I'd be fine. It would just override the pain. Just before the fight Jason told me to reconsider... I think by then they all knew I was going into that fight and, on 22 September 2000, that's exactly what I did.

Jason Godsey had to go over to Japan to corner Chris Lytle, one of his fighters, so Tony Ross cornered me in his place. He'd already been with me in the last UFC and knows me well, along with Paul and Leigh. I knew I'd have plenty of help from them. We all had different flights into Louisiana and met up in New Orleans once we'd all found our bearings. I also met up with the Japanese lads and it turned out that I was sharing the same dressing room as Yuichi on the night. Once I'd got settled, I met up with people like Frank Shamrock, Dan Severn, Pedro Rizzo and Tito Ortiz.

I went in there with a nine and one record. That's nine wins and one defeat – my UFC 24 fight against Scott Adams. I was also going in there to build on my Nate Schroeder fight. Was I doing the right thing here? Who knows? Tedd Williams was not the sort of opponent who would mess around. This was his second UFC – he won his first with a first-round knockout; he was California State Judo Champion as well as a college wrestler. He'd dropped a few pounds in training and was looking in good shape; I still came in at 221lb – looking good, but not quite feeling it. Backstage, warming up on the pads, I tried to throw a punch and it had all the power of a wet fart. My side hurt like hell, but I was still sure the adrenaline would sort it out. All said, I never would have gone in there if I thought I was wasting my time. I could feel the adrenaline starting to work its magic on the way down to the ring, hearing the crowd behind me gave me a real sense that I belonged here. This is the buzz I needed. I fed from the crowd and my corner team absorbing the atmosphere and the energy... I felt ready.

Our referee was John McCarthy. He signalled us to fight by saying, 'Let's get it on!' We touched gloves in the centre of The Octagon and went straight in there with a few punches to test the water. The pain was still there and was restricting my movement and my power. In practice I'd learned about being up against the cage wall and it was all upper body movements from that position. During that first round Tedd had me up against the cage, but went straight for my legs, and that's something I hadn't practised at all. He took me to the ground and fucking kneed me in my bad side. I was still calm and comfortable with the fight at this point, but my awareness of danger was in overdrive. I got my feet up against the fencing and pushed, forcing him to go round to the other side. I knew I couldn't move, so all I could do was defend. He was letting loose with a few elbows to the head along the way, and some knees from the side mount. His knees didn't seem to be connecting enough to do any damage, though. I was basically defending on the ground of four minutes. Tedd was dictating the fight, for sure, but I was making him work hard. I was as comfortable as I could be for someone with 260lb on them trying to knee and elbow them into submission. I came out of that round a frustrated fighter. I walked over to my corner shaking my head – I've always been my own worst critic. I wasn't doing too badly for a bloke who should probably not even have been standing up, never mind even dreaming about fighting. He'd definitely won the round and I knew there was a lot of work for me to do to turn things round. I promised myself not to get beaten right then.

At the start of the second round, I thought to myself, It's not going to the ground again. He came forward and I kneed him in the face, but because he was coming at me, his momentum took me on to my back and right back up against the cage wall. Fuck. I got to my feet, but he was going for my legs again. In this position I heard Tito Ortiz shout, 'Push his head down.' So I did – grabbed the back of his head and pushed it down. He couldn't take me down and I'd learned a new move in seconds right when I needed it. Cheers, Tito!

I could feel Tedd starting to tire now and it was my turn to take over. I pushed clear of him and he shot low for a single-leg takedown. He got my leg but I sprawled, hitting him hard and making him turn over to the guard. This is where the phrase 'heavy handed' comes from. I hit him with the big guns and turned the fight right round. He was coming in for the clinch, but I was holding him back with my forearm across his throat. He was taking damage and was not moving his hips at all – this was the opening I needed and took full advantage. More big blows and the strain was starting to show. I passed the guard and landed three knees to the head; as I did this I felt my side rip again and got back into his guard. Half a minute to go and Tedd was really hanging on. I was happy to keep it there till the end. At the end of the round he was slow in getting up and I knew I'd evened the score.

Going into the final round I knew I'd win it. I had loads left in me and I could sense that Tedd was worn down. We touched gloves in the centre and Tedd was taking steps back instead of forward. Exchanging a few punches, we went in for a clinch; I broke it off and kneed him in the face. For a few seconds it looked like he was gonna topple over. He tried to take me down but I was right on top of him and followed in with a few more knees. Back to our feet in the centre of the ring and I let loose with some heavy punches. The pain was unbearable, but I had to ignore it for another four minutes. I doubled up in pain for a second before composing myself and going straight into Tedd. A few more knees to the face and he took it to the fence again. In this position I knew he was using up a hell of a lot of energy. I pushed his head down and still he was trying for my legs. We ended up on the canvas and I rocked him with two right knees to the head. Now it was his turn to be up against the side of the cage. I was in his guard and in full control; Tedd was hanging on for all he was worth. I was driving him into the fence and kept up the bombardment of rights and lefts. Normally I would have been looking for a submission, but my side was starting to tighten up. From outside the ring I could hear my corner team shouting encouragement: 'It's the Freeman show!' Too right it was ... thirty seconds ... fifteen seconds. I made sure the round was mine, pounding and pounding, only stopping on the buzzer to end the fight. I got to my knees and knew I'd won.

Looking back, I think it probably was stupidity to walk into a fight like that with a fighter of such high calibre, but I came out on top. Tedd is awesome and up till then had had a perfect record. I would never go into a fight underestimating my opponent; my big mistake here was underestimating the pain in my side. In UFC rules, the winner of each round gets ten points and the opponent gets nine or less. They base their judgement on effective striking, grappling and assertiveness. I felt sure that round two and three were mine, I was just waiting for the confirmation. Then came the announcement from Bruce Buffer: 'The winner, by a unanimous decision – from England, Ian "The Machine" Freeman.'

On hearing the result, I congratulated Tedd Williams on his performance. I now knew why they call him 'The Gladiator'; his spirit is unbreakable.

I rested up well after the fight and took a long-overdue vacation. I couldn't wait to get back into training, but I wanted my to make sure I was fully healed first. I had my rib injury checked over on my return and was told there was no permanent damage; before long I was back in training. The response I got from this fight was better than I could ever have imagined. It was hailed as my best fight to date – and that was by people who had no idea about the injury. It proved I could come back from being behind on points, that I could turn things around and not back down. One thing it looked certain of doing was putting me in the run-up to a title fight. The hype was phenomenal ... first British UFC fighter, first to win, and now being recognised as a major presence. It was amazing. Amazing to hear all these names being put forward as possible opponents. All huge men, brilliant fighters, and I couldn't wait to be given the chance to fight them.

When the news of my win spread, I was getting phonecalls from all over the place, emails from well-wishers; it's been great.

* * * * *

While I was checking out more media coverage, there was someone else who was gaining front-page headlines at around the same time. On Sunday, 1 October 2000, Reggie Kray lost his battle against cancer. He'd been freed from Wayland Prison in Norfolk on 26 August, on compassionate grounds, and spent his last Thirty-five days bedridden in a hotel. As he died, his wife Roberta and some of his close friends surrounded him. I spoke of Reggie earlier on and to me it still didn't seem as though he was actually granted freedom. His bladder was another life sentence, but one that he could never walk free of. There are people on both sides of the fence who think Reggie had paid his debt and should have been let out, and those who say he was an evil killer who should have been locked up forever. We all have our own opinions, but I'm sure we'd be united in saying that cancer is the most fucking evil killer of humanity. No one is safe from it.

I received a call from Stevie Wraith to see if I wanted to go down to the funeral with him and I told him of course I would. I went down with him and mutual friends to Charlie's funeral and was quite looking forward to meeting up with the lads again. The thing was, Stevie didn't want to go down to Dave Courtney's house this time round – which made me wonder why. Dave's a good mate and I wanted to catch up with him. I said I'd go with Stevie, but wanted to drop in at Dave's at the same time. Stevie suggested just meeting up with him at Bethnal Green, and I guessed something was up. I made a few enquiries and found out one possibility why Stevie wanted to stay low profile. He'd had some kind of disagreement with Roy Shaw and Roy had said that he was gonna knock him out when they next met. Stevie didn't tell me any of this and once I'd found out about it I even gave him the opportunity to tell me. Still nothing. The reason why he wouldn't tell me: basically he wanted me beside him and, if anything kicked off, he assumed I'd jump in and try to stop it. Bullshit. I wouldn't stop anything. Roy is a friend of mine; we are both fighters with respect for each other. If Stevie had the balls to tell me this, to ask me if I'd help try to smooth things over and tell me he didn't want any trouble instead of expecting me to fight for him, then I would have appreciated his honesty. I'm not gonna be taken for a mug.

It happened that the funeral was on 11 October. '*Happy birthday dear I-an ... Happy birthday to you.*' I travelled down on the train the day before with Ray Cann, who'd done my awesome 'The Machine' tattoo. We were picked up at King's Cross station and taken over to one of Dave's pubs, where we stayed for some time. We caught up with everyone, had a laugh and enjoyed meeting up with people from all over the country. This time there were a lot more new faces than at the previous funeral – big bodybuilders and doormen. I was knackered from travelling and needed some sleep. They were all drinking and, me not being a drinker to start with, I just couldn't be bothered with it. I went to Dave's and got some sleep.

Around twenty lads rolled up at Dave's house in the early hours, three of them crashing out on the floor of the bedroom I was in. Just my luck. Being drunk, they were asleep in no time and one of them started snoring like a fucking walrus. Huge bastard, he was. You've heard nothing like it ... and I hope you never do.

I couldn't waste any words here: 'Shut the fuck up!' seemed to work for all of five minutes, then he rolled over and started again. Can you think of anything more annoying than that? I sat up and was about to throw my pillow at him. Bad move as I'd have to get up and climb over them to get it back. What else is nearby ... an alarm clock ... *Bang* ... bounced straight off his head and was reinforced with, 'Will you shut the fucking fuck up!' I ended up by stuffing toilet roll into my ears and eventually got off to sleep.

In the morning we had a laugh about the snoring, enjoyed some bacon sarnies – thanks, Jen – and dressed for the big day. There were forty of us all kitted out in black suits, crombies and shades. Then Dave spoke up about our floral tribute for the funeral. We all gave five quid each towards it – a dove that must have taken hours to construct. When it arrived, we all gathered round to have a gander ... it looked like no dove I've ever seen. No disrespect to Dave here, 'cos it wasn't him who made the thing. Let's just say it wasn't unlike a duck. Anyway, our cars arrived and they really made up for the floral duck. Big 1920s-style classic gangster type, real *Untouchables* stuff. Dave was in the white one at the front and I got in the second blue one along with Mad Pete, Dale Henderson and Tony Malloney. We drove over to the funeral parlour in Bethnal Green and went to the same pub as last time. There were quite a few people around but it didn't really look as if there were as many as there had been for Charlie's. Dave had been invited to the Chapel of Rest but could not get the rest of the lads in, so he'd decided to stay in the pub with us. It was pointless most of us standing outside and it was better to stick together.

The funeral itself was impossible to get into; again people were being refused entry, so we made our way up to the graveyard. Even at the graveyard entry was restricted. There was all kinds of politics, disagreements and plenty of confusion to go around. Apparently, Reggie had asked some close friends to carry his coffin, but that dying wish had been ignored. He was laid to rest with the gates locked in front of a handful of people. As soon as the gates were opened, there was a flood of people all rushing to get through at once. It was a nightmare. I turned to Ray and we basically read each other's mind. It was time to call it a day. We'd paid our respects and we didn't feel like wading through the circus up to the grave. It was time to leave. We got a lift back to the train station and were off. Old friends of the Kray family felt let down and had boycotted the funeral. Media coverage was disrespectful and I don't think things went as everyone would have hoped. It was definitely the end of an era, whether good or bad. It felt sad to think that he was the only one of his brothers to die a free man.

Glory Days

FEW YEARS PASSED since my first UFC. I was now the holder of two world championship belts, endorsing products, appearing on local and national TV and being offered film roles. Now all I needed was a big fight in front of a home crowd...

Saturday, July 13th 2002, was the first time the UFC has ever ventured outside the USA and came to the Royal Albert Hall. Beamed all over the globe on satellite and cable TV, the 'Brawl in the Hall', UFC 38, could potentially reach millions. There were promotions absolutely everywhere. Nationally, the buzz was phenomenal. We had our own fighters taking on the best from around the world; Mark Weir, James Zikic and Leigh Remedios were also attracting a lot of attention and this was definitely our chance to show everyone just what we were made of. I think it was important for the UK to show just how big MMA is over here and to hopefully open the floodgates for similar events. As far as we were concerned, all eyes were on us and we needed every aspect of the event to be a success.

My opponent was to be Frank Mir – the unbeaten UFC golden boy, hailed as the next big thing. Mir is a technician as well as a fighter with an awesome reputation. He's a name and was being closely watched by the UFC. This could be my chance to get my foot firmly wedged in the door once and for all and I was gonna go for it.

To train for this fight I asked a good friend of mine, UFC Champion, Josh Barnett. Josh is an awesome fighter from Seattle, Washington, and someone I have tremendous respect for. He said he'd train me on one condition … that I *never* quit. It sounds simple enough, but Josh was deadly serious. If he was going to help me, then it wasn't going to be any half-arsed sparring session. It was on his terms – he said he'd put me through gruelling, intense routines and push the pain barrier to the limit. He said the day I give up would be the day I went home. If I were prepared to put up with that, then he'd love to train me.

I spent four weeks in Seattle with Josh training every day and every night with one day off a week. I immediately found out how serious Josh was. He was determined to push me just like he said. We trained relentlessly at Matt Hume's gym, the AMC. It was weights in the morning for around two hours and then fighting and grappling at night for a further two to three hours. *Every* day.

I was staying in a Travel Tavern type hotel, like Alan Partridge used to stay in before he got his second series. By the end of it I was having nightmares about being introduced into The Octagon for my fight as Ian 'Ahaaaaa' Freeman. My room was pretty basic with a bed, TV, fridge and microwave. And yes … it is true you can watch TV on the toilet if you angle the mirror.

Remember when you were living at home and your mother

used to always say, 'You treat this house like a hotel'? Well that's what I did. It was a place for me to eat, sleep and shit in between training. I'd wake up at 9 am and head over to the gym to meet with Josh and do a two-hour workout. After that, I'd drive back to the hotel and make myself some food. All I lived off while I was there was jacket potatoes. It was like doing a full circle back to when I first had my flat all those years ago. Talk about boring. Having just a microwave to make food with you're quite limited as to what culinary masterpieces you can rustle up, so I usually mixed 'n' matched with tuna and instant pasta. (There's an idea for Jamie's next book – training food with a microwave). I'd have a nap till around 4pm then would have some pasta and be back in the gym from six 'til nine in the evening.

I grappled with some fucking awesome fighters. Frank Mir is well known for his groundwork so Josh was making sure I was prepared. I trained with Alan Gomez from Brazil, Aaron Riley and Bob Sapp, who at 360 lbs is a *big* star in Japan. We did a lot of work on take-downs and I also grappled with a mate of Josh's called Reece, a state champion wrestler. This was just the sort of training I needed ... being up against freestyle wrestlers is brilliant coz it was all about taking down and defending. It would be take-down, take-down, take-down, non-stop. We worked on fitness too and although I felt tired by the end of each night, I was getting faster and my game was improving all the time.

At the end of the first week I phoned Angie. I was ready to pack it all in. I felt like crying. I missed her and the kids. I missed everything ... I missed having a normal life. I just wanted to come home. Of course I knew I couldn't give up – I don't know how to. If I gave up training after a week I may as well have given the fight up.

I stuck it out. There was too many people involved that I couldn't let down. They would forgive me in the end – the one person who I knew wouldn't forgive me was me. No matter how hard you plead with your conscience, you never win. It's a fact of life. Even though it felt like hell at the time, I had to grit my teeth and get on with it. I had to look at my situation differently: Training isn't supposed to be easy … if you don't train, you won't win … your family are always there for you … you're not there for a holiday. Deal with it.

And that's exactly what I did. I had no other life outside of training. Saturday nights had me pacing the room practically wearing the carpet out. I'm the kind of person who can't just sit still or watch TV on a night. I'm usually around people. I need to be doing something or at least talking and having a laugh. I'd sometimes go to a diner for a change of menu and scenery, even if just to see that other people existed – then I'd spend Sundays just resting up and chilling out. One thing America doesn't understand is Sunday lunch – ask for Yorkshire pudding and they think you're mad. So, my one luxury was Gatorade. And lots of it.

It was like starring in *Groundhog Day Part Two*. Wake up, eat, drive to gym, train, drive back, sleep, wake up, eat, train, drive back, eat, sleep. It was paying off though. The guys in the gym were transforming me. Josh knew what I needed to learn and they made sure I learnt it. They started me on a lot more defensive work from the wall. The idea behind it is to prepare for fencing of the cage – fighting up against it, keeping your balance, losing your balance, using it to your advantage and ground work against the fence – the fence is just as important as your ground work and stand-up and, with the help of my training partners, I knew it was something I could use as part of my weaponry.

When I left Washington, I knew I was ready. I owe a lot to Josh and he knows I how much appreciate it. He pushed me to the limit and when he knew I was wrecked, he pushed me even further. Sadistic bastard! I hated him at the time and I think he probably knew it. Not that we fell out – let's call it a friendly hatred. He was brilliant; not many other people would give their time up like that. He got me into peak condition in those four weeks ... not just physically but mentally, and that's what makes all the difference. I'd come a long way and that in itself was a credit to Josh and the others. They say 'No pain, no gain' and they always seem to be right. Whoever *they* are. Does *anyone* know them?

The journey home always takes twice as long, but is always worth it. I rested up for five days before taking my regime back up. If I'd trained those four weeks and then went straight into the fight, I would have been fucked. I was hurting when I arrived home and was absolutely exhausted – I had jetlag to get over and needed to allow my body and mind to fully recover before getting back into it.

With three weeks left 'til the fight I spent my time at Spartan Kickboxing in Hylton Castle, Sunderland. My mate Paul Greaves owns it and literally let me have the run of the place for two weeks. It seemed all my mates were doing all they could to help me – it was excellent. I teamed up with Colin Sexton, Wayne Lasceslls, Rob Hewitt, Pud and Jimmy Welsh who put me through as much pain as they could dish out. I felt on top form ... like a different fighter altogether. The lads couldn't believe how much I'd improved – I was all over Wayne, a big fucker at around 290 lbs, he could tell that I was stronger and quicker within seconds. We'd fight in the mornings for two hours and in the evening it was weights and cardio. We did this for two weeks solid – no breaks, no excuses.

In the fight build-up, a reporter for *The Times* came to the gym to watch us training. *The Times!* Have I gone all highbrow or what? The UFC was getting some excellent coverage and what better way to do it than have The Machine in the Sunday Supplement? The reporter came up and interviewed me and watched a training session. I did forty-eight minutes full-on grappling where a fresh training partner would come in every two minutes in a rota system. This included groundwork and against the wall, as I'd been doing in America. After that I went straight over to the dummy and hit it around for five minutes – a grappling dummy, not the reporter.

Speaking of dummies and reporters ... FHM magazine decided to get coverage of the UFC as well. In the week before the fight I went down to London to train and do my final preparations and there were a few days of press conferences we had to attend. I trained with boxing coach Terry Coulter, Lee Murray, London Shootfighters and trained in Peacock's Boxing Gym. Around this time, a lot of the UK press wanted to interview the British fighters, take pictures and all that caper. If you imagine speed dating but being interviewed instead, that's what it was like. It was hectic but it was all part of the job as a fighter – and hopefully to quash some of the misconceptions about us at the same time in our national press.

So I'm sat there being interviewed by this bloke for FHM. I couldn't be bothered with it in the first place as they all tend to ask us the same questions over and over and you have to reply like it's the first time you've said it. He asked all the usual shit and then launched into some not so usual shit. I don't know if he had a death wish or what. I gave up hitting arseholes a long time ago and I had to fight the urge to come out of retirement. He asked me who would win a fight – me or a grizzly bear. A grizzly-fucking-bear? He was obviously looking for the kind of reaction he could write about – how we are all hot-headed psychos who start fights with people for no reason. I told him I wouldn't fight a grizzly bear. Was this tosser for real? I told him to ask sensible questions or not to ask any at all.

He apologised and composed himself: 'Who do you think would win – you or a shark?'

Some of the other fighters looked over at this point. I wasn't angry, I was pissed off at having to sit and listen to some prick trying to be clever. I told him I'm a professional athlete and I wasn't prepared to listen to anymore of his rubbish. He asks normal questions or he leaves. I'm sat amongst people like Carlos Newton and I know I have respect ... this idiot didn't know the meaning of the word. He apologised again and asked me 'Who is the smelliest person you've fought?' It would have probably been easier to knock him out after the first question.

It takes three years to get a journalism degree, you know. And that's assuming he passed first time round. I bought FHM when his article was in – and surprise, surprise – he'd made up all my answers himself. Now I *had* reacted the way he wanted. He went into detail about everything I said to him and my threatening behaviour, which may just have been funny if it wasn't lies. I bet he tells people that he was interviewing me and I just exploded, threatening him and snarling at him like the animal he'd love to think I was. There were six people in the room at the time it happened and I know who they thought looked the foolish one. Maybe behaving like a prick enhances your career ... I'll ask David Blaine if we ever meet.

There was another press conference prior to the fight too. This was a proper one – like the kind you've seen on TV (with real journalists this time!). There were people there from all over the world – Sky TV, BBC, ITV, CNN, ABC, XYZ, etc ... cameras and production people everywhere. It was held at the Park Lane Hotel in London, and more controversy was being served up.

It was hype in all fairness – boxing promoter Frank Warren had been slagging the UFC off big style. He'd been going around saying that one of his boxers could beat a UFC fighter and reckoned he could prove it. Just a bit of background here – the boxer/MMA fighter debate, unlike the MMA fighter/grizzly bear debate is nothing new. No disrespect to any boxer but unless they can ground 'n' pound, then their chances of winning are halved immediately. Then they need to know how to get out of submission moves. In a boxing match, they would obviously stand a good chance. That isn't what the argument was though. Warren was saying that boxing can beat MMA. I've said it before ... a stand-up fighter is a fish out of water on the ground. You can't box yourself out of everything and it looked like Warren was digging his own hole.

At the press conference there was a stage with our table on top and from left to right facing the press were Frank Mir, Matt Hughes, UFC co-owner Lorenzo Fertita, Carlos Newton, me, and UFC President Dana White. Hughes and Newton were there because of their big welter-weight grudge match topping the bill and myself and Mir because it was the biggest ever British fight. As it got underway, Dana White stood up to reply to Frank Warren's suggestion. He opened up a huge sports bag and poured $100,000 onto the table, throwing the gauntlet down to any boxer who could defeat MMA. Hands up ... has anyone seen $100,000 sitting two inches away from them on a table before? Neither have I – that's why I picked up a ten grand bundle and legged it off the stage. Quite literally. I was just doing it for a laugh – fuck knows why. The press thought it was all part of some act, even when I disappeared behind the black velvet curtain, which was directly behind us. Now, unknown to me, behind the curtain was a four feet drop. I just thought I was going to hide for a few seconds until I stepped through and vanished ... that was when the money went up in the air and scattered all over the stage.

When I sheepishly reappeared I had black velvet from the curtain stuck to the stubble on my head and face and Dana White was picking the notes up. Thank God they thought it was a set-up – boy would I feel a right twat if they knew any different. It broke the ice anyway.

I've mentioned hype already and that's all Frank Warren's outburst was. Maybe he was a bit put out that the UFC had rolled into town and stole some of his thunder. Let's face it; MMA for the masses is different and exciting. For a new spectator, it has all the hysteria of Bruce Lee in the 70's. It's constantly slated as being barbaric ... the most violent sport in America ... banned in some states ... it puts boxing in the shade. I don't seriously think Warren believed what he was saying. I also box and I know for a fact a good boxer can't beat a good all-round fighter.

One thing about such outbursts is that they usually come back to haunt you. Someone will always remember and bring it up, believe me. I remember mouthing off on a documentary once when I'd been beaten in a fight. I was wound up, a bit disappointed with my performance and let rip on camera. I thought I meant it all at the time. I never imagined that people would be discussing it for so long afterwards. Talk about backlash. It was weird. The MMA forums were debating whether I was right or wrong to say it. No one was questioning whether it was right or wrong to be filmed coz it made good TV. It was more or less a throwaway comment as far as I was concerned. Now I know anything said into any recording device can have its comebacks.

As fighters, we were all doing our own bit to hype ourselves up before our matches. We'd done the press conferences to death and had been interviewed for official UFC promotional products amongst others. I'm sure you've seen the WWF entertainers doing their piece to the camera to hype a fight – flexing and shouting and in danger of bursting a kidney before they even get in the ring. We do that for the UFC but in a more civilised manner. There's a great deal of camaraderie in fighting. We're athletes foremost and outside the ring a lot of us are good friends. We don't go around bitching and dissing each other. Well, most of us don't.

When you think big arse you think of J-Lo, right? Not me. Frank Mir is the biggest arse I'll ever know. He was arrogant, cocky and a total prick. And I'm sure those were his good points.

I hate to say it. Maybe his mother should have confiscated his Eminem CDs. He didn't even want to talk to me before the fight – no friendship, no nothing. He was walking around and looking down on everyone like he was top boy. I'll be the first to admit that there's a fair bit of vanity connected to what we do. You are competing to be the best and in front of a crowd, it goes without saying ... like being an actor or in a band. Mir is a good fighter but he lost my respect by the way he conducted himself. It was a let down. I'd seen his fights – Pete Williams in 46 seconds, the Mark Coleman knockout, the Roberto Tavern arm-bar – all impressive victories and then to see him acting like his shit didn't stink got me radged to fuck. We're all rivals ... but only in the cage. He couldn't seem to differentiate.

In his pre-fight sound bites, he was quoted as saying, 'If Freeman beats me, I'll swim home' and 'Ian Freeman is the right opponent to show off my stand-up skills'. I was a bit more reserved. There was everything resting on this fight for me and I was under a lot of pressure. In my interview I said I could win fights in America all the time and no one over here knows about it. If I lose once in the UK then everyone thinks I'm a failure. I know people have slated me in the past for not fighting in the UK – now that I was, I had to live up to their expectations. The only reason I've never fought in the country for so long was because of simple economics.

Going into the fight I was more composed than I have ever been. I was in the UFC and on home soil. I had Angie, Josh and Carl with me in my corner and I had the well wishes of my family with me in my head. I was ready. The adrenaline was pumping; I was raring to get into the cage and show everyone that The Machine can destroy anything in his way.

I weighed in at 219 lbs with Mir tipping the scales at 237 lbs. Mir's a big lad – 6'3" 23 years-old, undefeated in four fights and was looking in good shape after dropping a few pounds. This was his first fight away from home and he was said to be at his most confident. I was going in as the underdog, written off before the fight even started so I had a lot of work to do. I had an advantage – I didn't have to win the crowd over. My first home fight in a long time and I was feeding from their energy ... the atmosphere was electric, completely different to fighting overseas. Walking down to the cage was something else; the venue looked massive when I walked around it empty and full to capacity it's an unbelievable sight – it could be too easy to get overwhelmed by the whole thing.

Once inside the cage I felt calm. Mir was already in there warming up. This was it. We sized each other up from our respective corners and then Big John McCarthy got it underway with his usual, 'Let's get it on!' We touched gloves and you could tell straightaway what sort of fight it was gonna be ... no messing and no sussing each other out; it was all-out war. We clashed right in the centre – Mir with a kick and me with a big right. We both connected but my punch had the edge. He followed with a few more high kicks but they didn't do anything. I was steaming into him with punches and was in his guard against the fence before you could say, 'Freeman is the right opponent to show off my stand-up skills'.

Mir is dangerous on the floor – everyone knows it. He was trying to work a submission as soon as I was on him, going for a quick win. I had to watch what I was doing – he'd seize upon anything and turn it into a match winner if I wasn't careful. I landed a few lefts and a right. He was thinking all the time – I could see it in his face. I'd moved him over to the fence, still in his guard, and he was trying to get his left leg over and between us for an arm-bar. No way could I let him catch me.

We'd shifted out from the fence and Mir turned his attention to my knee. He was definitely working for submissions. I was answering all his attempts with big punches. He got a knee-bar on and it hurt like fuck. The pain shot straight through me; he could snap my knee unless I got out. Still clinched, we rose to our feet and I got in three knees to his ribs. He was hanging on round my neck trying to guard his face – the knees had winded him big style ... I landed a few uppercuts cracking him on the chin and hit him a few times in the face from the side.

We exchanged punches toe to toe. I had the upper hand; I knew my punches were taking it out of him. I was connecting while his were bouncing. He surged in with a knee to my stomach and went for the clinch. I was certain he was hanging on in more ways than one. I couldn't let up, I hit *him* with a knee and he tried to grab it. If I didn't know he was trying to fuck my knee up already, it was obvious now. I hit him with some more big uppercuts – they were connecting for sure, his head was snapping back with each one and the crowd loved it. He came forward and shot in against the fence ... going for my right knee again. I was pushed up into the mesh with him part head-locked at waist level. He had hold of my leg and sent us crashing to the floor as I lost my balance.

He was looking to turn *everything* into a submission. This is where he could be at his most dangerous – he could capitalise on the slightest mistake. The way I saw it, he *needed* a submission. It'd be his only way out because he couldn't take hits like this forever. He got a heel-hook on – my knee gripped between his legs and twisting my ankle for all he was worth. *Fucking hell.* I responded with four or five heavy shots to his face. The pain was fucking incredible ... you don't know the true meaning of pain until you've been heel-hooked. I pounded into him instinctively, his grip loosened and I was able to kick him in the face to make sure. He didn't get enough leverage to finish the job ... I was up on my other knee with him beneath me ... punching the fuck out of his face, each one of them counting, each one rocking him. He managed another inside heel-hook on and pulled; I forced my way back to the same position and landed more massive shots to his head.

It was a race against time ... he wanted the submission before I took his head off and I wanted to knock him out before he pulled my foot off. It was explosive. We were both hurt, both doing our best to survive. The punching worked – I was out of his hold and in his guard and I cracked him a few more times before standing up. I wanted him on his feet and once there he shot straight for my legs – I knew he'd be after my knee again. I sprawled and got in his guard. *Bang* ... my first left connected brilliantly; his head bounced off the canvas and a right knocked it the other way before he knew what was going on. I was elbowing and smashing my forearm into his face while he tried to hold on to me, grabbing my arms was all he could do to stop it.

I was all over him – he was mine now. I was knelt over him then switched and had him on his front, cracking into his face from the side and working him into the fence. He was taking too many shots. We both knew it. And now we both knew that he was never going to get a quick reversal and tap me. I was in full control, dropping forearms into his face over and over and the punching met no defence. All he could do now was hang on and pray for the bell. I wouldn't give him that chance. I made to stand up and he went for one last desperation knee-bar.

I stood across the ring, composing myself for my next assault. I had no idea how much of the round was left; all I knew was that I wanted to end it on my own terms. Big John McCarthy signalled to give Mir a chance to get to his feet. He'd already lost his mouthpiece and was bleeding from the mouth, nose and head ... looked like he didn't know where he was. He stood up and staggered ... McCarthy followed him, asking if he was ok to fight on but he fell to his knees before reaching the fence. He was propped up against it when McCarthy asked him again. I don't think he could answer. It ended there and then. First round win.

*****

It's one of the proudest moments of my life. To shout 'Yo England, I did it!' is something I'd waited a long time to do. I'd destroyed the UFC poster boy (wasn't he supposed to be swimming home?) in less than five minutes and was on top of the world. The last time I'd fought in this country was to a few hundred people ... now I'd just clocked up my best win in front of thousands upon thousands ... and in the Royal Albert Hall.

That was the best feeling in the world – winning a fight like that and being able to dedicate it to my dad who was in hospital. If it wasn't for his influence, I would never have been a fighter and would never have enjoyed moments like this. You want to know the worst feeling? It was the feeling that hit me around five minutes after. I found out that my dad had died the day before the fight. He never got to see it.

There's no way of dressing it up with words – it was like having my heart ripped out. Going from such a high to a low in seconds sent me into shock.

My dad had been taken ill in the run up to the fight. This is something that only close friends know until now. On top of all the training, all the physical torture I was putting myself through, I had the mental torture of knowing my dad was terminally ill. There was nothing I could do, nothing anyone could do. It started when I was in America. He lost his sight after a suspected stroke that happened in his sleep. He was taken to see a specialist and after a scan it was discovered he had a shadow on his brain. My mam was told to be prepared for the worst.

It turned our family upside down. How *do* you prepare? It's impossible. It's not real. You can't look at someone and imagine life without them – humans aren't equipped to deal with things like that. That was when I nearly packed it in to return to England. I had no idea what to do and could only do what I thought was right. I knew I had the support of my family whatever I did. I had to be strong. The worst part was being so far away and being powerless to help. Staying over there was a hard decision to make and it got even harder when I returned home.

With just one week to go before the fight, he was taken back into hospital. It was when I was in London doing all the promo and last minute prepping for the fight. We all knew that this time it was serious. A few days away from the biggest fight of my life and my dad was dying. There were so many questions and answers and I had no idea where to begin.

I'd sat down and discussed it with my mam before I left for London. I broke down. Being pulled both ways something had to give. I was losing my dad and didn't know how to deal with it. My mam knew what I had to do. She told me that there was nothing else in the world that my dad wants other than me to follow my dream. Do it – *do it.* Do it for your dad.

The hardest part for me wasn't just trying to cope; it was trying to block it all from my mind. While we were in London I told Angie I didn't want to know anything. Good news or bad news, she couldn't tell me. Even good news going into the fight would affect me. You can't take any personal business into the cage and not expect to get taken apart.

I managed to stay switched off from emotion during my fight and as soon as it was over, I needed to know. The very second I saw Angie in the cage; I asked if he was still alive. She said, 'As far as I know, yes' – it was actually picked up on camera. How I kept it together in my post-fight interview is anyone's guess. To be honest, as soon as the fight was over, I switched off from it and switched back to thinking about my dad. The fight was just something I had to end as quickly as possible to get back to reality. Mir didn't stand a chance.

Never-ending story

ITS ALWAYS HARD to decide when something like this stops. As far as I'm concerned, it's never gonna stop. I know I'm going from strength to strength with every fight and, as I said, I'm going all the way and taking all my friends, family, fans and fighters with me on a non-stop journey.

Winning the UFC seems the right place to end my story. There've been other fights since and there're gonna be hundreds more to come. It's just that I'm thinking how dramatic it will all look on celluloid on the big screen if ever they make a film!

No, really, I always wanted to leave my story on a high and that one from my point of view is the maximum high. I'd been watching the UFC for years since taking up jiu jitsu when there was only two of us in the class. It wasn't exactly a childhood dream, but being in The Octagon is something that every fighter has at least one fantasy about. That fantasy for me became a reality. I can't stress enough the tremendous respect I have for each and every MMA opponent of mine past, present and future. I've made a lot of good friends through this sport and I hope I continue to do so for a long time to come. You can't always have things your own way, though, and my first defeat just made me more determined than I have ever been in my life. If there is one thing I can teach you from my story it's never to give up. I've been fighting for most of my life – fighting for peace. For peace of mind and peace on the streets. On the streets it's a never-ending battle.

I'm known too well now to even sneeze in someone's direction. Last time I farted in public I was up in court for affray. Being known means that if I sort a fight out it's just an excuse to bang me up. All people (and especially the newspapers) see are the bad things. You can't make an omelette without breaking eggs in the same sense that you can't stop two gangs fighting in a bar without having to use force in one way or another. It can be a violent job. If it's seen as a bad thing to stop fights, then I'm a bad man. If people bothered to look a bit further, they would see a very different story.

One time I was standing talking to Ian and Kev at the door of Boulevard when one of the front windows got smashed in. We didn't see how it happened or who did it, but rushed in to see what was going on. A lad fell back and was hanging out where the window had been. Then a sheet of glass from the top of the frame gave way and came heading straight for his throat. I reacted on the spot and dragged him to safety. The glass shattered right where he had been lying; it would have sliced his head clean off like a guillotine. People just looked on in shock. That was a real hairy moment. You never seem to make the headlines when you save someone's life – or at least I haven't yet. People are eager to think the worst of you and don't understand that the job involves saving more people than you have to beat up. It's the jerks who kick off in pubs that are the danger to others.

If ten people come up to my door and one says, 'I want to fight you one on one', you know for a fact you're going to get jumped on by all of them. I'd rather get jumped by all of them than back down. It's happened before and people never learn. I will not back away from any challenge – I don't know how to. If there is a challenge in the ring, I'll say yes if the money is right. Gone are the days when I'll risk injury for the sake of getting my petrol money back at the end of the night. If it's a personal street challenge, then I'll take it on without hesitation. On the street and with my lads I can say this with confidence: it's nice to have power but you don't get it by being a dickhead, you don't get power by being a liar and you certainly don't get it by being false. You've got to prove you can walk the walk and that way you will earn and gain respect. It takes a long time. For me it's taken fourteen years, and sure it's been hard. I've sweated blood for my lads. If anyone just jumped in and tried to talk the talk, they would either be lynched or laughed at – and I think they would be lynched. My lads always know that they have got me to back them up one hundred and ten per cent. It works both ways. It's a business. It's respect. Every story you have read about me fighting someone has always been for a reason. The reason is always that they are bullies, troublemakers or a danger to the public.

My lifestyle now is one of high living, with movie roles, photoshoots, guest appearances and travelling the world, but my life is still with the streets. Most of the pubs mentioned in this book I no longer have any connection with, other than to say I am still close friends with the owners and managers. I now delegate most of my work to the pub and club scene, but if things get out of hand then I'm in there sorting out what needs to be sorted. I'm still very much available for work, and still help people out with their business. As you may have gathered from this book, I am no angel and I don't intend to state otherwise, but what I can say is that no one was hurt without asking to be hurt.

Maybe my younger days were all due to my inner feelings from the attack and maybe I needed help; but again I've never hit anyone for no reason. You leave me alone and I leave you alone. You're nice to me, then I'm *double* nice to you. You fuck with me or my family, then I make sure you never do it again. Simple mathematics, isn't it? I want everyone out there to be my friend and shake my hand. I want everyone to understand that life has its paths and you choose which path you take. I was lucky and I chose the path of a professional fighter before I ended up in jail. Now I have a career, a new lifestyle and a goal. Whenever I went to court, the magistrates never looked at my private life to see if I had any mental scars that might have made me violent, or offered some kind of answer to why I was there. Maybe if they had, they could have ordered counselling a long time ago. But no, all they ever did was look down their noses at me and presumed that I was as guilty as hell.

People have asked why I do it. I think it's because I *can* do it. You hear about all the other big boys and there is one thing we all have in common. It's a drive, a passion, and a quality that only leaders have. It's a quality you can't quite put your finger on. It's something we are born with and being a mechanic or an office clerk would be going against the grain. If anything, I see my job as being like an unofficial policeman. Cut the laughter and I'll explain. I'm basically a policeman but without any written law. The peace I keep, granted, may be outside the bounds of the law. I don't deny that sometimes it is called for. I've got morals; I don't do drugs, I don't agree with them; I don't condone wife-beating or child-beating. I have to keep a lot of people in order as part of my job, thinking on the spot and handling anything from one or two people at once to full-on gangs of men trying to smash up pubs, clubs and people. I know the police don't always approve of my methods, but a lot of the time we are doing a similar job. I am keeping those types out of my bars and they are trying to take them off the streets. There are others like me in towns and cities the world over. It's all we know. It's all *I* know. It's everything.

I think my story will show people that I was not born with a silver spoon in my mouth and it was not just luck to be asked to fight in the UFC. I damn well worked hard to get where I am today and no man will ever take it away from me. It seems like a lifetime ago to think back to the days when I was your average nine-to-five salesman before that incident that changed my life. It was so horrific – I'd lost my will to live, and writing this book has brought a lot of those memories back. Eventually I managed to get out of that hole I'd sunk into, but it was a journey to hell and back and everyone paid the price. Give me respect and you'll get it back. I can be a good friend or your worst enemy. If anyone still has any problems with that, then The Machine is the man to see.

There are names I have mentioned, names I should have mentioned and names I have not mentioned at all. I apologise if you are a friend of mine and there is no mention of you in this book – there were too many stories to go into this one, so you could be in the next. People's names have been left out through respect or for protection, depending on the circumstances.

I've talked about the paths that have to be taken – I have chosen my path and in the past it might not have always been the right one. Let's just say I was finding my feet. You may have chosen your path already. I know where I'm going now and, once you realise that too, then nothing will stop you. Whatever path you choose, good or bad, make sure you leave the innocent alone. Take chances for the good, not the bad, and never give up your dreams.

Winners never quit and quitters never win.